THE SEVEN CULINARY WONDERS OF THE WORLD

This book was designed and produced by

White Lion Publishing
The Old Brewery
6 Blundell Street
London N7 9BH

Senior Editors	Carol King, Hannah Phillips
Editor	Abi Waters
Senior Designer	Isabel Eeles
Production Manager	Rohana Yusof
Editorial Director	Ruth Patrick
Publisher	Philip Cooper

Published in North America by Smithsonian Books

This book may be purchased for educational, business, or sales promotional use. For information, please write: Special Markets Department, Smithsonian Books, P.O. Box 37012, MRC 513, Washington, DC 20013

Cataloging-in-Publication Data
Names: Linford, Jenny, author. | Pattullo, Alice, illustrator.
Title: The seven culinary wonders of the world : a history of honey, salt, chile, pork, rice, cacao, and tomato : featuring 63 international recipes / Jenny Linford ; illustrated by Alice Pattullo. Description: Washington, DC : Smithsonian Books, [2018] | Includes index.
Identifiers: LCCN 2018011526| ISBN 9781588346421 (hardcover)
Subjects: LCSH: International cooking. | Food—History. | LCGFT: Cookbooks.
Classification: LCC TX725.A1 L534 2018 | DDC 641.3/009—dc23
LC record available at https://lccn.loc.gov/2018011526

Manufactured in China, not at government expense

22 21 20 19 18   5 4 3 2 1

THE SEVEN CULINARY WONDERS OF THE WORLD

A History of Honey, Salt, Chile, Pork, Rice, Cacao, and Tomato

JENNY LINFORD

ILLUSTRATED BY
ALICE PATTULLO

Smithsonian Books
WASHINGTON, DC

CONTENTS

INTRODUCTION

The ingredients we eat every day play a special part in our lives. To begin with, we have an intimate relationship with them, consuming them in order to sustain our bodies physically. Our relationship with key ingredients we eat today is in many cases a long one, developed over thousands of years. These are foods that over their history as part of the human diet have acquired cultural and religious values and taken on symbolic and superstitious meanings.

The seven foods explored in this book are ones that we now take for granted. Pork is, nowadays, a commonplace meat, widely found in various forms, whether as bacon strips and sausage patties served for a diner breakfast, the ham sandwich eaten for a quick lunch by office workers, or the hot dog devoured while watching a baseball game. Honey, bought in jars from supermarkets, is enjoyed for its sweetness, drizzled over pancakes in the morning or blitzed into fruit smoothies. Salt is cheap and ubiquitous, placed on our tables so that we can season our food to taste. In the world of food manufacturing, salt is one of the most widely used additives. It is used as a flavor enhancer to increase the "tastiness" of processed foods and also for its preservative effects. While we expect it in overtly salty foods such as potato chips, it's also, more surprisingly, present in other everyday manufactured foods, such as bread, tomato ketchup, and cakes. Around the globe, chiles are used to zip up dishes from beef tacos to curries—a handy way of adding heat. Rice is now a pantry staple, a filling carbohydrate that can be conveniently stored and cooked when needed. Made from cacao, chocolate confectionary in the developed world is affordable and widely available, found in gas stations and grocery stores. Chocolate bars are bought, almost absentmindedly, as a sweet treat, devoured in minutes. From the slices of firm-fleshed, bland fresh tomatoes found in salads, sandwiches, and burgers to *passata*-topped pizzas, tomatoes, too, are widely present in our diet. These are now foods that we barely think about.

All of them, however, are remarkable ingredients in their own right, with fascinating stories behind them. Furthermore, they are foods that have traveled the world, reflecting our omnivorous curiosity as a species. Alongside an understandable wary resistance to new foods, there has also been a human willingness to experiment—to plant, for example, seeds of "exotic" plants, such as chiles, rice, or tomatoes, brought on long sea voyages from the other side of the world. The international range of recipes within this book—Malaysian *nasi goreng*, Italian *sugo al pomodoro*, Portuguese salt cod croquettes, Chinese *char siu*, North American brownies, Greek baklava, Israeli *zhoug*—reflects this open-minded interest in food and the way in which our seven ingredients have traveled the globe and become an intrinsic part of many national cuisines.

Tracing the histories of these foods makes it clear what an ingenious and curious species human beings are. We have acted upon the natural world we found ourselves in, using its resources and shaping them in order to nourish our population. Salt was found in the sea and the land. Wild animals and birds—among them pigs, sheep, cattle, and chickens—have been domesticated to provide us with meat, milk, wool, fertilizer, and leather. Wild plants—often initially unprepossessing and hard to cultivate—have been bred over generations to have traits we consider desirable, such as good flavor and texture, higher yields, disease resistance, and ease of harvesting. We even developed a way of working with bees in order to be able to gather their honey easily and safely.

Among the earliest animals to be domesticated was the pig, descended from wild swine. In the ancient world, there was considerable respect for the pig's wild ancestors. Powerful, fierce wild boars charge ferociously through ancient Greek and Roman myths, Celtic legends, and Arthurian tales. The domestic pig's ability to scavenge for food and fend for itself until slaughtered, however, made it a useful animal to keep. Pork is the world's most consumed meat, yet, fascinatingly, it is also considered taboo by two major religions, namely Judaism and Islam. The killing of a pig in rural communities around the world was often an annual event, celebrated with a special feast of fresh pork, a rare treat, eaten with relish on that occasion. It is in the world of charcuterie that pork comes into its own, the ample flesh enjoyed in many diverse forms, from fresh sausages to preserved hams and salamis.

Honey was humankind's first sweetener. Collected from the hives of wild bees, it has been eaten for thousands of years. The earliest depiction of humankind's appetite for honey is a cave painting of a human being collecting honey, dating from 8,000 to 10,000 years ago. Sweetness is one of the five fundamental tastes our tongues recognize, and we are biologically programmed to like it. Honey was for centuries considered something wondrous, seen in many cultures around the world as a gift from the gods. Beekeeping to this day continues to interest people, a fact linked to our respect for bees and fascination with the complex workings of their colonies.

Salt is needed by our bodies, so it is vital for life. Saltiness, like sweetness, is one of the five tastes our tongues recognize, a key flavoring that we crave. For several centuries, salt was very valuable indeed. Such was its economic importance that, famously, the word "salary" derives from the Latin *sal* for salt. It is a mineral that humans extracted with much work, either from the sea—through the process of evaporating brine—or as rock salt, hewn from the ground with hard, physical labor. As well as being used as a seasoning, salt is essential for making many of our great preserved foods, from ham and cheese to pickled and fermented foods, such as kimchi and soy sauce.

Chiles, thought to originate from Bolivia in South America, are today cultivated around the globe. It is estimated that around one-quarter of the world's population eat chiles in some form every day. Compounds called capsaicinoids contained within chiles, particularly in the seeds and the surrounding tissue, are what cause that unique chile burn. Fascinatingly, rather than avoiding a fruit with this punishing effect, human beings have instead sought it out, relishing that heat sensation. Following the Spanish invasion of Mesoamerica, chiles were spread through trading routes and introduced to other parts of the world, including Europe, Africa, India, and Southeast Asia. An extensive use of chiles is now a trademark of a number of cuisines, notably Mexican, Indian, and Thai. We continue to be fascinated by the heat effects of chiles, growing new cultivars that now reach extraordinary, record-breaking levels of ferocious hotness.

Despite its ubiquity as confectionary in the developed world, chocolate made from cacao retains a sheen of glamour and is still seen as a treat. Its history as a supposed aphrodisiac resonates in its current popularity as a Valentine's Day gift for lovers. Cacao is native to the Americas, highly valued by the historic Olmec, Maya, and Aztec civilizations, by whom it was used as a currency and required as a tribute. Drinks made from ground cacao beans were prepared with great care and drunk by the privileged elite of Maya and Aztec societies. It was through the Spanish conquistadors and their invasion of Mesoamerica that cacao was introduced to the continent of Europe and other parts of the world. For most of its history, cacao was consumed as a beverage rather than a food. It was the Industrial Revolution and the development of particular machinery that allowed the beans to be processed and transformed into eating chocolate with the smooth texture we now expect from it.

Rice, a cereal, is one of our major food crops, an important source of calories for over half the world's population. Cultivated rice is derived from wild rice, but where this cultivation first took place remains unconfirmed, with both China and India vying for this honor. To this day, rice remains a staple in both these great countries, central to their cuisines. In order to grow rice successfully, farmers in Asia developed a system of growing rice, which is a semiaquatic plant, in flooded plots of land called paddy fields. Growing rice in this way involved the setting up of complex irrigation systems to allow the water to be shared fairly among many farmers. This required a high level of social cooperation, with the term "rice-growing societies" used by social historians studying the impact of the crop on shaping the society around it.

The tomato, originally from South America, has been extraordinarily successful as a globe-trotting ingredient. Its adoption as a culinary mainstay, however, came comparatively late in the day, as it was initially regarded with skepticism. It was introduced to Europe by the Spanish. As an exotic novelty, it enjoyed a reputation as an aphrodisiac; hence its nickname "love apple." Its bright, colorful fruit meant it was initially cultivated for its appearance rather than for eating. The nineteenth century, however, saw the rise of both tomato growing and the tomato canning industry in Italy. Today the *pomodoro* is regarded as typically Italian, used in dishes from pasta sauces to pizzas. As travelers to Italy know, the taste of fresh tomatoes there, grown in warm sunshine and good soil, is hard to beat.

The journey of each of these historic ingredients follows roughly the same overall arc. Initially, these were foods that were highly prized—the stuff of legend, costly, and luxurious—but, over the centuries, thanks to human inventiveness and endeavor, they became widely available and affordable. The exotic glamour that attached to them has diminished considerably. It is, however, when we take the trouble to learn the history of these ingredients that we remind ourselves afresh of quite how extraordinary these everyday foods are. And this allows us to appreciate these seven ingredients for the seven wonders of the world that they are.

PORK

The pig occupies a special place in human history; our relationship with this animal is a long and enduring one. Along with the dog, it was one of the earliest animals to be domesticated. It is from the wild boar *(Sus scrofa)* that all domestic pigs are descended.

Where this domestication first took place is uncertain. Archaeological evidence suggests pig domestication may have taken place in China in 8000 BCE. In the Middle East, archaeological evidence in the form of the bones of domesticated pigs has been found at various sites. Significantly, pig bones were excavated at Hallan Çemi in Turkey, a site dated to around 8000 BCE. The evidence of these bones suggests that wild boar were living alongside people in the village.

The reason for this early close relationship between people and pigs rests in the innate nature of the wild boar as a curious, confident creature. Pigs, famously, are great omnivorous scavengers, whose natural habitat was woodland. Early human settlements, however, with their refuse heaps and crops, offered rich pickings for these animals, which gradually became accustomed to humans. It is thought that wild boar piglets, which humans captured and reared, were the ancestors of what became domesticated pigs. The pig's usefulness as a sacrificial animal is thought to have played a part in its

Unlike other livestock animals, such as cattle, sheep, or goats, reared for milk or wool as well as for their meat, the pig is farmed solely for the meat it produces—pork.

domestication. Pigs were sacrificed to the gods in ancient Greece and Rome, as well as in China. "The young of the hog is considered in a state of purity for sacrifice when five days old," observed the Roman author Pliny the Elder in his *Natural History* (77 CE).

Primarily, though, unlike other livestock animals such as cattle, sheep, or goats, reared for milk or wool as well as for their meat, the pig is farmed solely for the meat it produces—pork. As is explored in the "Charcuterie" section of this book (see pp. 29–41), the meat obtained by slaughtering a pig was used with great ingenuity by people around the world. Pigs have long been an important source of meat in many countries. The role of the pig in Chinese life was historically so central that the Chinese ideogram for home consists of the character for "roof" over the character for "pig." The figure of the swineherd, whose job it was to look after pigs, runs through European literature and folklore, from Eumaeus in Homer's *Odyssey* (675–725 BCE) to Hans Christian Andersen's story "The Swineherd" (1842).

The pig's omnivorous nature and its ability to gain weight made it a useful animal, as it was able to forage and could also be fed simply on scraps and leftovers. Biologically speaking, the pig is admirably equipped for life as a forager. Its sharp teeth allow it to devour a large range of foods. It is, however, the pig's snout that is a remarkable asset, both tough enough to enable the animal to dig effectively with it into hard ground, and very sensitive, like a cat's whiskers. At the end of the snout is a rigid nasal disc, strong enough to be used for digging but packed with sensory receptors, which give the pig a remarkable sense of smell and enable it to sniff out food. The ability to smell out edible tubers and roots deep in the earth led to the use of pigs, as well as dogs, to track down the intensely aromatic truffle, the valuable fungus that grows underground. The fifteenth-century Italian Renaissance historian and writer Bartolomeo Sacchi Platina wrote a description of hunting for truffles with pigs and hounds, and the use of truffle pigs to find this highly prized delicacy is a custom that continues to this day.

In China, domesticated pigs were confined within pig houses, enabling them to put on weight quickly and easily. Pigs were valued for their ability to consume waste, including human excrement, and transform it into meat that humans could consume. During the Han dynasty (206 BCE–220 CE), the raising of pigs was encouraged. So highly were swine regarded during this era that funerary pigs were buried in graves to accompany the dead in their afterlife.

Within Europe, two different types of domesticated pigs were bred: short-legged "sty" pigs, which could live in confined spaces, and longer-legged range pigs, which roamed the woods with a swineherd in attendance. In Europe, there was a long tradition of grazing pigs in forests, where they could be fattened up on the natural seasonal bounty of fruits and nuts, such as beech nuts, hazelnuts, and acorns. There was an economic value to this practice, and it was recorded as such in England's *Domesday*

Book (1086). One entry, for example, about the land of St. Peter of Westminster in "Ossulstone," records: "Meadow for eleven ploughs, pasture for the livestock of the vill [meaning small village], woodland for 100 pigs."

Over the centuries, as the forests were chopped down to make way for human habitation and agriculture, access of pigs to the woodland to feed on mast (the fallen nuts) was granted seasonally, usually beginning on St. Michael's Day, September 29, and ending on St. Andrew's Day, November 30. Nowadays, the pannage tradition (see p. 24) is still to be found in Spain in the creation of the *jamón ibérico de bellota* from pigs grazed in acorn woods (see p. 38). In areas of apple cultivation, the tradition also grew up of the "orchard pig." In Gloucestershire, Britain, the traditional breed of pig, the Gloucestershire Old Spot, was allowed to graze in apple orchards, where it fed on the generous amount of windfall apples.

The pig's toughness and flexibility when it came to eating scraps made it a useful meat animal to take on long ship voyages. The animal's fertility—with sows producing a number of litters each year—allowed it to reproduce successfully and thrive in the countries to which it was introduced.

SALADE AUX LARDONS

Serves 4
Preparation 10 minutes
Cooking 8–9 minutes

Lardons is the French word for small strips of bacon or belly fat. In this classic French bistro salad, fried *lardons* and poached eggs transform a delicate lettuce into a satisfying dish, filled with flavor and texture.

6 tbsp olive oil
1 tsp Dijon mustard
8 oz slab bacon, cut into
   1-inch cubes
5 tbsp red wine vinegar
4 fresh eggs
2 heads frisée, trimmed,
   torn into 2-inch pieces,
   rinsed, and dried
Salt and freshly ground
   black pepper

1 Mix together the olive oil and mustard to form a dressing. Season with a little salt, bearing in mind the saltiness of the bacon, and lots of freshly ground pepper.

2 Fry the bacon in a skillet over medium heat, stirring often, for about 5 minutes until crispy. Add the red wine vinegar to the skillet and cook for 1 minute, stirring now and then, to slightly reduce the vinegar. Set aside and keep warm.

3 Bring a saucepan of water to a boil, then reduce the heat to a simmer. Carefully break each egg into a ramekin and slide it into the simmering water. Poach the eggs for 2–3 minutes. Carefully remove with a slotted spoon and dry on paper towels.

4 Pour the olive oil dressing over the frisée and toss thoroughly to coat. Divide the frisée among four serving plates. Add the warm bacon mixture to each serving, tossing lightly. Top each serving with a poached egg and serve at once.

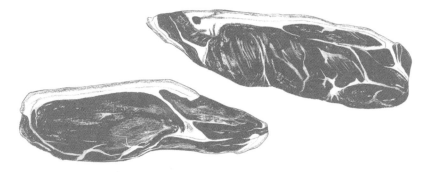

Archaeological and DNA evidence show that pigs were taken to the Pacific islands by migrating people. It was the explorer Christopher Columbus who introduced pigs from Europe to the New World in 1493. Brought to Hispaniola, in the West Indies, the original group of eight animals thrived and multiplied, becoming a plentiful, feral presence on the island. The Spanish conquistadors introduced pigs to Central and South America. It was the Spanish conquistador Hernando de Soto's expedition of 1539 to 1542 that introduced pigs to Florida, in what is now the United States. Another significant porcine introduction to North America was by the English explorer Walter Raleigh, who took pigs to John Smith's Jamestown settlement in 1607, where they multiplied hugely.

Pigs thrived in North America, valued as a useful animal by settlers, and salt pork, a preserved food made by salting fresh pork, became an important part of North America's diet. In the nineteenth century, the Norwegian Ole Munch Raeder, who chronicled life in North America, wrote: "I cannot refrain from saying a few kind words on behalf of the favorite pet of the Americans, the swine. I have not yet found any city, county, or town, where I have not seen these lovable animals wandering about peacefully in huge herds."

The eighteenth and nineteenth centuries saw the development of different pig breeds, with much experimentation done in Britain. The twentieth century, alongside the development of large-scale industrial pig farming, saw the rise of pigs bred to produce lean meat, as its fat—prized for so long—fell out of dietary favor. Today, pork is the most consumed meat in the world, with China near the top of the table in terms of per capita pork consumption.

THE BOAR IN LEGEND

Humanity's long relationship with the pig is reflected not only through its role in agriculture but also in folklore and mythology, signifying the animal's historic importance.

The Chinese zodiac, which traces its origins back to at least the Han dynasty (206 BCE–220 CE), features twelve animals. Among them is the pig, the last of the twelve. According to tradition, the reason for this position in the cycle is that, when the Jade Emperor summoned the animals, the pig—either through laziness or stoutness—arrived last. Those born in the Year of the Pig are thought to be diligent, compassionate, and generous, with a capacity for concentration.

In ancient Greek mythology, the pig appears in a more formidable form, as the gigantic Erymanthian boar. One of the Twelve Tasks of Hercules was that the Greek hero was commanded to seek out and capture alive the huge, ferocious boar, which lived on Mount Erymanthos and caused much destruction to the crops and herds of the people of Arcadia. Hercules chased and captured the boar, duly bringing it back as instructed to King Eurystheus. At the sight of the boar, the cowardly king was so terrified that he leapt into a huge storage jar to hide from it.

The hunting of powerful wild boars is a recurrent theme in ancient legends. The Roman poet Ovid, in his famous *Metamorphoses* (c. 800 CE), recounts the complex tale of the Calydonian boar. In this Greek myth, the goddess Artemis calls up the monstrous boar from the underworld to ravage the kingdom of Calydon, as its king has failed to honor her. A group of Greek heroes, together with the virgin huntress Atalanta, succeed in killing the boar, but fall out among themselves with tragic and fatal consequences. It is a story that was retold over the centuries and depicted in numerous ways, on vases, on sarcophagi, and in a well-known painting by the Flemish artist Peter Paul Rubens, *The Calydonian Boar Hunt* (c. 1612).

The boar plays an important part in Celtic mythology. In Irish legend, the tale of the warrior Diarmuid and Gráinne is a romantic but ill-fated love story, which exists in many versions. Diarmuid elopes with Gráinne, the intended wife of his friend and leader Fionn Mac Cumhaill, but is forgiven by Fionn. Years later, however, Diarmuid meets his death by being gored by a giant enchanted boar, having been warned as a child not to hunt boar as this would lead to his death. In one version of the story, Fionn has the power to heal lives by letting the injured drink from his hand, but rather than acting promptly to save the wounded warrior, Fionn, remembering the dishonor he suffered, lets the water trickle through his hands and is too late to save Diarmuid.

The hunting of powerful wild boars is a recurrent theme in ancient legends. The Roman poet Ovid, in his famous Metamorphoses *(c. 800 CE), recounts the complex tale of the Calydonian boar.*

In Welsh mythology, Twrch Trwyth is a supernatural creature, a man turned into a wild boar. The story of Twrch Trwyth is contained in the tale of the hero Culhwch and his beloved Olwen, daughter of a giant, found in *The Mabinogion,* a collection of stories from the historic oral tradition, compiled in Welsh in the twelfth and thirteenth centuries. In the best heroic tradition, Culhwch is set various tasks he must complete in order to be granted Olwen's hand, among them obtaining the comb and scissors that

ROAST PORK BELLY
WITH APPLE SAUCE

Serves 4
Preparation 15 minutes
Cooking 1½ hours

Roasting a piece of pork belly is an excellent way to enjoy both tender, succulent roast pork and crisp, golden-brown crackling. The apple sauce, which in Britain is traditionally made from Bramley apples, is a very good accompaniment, as it cuts through the richness of the meat.

4-lb piece of pork belly, skin scored with a sharp blade

1 large garlic clove or 2 small garlic cloves, peeled and cut into slivers

2 tbsp fennel seeds, crushed (optional)

Salt and freshly ground black pepper

APPLE SAUCE

1 lb cooking apples, peeled, cored, and finely chopped

2 tbsp water

1–2 tbsp sugar

1 Preheat the oven to 425°F. Pat the pork thoroughly dry. Using a small, sharp knife, cut little slashes in the fleshy side of the pork belly and insert the garlic pieces into the pork to flavor it. Rub the meat with crushed fennel seeds, if using, and season with salt and pepper. Season the skin well with salt, rubbing it into the slashes.

2 Place the pork on a rack in a roasting pan and roast for 30 minutes. Reduce the oven temperature to 375°F and roast for a further hour until the crackling is crisp and golden brown and the pork is cooked through.

3 While the pork roasts in the oven, prepare the apple sauce. Place the apple and water in a small, heavy pan. Cover the pan and cook over low heat for 10 minutes, stirring now and then, until the apple pieces have softened.

4 Add the sugar and mix in well with a wooden spoon. Transfer the apple sauce to a serving bowl and set aside to cool to room temperature.

5 Serve the roast pork belly hot from the oven, with the apple sauce on the side.

are found on Twrch Trwyth's head. So difficult are these tasks that he has to ask for help from his cousin King Arthur, who agrees to aid him. King Arthur and his knights hunt Twrch Trwyth, with Arthur losing many of his men to the savage beast. Finally, however, the boar surrenders the comb and scissors, loses his tusks, and is driven to his death off the coast of Cornwall.

TABOO

Strikingly, despite the fact that pork is the most widely consumed meat in the world, it is also a meat with taboos attached to it. The consumption of pork is forbidden in two of the major religions: Judaism and Islam. Within Christianity, the Ethiopian Orthodox Church forbids the consumption of pork, and the Seventh-Day Adventists avoid eating it. This means that around one-fifth of the world's population does not eat pork for religious reasons.

Throughout the pig's long relationship with humans, there has often been an ambivalence in how it has been regarded. Swineherds in ancient Egypt were considered a separate caste, contaminated by their contact with pigs. Pork was a food eaten by the poor, such as the laborers working on the pyramids, and was not eaten by the elite in Egyptian society, including priests. Hence "unclean" has become a word often associated with pigs. Indeed, after the fifth-century Greek historian Herodotus visited Egypt, he wrote of its inhabitants: "The pig is regarded among them as an unclean animal, so much so that if a man in passing accidentally touches a pig, he instantly hurries to the river, and plunges in with all his clothes on."

The omnivorous nature of the pig when it comes to food, and its ability to forage, was central to the pig being regarded as a useful animal by human beings. The pig's ability to scavenge and eat waste was historically regarded as a practical way to keep settlements and villages clean.

The omnivorous nature of the pig when it comes to food, and its ability to forage, was central to the pig being regarded as a useful animal by human beings.

However, this very willingness to eat waste, such as excrement and carrion, led to the pig being regarded in an adverse light, while pork, in certain societies, became a meat with a stigma attached.

In Judaism, the prohibition against the consumption of pork is found in the Bible. When God spoke to Moses, he laid out strict rules as to how the Hebrews should behave in order to remain his followers; these included dietary strictures.

In Leviticus 11:1–2, these stipulations are clearly explained:

Now the Lord spoke to Moses and Aaron, saying to them, "Speak to the children of Israel, saying, These are the animals which you may eat among all the animals that are on the earth: Among the animals, whatever divides the hoof, having cloven hooves and chewing the cud—that you may eat. Nevertheless these you shall not eat among those that chew the cud or those that have cloven hooves: the camel, because it chews the cud but does not have cloven hooves, is unclean to you; the rock hyrax, because it chews the cud but does not have cloven hooves, is unclean to you; the hare, because it chews the cud but does not have cloven hooves, is unclean to you; and the swine, though it divides the hoof, having cloven hooves, yet does not chew the cud, is unclean to you. Their flesh you shall not eat, and their carcasses you shall not touch. They are unclean to you."

Furthermore, in Deuteronomy 12:23, there is this instruction: "Only be sure that thou eat not the blood: for the blood is the life; and thou mayest not eat the life with the flesh."

Animals that eat blood, such as pigs, which are carrion feeders, were, therefore, not to be eaten, as this would contaminate those who ate them. In this way, many centuries ago, not eating pork, along with the observance of other dietary rules (such as not combining meat and dairy), became an important, defining part of Jewish identity.

In Islam, the eating of pork is *haram* (strictly prohibited). The Qur'an, the Islamic sacred book containing the word of Allah (God) as dictated to Muhammed by the Archangel Gabriel, explains what behavior is *haram*, or forbidden to those practicing Islam. Within the Qur'an the prohibition on the consumption of pork is explicit and occurs several times. One verse, Qur'an 2:173, for example, says: "He has only forbidden to you dead animals, blood, the flesh of swine, and that which has been dedicated to other than Allah."

The primary reason given for avoiding pork within Islam is that the pig is seen as impure, an animal that lives in dirt and excrement and that eats waste. It is regarded as a contaminated animal and one that would contaminate those who consumed its flesh. Pork in the Islamic world is also regarded as an unhealthy meat, filled with toxins and carrying disease.

In times of religious tension, the pork taboo took on a special importance. The Spanish Reconquista—the retaking of the Iberian peninsula from the Muslims who had invaded it in 711 CE—was a centuries-long struggle, completed in 1492 with the fall of Granada. After the Reconquista, the eating of pork, forbidden under Islam, became central not just to Spanish

PORK TONKATSU

Serves 4
Preparation 15 minutes
Cooking 12–16 minutes

This classic Japanese pork dish is a much-loved family favorite. The combination of deep-fried, panko breadcrumb–coated pork with tangy *tonkatsu* sauce, steamed rice, and crunchy white cabbage is a simple but satisfying one.

TONKATSU SAUCE
4 tbsp tomato ketchup
1 tbsp Worcestershire sauce
1 tbsp dark brown sugar
1 tbsp dark soy sauce
1 tsp balsamic vinegar

4 pork loin steaks, each
   weighing about 8 oz, trimmed
   of any fat
Sunflower or vegetable oil,
   for deep-frying
3 oz panko breadcrumbs
6 tbsp all-purpose flour,
   seasoned well with salt
   and pepper
2 eggs, beaten

TO SERVE
Steamed rice
Finely shredded white cabbage

1   First, make the *tonkatsu* sauce by mixing all the ingredients together in a bowl.

2   Place the pork loin steaks between two large sheets of plastic wrap. Use a meat mallet to beat each steak to tenderize and flatten it to ½ inch thick.

3   Heat the oil for deep-frying in a wok or deep saucepan until hot. Test the heat by adding a pinch of panko breadcrumbs; if they sizzle, the oil is hot enough.

4   Coat the pork loin steaks first with the seasoned flour, then with the beaten egg, and finally with the panko breadcrumbs.

5   Add the breaded pork to the hot oil and fry in two batches for 3–4 minutes until golden brown on one side. Turn over and fry for a further 3–4 minutes until golden brown on the other side and cooked through. Remove and drain on paper towels.

6   Cut each pork *tonkatsu* into slices crosswise and serve at once with steamed rice, shredded white cabbage, and the *tonkatsu* sauce on the side.

cuisine but also to Spanish identity. There was a forced conversion by the Catholic authorities of Muslims and Jews in Spain, and the eating of pork became a way of testing whether people were truly Christian.

The Spanish Inquisition, founded in 1481, investigated whether *conversos* (Jews who had converted to Christianity) had truly converted. An extensive Inquisition list of Jewish food practices contains "not eating pork, hare, strangled birds, conger eel, cuttlefish, nor eels or other scaleless fish, as laid down in the Jewish law." Whether people ate pork or not became central to the Inquisition. Unsurprisingly, pork eating was embraced by Spanish Christians as a way of expressing their faith.

THE CULINARY PIG

For centuries, the fatty texture of pork was considered one of its charms. However, in the twentieth century, the breeding of leaner pigs, and consequently drier, less flavorful meat, has eroded that appeal. Roasting is a traditional way of cooking pork in many cuisines, including British, French, and Chinese. In Western cooking, pork is often paired with apple, with the tang of the fruit cutting through the richness of the meat.

Among the particular culinary treats that pork continues to be valued for to this day is its crackling, the external layer of skin and fat, which when roasted becomes crisp and succulent. The English essayist Charles Lamb gives a famously eloquent description of the pleasures offered by pork crackling in "A Dissertation upon Roast Pig" (1906). He opines:

> There is no flavor comparable, I will contend, to that of the crisp, tawny, well-watched, not over-roasted, crackling, as it is well called—the very teeth are invited to their share of the pleasure at the banquet in overcoming the coy, brittle resistance—with the adhesive oleaginous—O call it not fat—but an indefinable sweetness growing up to it.

In China, where pork has long been prized, there is a particularly varied repertoire of pork dishes. *Char siu* (barbecued pork) is made by marinating cuts of meat in a salty-sweet marinade and then roasting it. The marinade imparts a reddish-brown color to the meat, though nowadays red food coloring is often used as well because red is an auspicious color in Chinese culture. *Char siu* (see p. 28) is often eaten simply with rice, but sliced *char siu* is also used to add flavor and texture to a range of dishes, including stir-fried rice or noodles.

Ground pork is widely used in a range of ways. It is employed as a filling for dumplings, to stuff dried shiitake mushrooms, in meatballs—such as

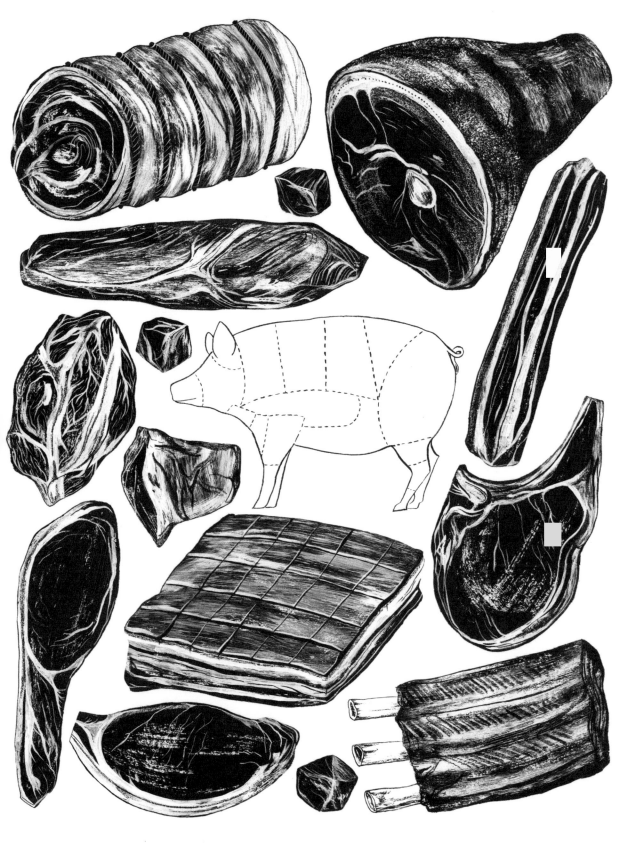

lion's head dumplings—and in a classic Szechuan cellophane noodle dish, picturesquely named "ants climbing a tree."

HOG KILLING

For several centuries, the annual slaughter of a pig during the winter months was an important event in rural households. European medieval illuminated manuscripts, known as books of hours, often depict the seasonal Labors of the Months, from digging in March to harvesting the grapes in September. Among the traditional labors shown are the gathering of acorns in November to feed to pigs and the killing of the pigs in December. The choice of December for this procedure was crucial for two main reasons: the pig was to provide food for the bitter, lean winter months to come, as well as for Christmas feasting, and, essentially, the weather in this month was cold enough to allow the meat to be stored and cured safely without going off. Pigs were traditionally fattened up in the fall months before their slaughter. This often involved the practice of pannage, a right granted to agricultural workers in Europe to release their swine into the woods so that they could eat and grow plump on the seasonal bounty of beech mast, acorns, and chestnuts. In China, the annual slaughter took place just before Chinese New Year, a lunar festival, falling in January or February.

Historic accounts of butchering the pig make clear that it was a noisy, strenuous business, with the pig squealing and resisting its fate. Flora Thompson, in her book *Lark Rise to Candleford* (1945), charting English rural life in the late nineteenth century from her own memories, describes how pig stickers—traveling butchers—would carry out the demanding task. Laura Ingalls Wilder based her classic of U.S. pioneering life, *Little House on the Prairie* (1935), on her experience as a child growing up in the northern Midwestern United States during the 1870s and 1880s. She describes the killing of the pig as part of the seasonal cycle, following on from the harvesting of fruit and vegetables:

> *Near the pigpen, Pa and Uncle Henry built a bonfire, and boiled a great kettle of water over it. When the water was boiling they went to kill the hog. Then Laura ran and hid her head on the bed and stopped her ears with her fingers so she could not hear the hog squeal.*

Killing a pig was often a communal affair, with family and friends gathering together to take part in a meal. There was good reason for this, as the process required a lot of work, with the gathering of the firewood for the scalding vat being the start of it. In some cases, a wooden scaffolding

BARBECUED PORK RIBS

Serves 4
Preparation 10 minutes
Cooking 2 hours 10 minutes

A tangy, salty-sweet barbecue sauce gives a delicious flavor to spare ribs, making them a tasty, finger-licking treat. This recipe uses a broiler to finish them off, but if the weather permits, cook the glazed ribs over the barbecue for an extra smoky hit. Serve the ribs with potato salad, sweet corn, and coleslaw.

3 lb baby back pork ribs
Salt and freshly ground
   black pepper

BARBECUE SAUCE
1 tbsp sunflower or
   vegetable oil
1 onion, peeled and chopped
2 garlic cloves, peeled
2 cups canned tomatoes
½ cup water
4 tbsp dark brown sugar
2 tbsp Worcestershire sauce
4 tbsp red wine vinegar
2 tbsp tomato paste
2 tbsp tomato ketchup
1 tbsp honey
1 tsp smoked paprika

1   Preheat the oven to 400°F. Season the pork ribs well with salt and pepper. Wrap them in two layers of aluminum foil, place on a baking sheet, and bake for 2 hours until the pork is tender.

2   Now make the barbecue sauce. Heat the oil in a pan, add the onion, and fry gently for 10 minutes until lightly brown. Add the garlic and fry for 1 minute until fragrant.

3   Add the canned tomatoes, water, sugar, Worcestershire sauce, vinegar, tomato paste, ketchup, honey, and smoked paprika. Season with salt and pepper. Bring to a boil, reduce the heat, and simmer for 5 minutes, stirring now and then. Use a jug blender or hand blender to blend the barbecue sauce until smooth.

4   Preheat the broiler until very hot. Unwrap the pork ribs, brush generously on all sides with the barbecue sauce, and broil for 5 minutes on each side until glazed. Serve the sticky ribs with the remaining barbecue sauce.

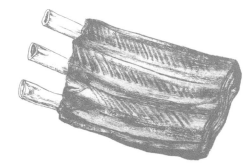

on which to hang the pig carcass (to make it easier to work with) was constructed. The freshly killed pig was hung on this with its head facing down, and its throat was then cut to release the blood, so as to cool the body quickly.

Next came scalding the pig, with the heavy carcass laboriously placed in the hot water. The aim of this immersion was to loosen the bristles on the skin, allowing them to be scraped off easily, leaving the skin smooth and clean. After the carcass had been thoroughly scraped, it was cut open and the offal inside was removed and prepared. The cleaned, gutted carcass was then butchered, with the various cuts cooked or cured in a variety of ways. Pigs were a valuable source of protein, and, historically, every part of a pig slaughtered in this way was used—an aspect that is explored further in this book in the section on "Charcuterie" (see pp. 29–30).

In addition to the practical reasons of offering help with the labor of slaughter and processing the carcass, the gathering of family and neighbors took place for celebratory reasons. The annual killing of a pig in rural communities, where life was hard and frugal, was an important event. It offered the chance to taste fresh pork and other delicacies available only once a year—a brief taste of plenty.

In Spain, the word *matanza* (from *matar*, meaning "to kill") is used to describe the traditional yearly slaughter of a pig. The *matanza* ritual celebration is a two- to three-day-long process that involves killing the pig and the subsequent butchering and transformation of the carcass. "The annual pig-slaughter was until recently the most important gastronomic event in the European peasant calender," observes British food writer and broadcaster Elisabeth Luard in her book *European Peasant Cookery* (1986).

SUCKLING PIG

Young piglets, slaughtered at two months, when they are still sucking their mother's milk, are known as suckling or sucking pigs. They have been regarded as a delicacy in many cultures around the world for centuries. The extravagance of killing a juvenile animal while it is so small, rather than rearing it until it could feed more people, meant it was a luxury. An entire suckling pig was generally roasted whole and has long been associated with feasting, known to have been popular in ancient Greek and Roman feasts. From an eating point of view, the flesh of suckling pigs is pale and tender, while the succulent crackling produced by the roasted skin is highly regarded.

In Chinese wedding banquets, where each dish served has a symbolic value, the suckling pig represents virtue and purity, with its serving at the marriage feast symbolizing fertility. On the Indonesian island of Bali (with a large Hindu population), a suckling pig dish called *babi guling* is served on special occasions such as weddings or blessings. For this, the piglet is stuffed with an aromatic paste of herbs and spices, then cooked over an open fire. In the French writer Gustave Flaubert's novel *Madame Bovary* (1856), the wedding breakfast features a suckling pig as its centerpiece: "The table was set up inside the cartshed. On it were four sirloins of beef, six fricassees of chicken, casseroled veal, three legs of mutton and, in the center, a beautiful roasted sucking pig, flanked by four chitterlings with sorrel."

Suckling pig, known as *cochon de lait*, is a feature of U.S. Cajun cuisine. Cooking the dish was traditionally a community event, in which a whole piglet, seasoned with spices and herbs, was roasted over a pecan wood fire. The town of Mansura, Louisiana, claims to be the capital of *cochon de lait*. Each year, Mansura holds an annual celebratory festival at which this historic dish is consumed with relish.

CHAR SIU
(CHINESE BARBECUED PORK)

Serves 4

Preparation 10 minutes,
  plus 4 hours marinating

Cooking 1 hour

1 lb 2 oz rindless pork loin
  fillet, cut into 2-inch-wide
  strips

3 tbsp light soy sauce

3 tbsp granulated sugar

1 tbsp Chinese rice wine

1 tbsp hoisin sauce

1 tsp Chinese five-spice
  powder (optional)

Honey, for glazing

This popular Chinese pork dish can be eaten either warm from the oven or at room temperature, often accompanied simply by steamed rice and blanched Chinese greens (such as bok choy, *choy sum*, or *gai lan*) tossed with oyster sauce.

1 Thoroughly mix together the soy sauce, sugar, rice wine, hoisin sauce, and Chinese five-spice powder, if using, to make the marinade.

2 Place the pork in a large bowl and coat evenly and thoroughly with the marinade. Cover and marinate in the fridge for at least 4 hours or overnight.

3 Preheat the oven to 400°F. Pour boiling water into a deep roasting pan to about an inch in depth. Place a rack above the water, layer the marinated pork strips on the rack, and brush well with the marinade. Reserve the remaining marinade.

4 Roast the pork for 30 minutes. Turn over the pork strips, brush with the remaining marinade, and return the pork to the oven. Reduce the oven temperature to 350°F and roast the pork for 30 minutes more until cooked through.

5 Remove the pork from the oven and brush the pork strips thoroughly with honey, coating all sides with a thin layer. Serve hot or at room temperature.

CHARCUTERIE

Historically, the killing of a pig was followed at once by butchering and processing the carcass before the meat could go bad. With admirable thriftiness, reflecting the value of meat and fat, a use was found for every part. Certain cuts and organs were set aside for immediate consumption, while other parts were transformed into items that could be preserved for the future. "Everything but the squeal" was used, as the expressive phrase goes. For example, after slaughter, the pig would be bled, resulting in a large quantity of blood that needed to be used very quickly before it went off. Blood sausages, such as black pudding, made by mixing the blood with chopped pork fat and cereal or chopped onion to bind it, and placing the mixture in the pig's intestines, were a practical response. The ancient Greek poet Homer even mentions blood sausages in the *Odyssey* (c. 675–725 BCE). Blood sausages are found across Europe, with France, in particular, having a rich tradition of *boudin noir* (black pudding). It is produced by butchers in numerous regional variations, such as the addition of chopped apple in Normandy or chestnuts in the Auvergne.

The term *charcuterie*, applied to the products made from pork, comes from the French *char cuit*, meaning "cooked meat." It dates to the fifteenth century, when tradesmen in Paris were allowed to prepare, cook, and sell pork flesh and fat. The tradition grew up of specialist shops called charcuteries that sold their own-made pork delicacies. These were wide ranging and included fresh and cured sausages, *crepinettes* (sausage-meat patties, wrapped in caul fat), *andouilles* (tripe-filled sausages), hams, pâtés such as *pâté de campagne*, *fromage de tête* (head cheese or brawn), terrines, and *rillettes* (made by cooking meat in lard, then pounding it into a paste and potting it). In addition, within this range were many regional variations, adding to the richness of French charcuterie. Creating this range of products took time and skill, and the French are justly proud of their charcuterie inheritance.

> *The term* charcuterie, *applied to the products made from pork, comes from the French* char cuit, *meaning "cooked meat." It dates to the fifteenth century, when tradesmen in Paris were allowed to prepare, cook, and sell pork flesh and fat.*

Italy, too, is a country with a proud tradition of pork charcuterie, including dry-cured ham (see p. 36). Among its specialties are the cured sausages known as salami, which require no cooking and can simply be sliced and eaten. *Salame milanese* is among the best known, as it is widely produced. A Tuscan specialty is *salame finocchiona*, distinctively flavored with fennel seeds. Salamis from the south of Italy, such as *salame napoletano*, are characteristically piquant affairs, flavored with chile. Among the most prized is *salame di Felino*, a refined salami flavored with wine and pepper, produced near Parma from the same breed of pigs from which Parma ham is made. Distinguished by its large size and bright pink color, *mortadella*, sold in delicatessens alongside salami, is a smooth-textured cooked pork sausage, originally from Bologna. It is flavored with peppercorns, and the best-quality mortadella is studded with pistachios. Mortadella is not only sliced and eaten, but also used in pasta fillings and meatballs.

Less well known outside Italy is *lardo*, a specialty made by curing pork back fat with salt and aromatic herbs and spices. The two best-known types of *lardo* come from Tuscany, where the fat is cured in marble containers, and the Valle d'Aosta, where it is cured in glass containers. It is classically eaten finely sliced, either on its own or with bread, as an antipasto.

Another historic Italian delicacy produced from pork is *culatello di Zibello*, made from the fillet of a pig's thigh. It was first mentioned in the fifteenth century, and where and how it is made is strictly regulated by a Protected Designation of Origin (PDO). The pork is salted and tied up with twine to form a characteristic pear shape, then aged in humid conditions for at least twelve months, during which time it develops a rich aroma, a soft texture, and characteristic sweetness of flavor.

CHINESE CHARCUTERIE

China, as befits the importance of pork within its cuisine, has a long history of pork-based charcuterie. Jinhua ham is a salt-cured ham, produced since the Tang dynasty (618–907 CE), which is when scholars have found the first recorded reference to it, in the city of Jinhua in Zhejiang, eastern China. The ham is historically made from the legs of China's *liangtouwu* pig (nicknamed "two ends black" or the "panda pig" because of its distinctive black and white markings), a slow-growing breed noted for the flavor of its meat. Production of the ham traditionally begins during the cold winter months with the salting of the fresh pork. The hams are then washed, shaped, dried, and matured for a number of months. The resulting ham is a highly prized delicacy, reputedly enjoyed by the First Emperor of the Song dynasty (960–1279 CE) and written about in the famous Chinese novel *Dream of the Red Chamber* (1791), by Cao Xueqin.

A deep red in color, Jinhua ham has a dense, chewy texture and complex, salty flavor. Classically, in Chinese cookery, it is used as a flavor enhancer rather than being eaten in its own right, as with Italy's Parma

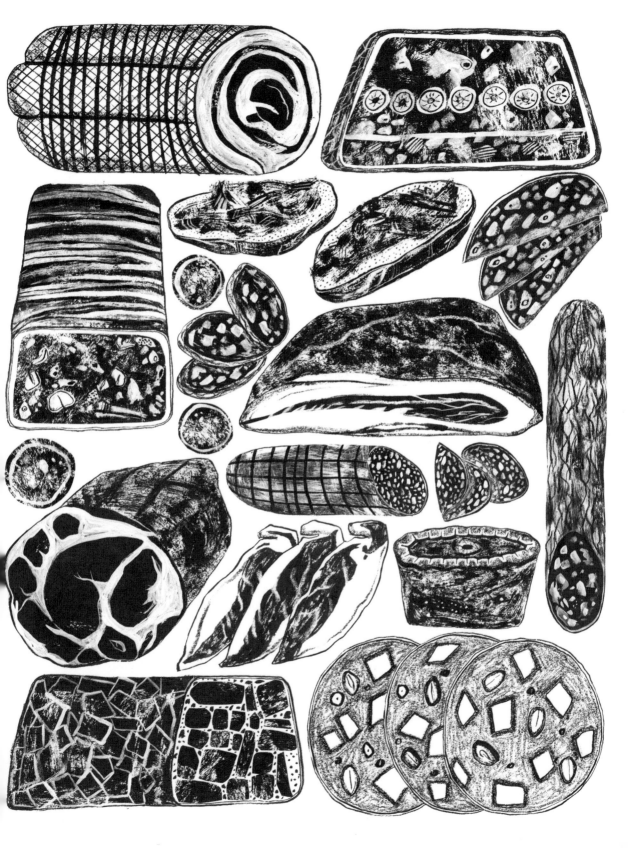

ham or Spain's *serrano* ham. It features in braised dishes and soups, such as "Buddha jumps over the wall," a tempting and luxurious soup filled with assorted expensive delicacies such as abalone and scallops.

A more affordable, everyday Chinese charcuterie item is the *lap cheong* sausage. A generic name meaning "waxed sausage" or "waxed intestine," *lap cheong* is a dried, cured, visibly fatty pork sausage flavored with salt and sugar, which help to preserve it. Sometimes it is also enriched with rice wine or rose liqueur. Variations include sausages made with pig or duck liver and spiced sausages flavored with aromatic Chinese five-spice powder or Szechuan peppercorns. *Lap cheong* sausage has a distinctive firm, chewy texture and is always cooked before eating, featuring in dim sum dishes such as lotus leaf–wrapped sticky rice parcels or turnip cake. *Lap yuk* is Chinese preserved pork belly—either air-cured or smoked—that is used to add flavor, richness, and texture to dishes like clay-pot rice or stir-fried rice.

BACON

A familiar presence on breakfast tables in Britain and the United States, bacon is a popular form of cured pork, made from the side of a pig. Different cuts of meat result in different types of bacon, with pork belly used to produce what is called "streaky bacon" (where the meat is streaked with fat), while leaner "back bacon" comes from the back of the pig.

Traditionally, bacon was made by dry curing the fresh meat with salt, then often smoking it to extend its life. In rural communities, bacon was an important food, used to add flavor to a restricted diet. The English pamphleteer, writer, and farmer William Cobbett wrote of its importance in *Cottage Economy* (1821), observing that the possession by cottagers of a couple of flitches (sides) of bacon "tends more to keep a man from stealing than whole volumes of penal statutes." In Britain, regional cures developed, with Wiltshire bacon (named after a county noted for pork production) being mentioned in 1794. Isabella Beeton, author of the Victorian bestseller *The Book of Household Management* (1861), describes the Wiltshire cure for bacon as using salt and sugar. In Scotland, Ayrshire bacon was a distinctive cure, in which the carcass was not scalded and the bacon was rolled into a round. In the county of Suffolk one finds the tradition of Suffolk sweet-cured bacon (sometimes called black bacon), with the use of molasses in the cure and hot smoking giving a sweet flavor and distinctive dark rind. The industrialization of bacon production saw the development of wet brining and the widespread usage of needle-cure methods, in which the pork flesh is injected with brine in order to speed up the time-consuming curing process.

SAUTÉED CHORIZO
WITH RED WINE

Serves 4
Preparation 10 minutes
Cooking 16 minutes

Tasty chorizo sausage, made from pork flavored with paprika, or *pimentón*, is a popular ingredient in Spain. This quick and easy recipe is for a classic tapas dish, enjoyed in Spanish bars with a glass of wine. When shopping for the ingredients, bear in mind that fresh cooking chorizo is needed for this recipe, rather than the dry, cured chorizo that can be eaten without cooking.

1 tbsp olive oil

4 fresh chorizo sausages,
  cut into 1-inch pieces

1 onion, peeled and sliced

1 garlic clove, peeled and
  chopped

½ cup red wine

Chopped parsley, to garnish
  (optional)

Rustic bread, sliced, to serve

1   Heat the olive oil in a heavy skillet. Add the chorizo and fry over medium heat for 5 minutes, stirring often, until lightly browned.

2   Add the onion and fry, stirring, for 5 minutes until lightly browned on all sides. Add the garlic and fry for 1 minute, until fragrant.

3   Add the red wine and cook for 5 minutes, stirring often to coat the chorizo in the red wine sauce.

4   Garnish with parsley and serve the chorizo at once, with rustic bread to mop up the tasty juices.

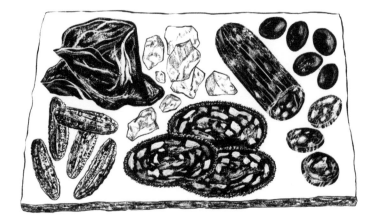

CHINESE PORK POTSTICKERS

Makes 20 potstickers
Preparation 25 minutes
Cooking 12 minutes

The Chinese have a great tradition of pork dumplings, which are added to soups, steamed, or fried. These small, flavorful potsticker dumplings, stuffed with a tasty pork mixture and served with a dipping sauce, make an excellent first course for a Chinese-inspired meal.

4 oz ground pork

1 scallion, finely chopped

1 garlic clove, finely chopped

1 tsp finely chopped ginger root

1 tbsp light soy sauce

1 tsp rice wine

1 tsp sesame oil

20 gyoza wrappers

1 tbsp vegetable oil

⅓ cup cold water, plus more
   if needed

DIPPING SAUCE

4 tbsp light soy sauce

1 tbsp Chinese rice vinegar

1 tsp sesame oil

1 tsp finely chopped ginger root

1   First prepare the filling. In a mixing bowl, mix the pork, scallion, garlic, and ginger together thoroughly. Add the soy sauce, rice wine, and sesame oil and mix in well.

2   Place a heaped teaspoon of the pork mixture in the center of a gyoza wrapper. Brush the edges lightly with a little water and bring the wrapper over the filling, pressing together the edges well and pleating by pinching with your fingers. Repeat the process until all the gyoza wrappers have been filled.

3   Heat the oil in a large, lidded, heavy, nonstick skillet until very hot. Add the dumplings, flat side down, in a single layer in the pan. Reduce the heat to medium and fry for 2 minutes until the bottoms of the dumplings are lightly browned.

4   Pour the water into the skillet over the dumplings. Cover at once, reduce the heat to medium-low, and cook for 10 minutes, checking halfway through. If, when you check at this stage, all the water has cooked off, add a further 2–3 tablespoons of water, cover, and cook for 5 minutes.

5   While the dumplings are cooking, mix together the dipping sauce ingredients.

6   Serve the freshly cooked dumplings with the dipping sauce in a side bowl.

In Italy, pork belly, the same cut used to produce streaky bacon, is seasoned with salt and spices, cured, and transformed into pancetta. It is produced in two forms: *tesa*, in which the piece is left in its original shape, and *arrotolata*, in which the meat is rolled up into a circular form. In the Italian kitchen, chopped pancetta *tesa* is used along with onion and celery in *soffrito*—the fried flavoring mixture that is the first step in creating many Italian dishes.

SAUSAGES

Among the classic products of pork charcuterie is the humble sausage. Fresh, cured, and cooked sausages are found in numerous forms wherever pigs are kept for meat. The word sausage comes from the Latin *salsicia*, which in turn derives from *salus*, meaning "salted," with salt being essential for preserving fresh meat. Pork sausages were made from chopped, salted meat, often stuffed into natural casing made from the pig's intestines. Sausage making traces its roots to antiquity. Ancient Greek writer Aristophanes mentions blood sausages in his play *The Knights* (424 BCE). In *On the Subject of Cooking* (c. 900 CE), a collection of his recipes, first-century Roman gourmet Apicius mentions *luganega* sausage, a mild sausage made to this day in Italy.

What is striking about the world of sausages is the huge variety of flavors and textures within it. Fresh sausages, designed to be cooked and eaten soon after making, are flavored in numerous ways, with national, regional, and individual variations. Spices and herbs are a traditional addition, the former valued for their preservative properties as well as for their flavor. Britain's Cumberland sausage is seasoned generously with black pepper and chopped sage. The chorizo (*chourico*) sausage found in Spain and Portugal has a distinctive orange-red color and flavor due to the addition of sweet or hot *pimentón* (Spanish paprika). In Thailand, pork sausages are flavored with aromatic lemongrass, kaffir lime leaves, galangal, and chile to spicy effect. Fennel or garlic are popular flavorings in Italy for fresh sausages, known as *salsicce*.

What is striking about the world of sausages is the huge variety of flavors and textures within it. Fresh sausages, designed to be cooked and eaten soon after making, are flavored in numerous ways.

Sausages play a central, much-loved role in German cuisine, with around 1,500 varieties to be found. These fall into three overall categories: *brühwurst* (scalded sausages, which require heating through before eating), *kochwurst* (fully cooked sausages), and *rohwurst* (raw). By far the most popular type of sausage in Germany is the *brühwurst*, an example of which is the *bockwurst*, made from a mixture of veal and pork and flavored with paprika and chives. It was German-speaking Central European immigrants who introduced this type of sausage into the United States during the nineteenth century, and to great effect. The U.S. hot dog traces its origins to the frankfurter (a slender, smoked pork sausage originating from Frankfurt) and the *wiener* or *wurstel*, a similar sausage made in Vienna from a mixture of pork and beef. In the United States, these types of sausages became known as "franks" or "wienies." Where and when the frankfurter or wiener was first placed in a bun, creating the hot dog, are disputed. Certainly by the late nineteenth century, frankfurters and wienies in buns were being sold in a number of U.S. cities. Today the hot dog is an iconic U.S. food, one that is also widely eaten around the world.

HAMS

Hams, historically made from the pig's hind leg, have long been esteemed. In *De Agri Cultura* (c. 160 BCE), the Roman senator and historian Cato the Elder described how hams were made by salting legs of pork, then drying and smoking them. Smoking was used to preserve the meat, but it was also valued for the flavor the process adds. Germany's Black Forest ham, named after the region where it originated, and France's Bayonne ham are two well-known examples of European smoked hams. In the United States, Smithfield ham is a historic product named after a town in Virginia. Genuine Smithfield ham is cold smoked over a fire made from oak, hickory, and applewood to create flavor and matured for at least six months.

Among the most highly prized of pork charcuterie items, however, are dry-cured hams. These are created from pork legs that are first salted, rested, and then carefully cured in specific conditions for a number of months. During this period, the ham dries out and changes in texture while also developing in flavor. Italy's Parma ham is a notable example of an air-dried ham. Also in Italy, one finds *prosciutto San Daniele*—from the Friuli Venezia Giuli region and named after the town of San Daniele, where it has long been produced—which is matured for at least thirteen months and characterized by a sweetness of flavor.

In Spain, *jamón* (dry-cured ham) is a much-loved food, central to the country's cuisine and with a legendary history of production. It is estimated that Spain produces more than 40 million dry-cured hams a year, while the average annual consumption of *jamón* for each Spaniard exceeds 7 pounds. Broadly speaking, there are two types of *jamón* in Spain, with the breed of

GLAZED BAKED HAM

Serves 8–10
Preparation 25 minutes,
  plus overnight soaking
Cooking 4 hours

A whole glazed baked ham is a splendid sight and traditionally has been associated with special celebrations, such as Christmas. Large enough to feed a crowd, the ham can be served either warm from the oven or at room temperature, making it an excellent dish for entertaining, as it can be made ahead of time.

One 11-lb raw smoked or
  unsmoked ham, bone in
1 onion, peeled and quartered
2 carrots, cut into chunks
Small bunch of parsley
2 celery sticks, roughly
  chopped

GLAZE
6 tbsp soft light brown sugar
2 tsp grated orange zest
1 tbsp mustard powder
Cloves for studding the ham

1 Soak the ham overnight in cold water to remove any excess salt.
2 The next day, drain and place the ham in a large pan with the onion, carrot, parsley, and celery. Cover the ham with cold water, bring to the boil, and cook briskly for 5 minutes, skimming off any scum that forms on the surface of the water. Cover the pan and simmer very gently for 3 hours 40 minutes, until cooked through.
3 Remove the ham from the water, reserving the water to use as stock for soups.
4 Preheat the oven to 425°F.
5 Once the ham is cool enough to handle, carefully cut off the skin, leaving a good layer of white fat. Cut a diagonal criss-cross pattern in the fat, forming diamonds.
6 Make the glaze by mixing together the brown sugar, orange zest, and mustard powder. Spread this mixture evenly over the fat. Then push a clove into the center of each scored diamond.
7 Place the ham on a baking sheet and bake for about 15 minutes to set the glaze. Serve warm from the oven or at room temperature.

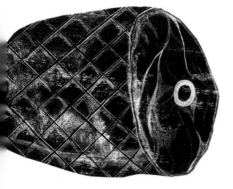

the pig being the starting point for differentiation. The first is called *jamón serrano* and is made from European white pigs (*cerdos blancos*), which gain weight quickly. The majority of dry-cured ham produced in Spain is *jamón serrano*, and while there are notable producers, it is regarded as the "everyday" *jamón*. The second type of *jamón* is called *jamón ibérico* and is produced from Spain's indigenous Iberian pigs, a dark-haired, black-footed breed, affectionately known as *pata negra* pigs because of their black hooves. This breed is slower to fatten and has smaller litters than the European white pigs. Only around 10 percent of Spain's *jamón* is *jamón ibérico*, and ham from these pigs is considered a delicacy.

The way in which the pigs are reared and fed plays a part in how the ham made from their meat is classified. *De cebo* is the term for farm-reared pigs fed on a diet of grain. *De recebo* is used to describe free-range pigs allowed access to pasture and fed on a mixture of grains with some acorns. The most highly prized is *jamón ibérico de bellota*. This ham is made from Iberian pigs that are allowed to wander freely through the *dehesa* (a woodland system containing holm and cork oaks found in the regions of Andalusia, Extramadura, and Salamanca). The acorn season, known as the *montanera*, sees acorns (*bellotas*) falling from the oak trees in large quantities to cover the ground from fall to spring. It is these acorns, eaten with relish by the roaming Iberian pigs, which give their flesh the particular sweet, nutty depth of flavor for which *jamón ibérico de bellota* is noted. The acorns, with their high levels of oleic acid, also have an additional benefit, creating a *jamón* that is high in unsaturated fats, which promote the creation of "good" cholesterol in the body and reduce the levels of "bad" cholesterol; the ham is rich in nutrients and very digestible. Curing the *jamón ibérico de bellota* is a skillfully controlled process, during which the salted meat is subject to different temperatures at key stages. It is matured for up to three years, by which time the ham has developed an extraordinary degree of umami-rich flavor. Traditionally, this most luxurious of hams is handsliced into small, fine pieces and served at room temperature, so that its full aroma can be released and appreciated.

PORK FAT

Historically, the pig was an important and invaluable source not just of meat, but also of fat, known as lard. In rural households, one of the tasks carried out after the annual slaughter of the pig was the rendering of fat from the carcass. This was done by cutting off the fat, chopping or mincing it, and then slowly and gently heating the solid fat, without burning

it, until it was liquid enough to be strained clean of any residue. Fat from different parts of the pig's carcass varied in texture and flavor and was valued accordingly. Traditionally, the most highly prized was the leaf or flare lard, made from the fat deposited around the kidneys and inside the loin, valued for its whiteness and neutral flavor. The layer of firm-textured back fat was also valued, used to help create charcuterie products such as salamis or rendered down into good-quality lard. The least-regarded lard was that extracted from the "soft fat" between internal organs and muscle layers.

Once rendered, the lard could be kept and used for several months. One of the side-products of the rendering process was the creation of cracklings—little, crisp, brown pieces of cooked fat and skin. In the United States, these were skimmed off, dried, ground, and stored, often used to flavor johnnycakes, the traditional corn-based hearth breads, something that U.S. writer Laura Ingalls Wilder records in her *Little House* (1932–43) series of children's books.

In many countries, including the United States, lard was an essential cooking fat for many centuries. In China, lard was used as a frying medium to add richness to certain dishes. In Central and South America, lard was widely used in cooking, for frying, and in dishes such as tamales. Accounts of domestic hog slaughtering in the United States make clear the importance of lard—this rendered fat would be stored and used for a year, until the pig-killing season came round once again. It was a versatile culinary fat, which was used in a variety of ways, as a spread, it was usually eaten on slices of bread. Its high smoke point means it is excellent for deep-frying, with North America's fried chicken classically cooked in lard.

Due to its crystal structure, lard makes an effective shortener for pastry, for which it was historically much used. In South America, lard is used to make the dough for empanadas, creating its characteristic tender texture. The British pork pie is a historic delicacy, associated with the market town of Melton Mowbray, Leicestershire, since the eighteenth century. The crust enclosing the pork filling is made from lard, flour, and hot water. Another historic British treat, found most commonly in rural areas noted for pig rearing, was the lardy cake, a rich creation made from a lard-enriched sweet dough enhanced with spices and dried fruits. Very much a luxury, this was a celebratory cake, often made at harvest time.

Fat's ability to help preserve foods also means that lard is used in this way. The southwest of France has a venerable tradition of confit, a word that comes from confire, *"to preserve."*

Fat's ability to help preserve foods also means that lard is used in this way. The southwest of France has a venerable tradition of confit, a word that comes from *confire*, meaning "to preserve." In making confit, cuts of meat from animals and birds that are naturally rich in fat—pigs, ducks, geese—are first cured with salt and then cooked very slowly and gently in their own fat. After cooling, the confit was traditionally placed in special clay pots and stored in a cool, dry place where it would keep for several months. Confit, with its distinctive melting texture, is very much a delicacy, eaten either hot or cold, often accompanied by a cleansing dandelion or chicory salad to cut through the richness.

In recent decades, the use of lard as a cooking fat has declined in many countries around the world, as people switch to oils and margarine, which are perceived as healthier options. Animal fats such as butter and lard are, however, making something of a comeback, as research suggests that their negative reputation on health grounds may have been misplaced.

TOAD IN THE HOLE

Serves 4
Preparation 15 minutes
Cooking 45 minutes

No one really knows how this much-loved traditional British sausage dish achieved its striking, idiosyncratic name, but presumably it's due to the appearance of the sausages peeping through the batter. It's a popular family favorite, enjoyed in households to this day.

1 cup all-purpose flour

Pinch of salt

2 eggs

1¼ cups milk

2 tbsp sunflower or
   vegetable oil

8 sausages

ONION GRAVY

1 tbsp oil

2 onions, peeled and
   finely sliced

1 bay leaf

Splash of dry red wine

1¼ cups chicken stock

Salt and freshly ground
   black pepper

1 Preheat the oven to 425°F.
2 First prepare the batter. Sift the flour and salt into a mixing bowl. Break the two eggs into the center. Gradually whisk in the milk, mixing well, until a thick, smooth batter forms. Set aside to stand.
3 Heat the oil in a small roasting pan on the stove, tipping the pan to coat it evenly. Add the sausages and roast in the oven for 15 minutes, turning now and then, until evenly browned.
4 Pour the batter into the pan around the sausages and bake for a further 30 minutes until risen and golden brown all over.
5 Meanwhile, make the onion gravy. Heat the oil in a skillet. Add the onions and bay leaf and fry over medium-low heat, stirring now and then, for 10 minutes, until the onions are lightly browned. Add the red wine and cook for 2–3 minutes until largely evaporated.
6 Add the stock, bring to a boil, reduce the heat, and simmer for 10–15 minutes, until the stock has reduced. Season with salt and pepper.
7 Serve the toad in the hole straight from the oven with the onion gravy on the side.

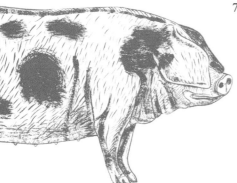

HONEY

Sweetness is one of the five tastes that our tongues detect and to which human beings are naturally attracted. Honey was for many centuries our primary sweetener and as such was hugely valued. In many cultures, honey was seen as a gift from the gods to humankind.

Honey—a natural sweetener—is made by honey bees. Of the 20,000 species of bee (members of the genus *Apis*), there are only seven recognized species of honeybee, the most common of these being the Western honeybee (*Apis mellifera*). It is solely these species that produce honey from nectar, storing it in their nests as a food source to see the bee colony through the winter. Honey—which is composed of 82 percent carbohydrates and 18 percent water—is predominantly made up of more than twenty types of sugars, mostly fructose and glucose, and, at lower levels, maltose, sucrose, and other complex carbohydrates. It is also acidic, with an average pH of 3.9, but this is masked by the sweetness. It is this industriously gathered, carefully stored sweet substance that humans have long prized, first gathering it from bees in the wild, then developing a system of beekeeping that allows for the harvesting of honey from groups of bees.

The human relationship with wild honey is an ancient one, but when or where human beings first started eating wild honey is information lost in time. Given our ability to taste sweetness and the pleasure it gives our bodies, human beings would naturally have relished honey when they came across this mysterious, astonishingly sweet substance inside wild bees' nests. In the same way that wild animals, such as bears or monkeys, seek out wild bees' nests to eat the honey found within, so, too, did human beings. One of the earliest depictions of honey gathering is a prehistoric cave painting in the Cuevas de la Araña (Spider Caves) in Valencia, Spain, thought to be around 8,000 to 10,000 years old. The image shows a human figure either using ropes or vines or standing on a ladder (depending on interpretation), taking honey from a wild bees' nest, while bees hover ominously nearby. Given the understandable aggression of hundreds of bees with the capacity to sting, facing the loss of their precious honey, this was dangerous work. Honey hunting still carries on to this day among aboriginal people in Africa, Asia, Australia, and South America. Contemporary photographs of the Gurung tribesmen of Nepal collecting honey from the Himalayan cliffs, as they have done for centuries, strikingly resemble that ancient cave painting.

Over the millennia, honey from the wild continued to be collected by human beings. It is in ancient Egypt that we first come across records of beekeeping or apiculture. Reliefs on the wall of the sun temple Shesepibre (meaning "Delight of Ra"), constructed around 2,400 BCE, show scenes of beekeeping, complete with hives and, possibly, the act of blowing smoke to tranquilize the bees. Honey was very important to the ancient Egyptians, with its use controlled by the authorities; government officials had titles such as "Sealer of the Honey" or "Overseer of All Beekeepers." The practice of beekeeping—in which human beings provided the bees with artificial hives, then took the honey that the bees stored there—became widespread in many countries. For example, it is known that beekeeping was practiced in the Levant by 1500 BCE, as Hittite laws lay down penalties for stealing swarms and beehives. In China during the sixth century BCE, the Chinese statesman Fan Li wrote about beekeeping in his book *Golden Rules of Business Success*. In Mesoamerica, both the Aztecs and the Maya kept stingless American honey bees. In medieval Europe, abbeys and monasteries were important centers of beekeeping; the honey was used for sweetening and to make mead (see p. 68), while the wax collected from the hives was used for candles.

So useful were honey bees that human beings introduced them to new territories around the globe through conquest or trade. The honeybee is not native to North America but was introduced from Europe by colonists in the early 1600s. Studies of the genome of the United States honeybee have shown it to be derived from three European subspecies. The Spanish are credited with bringing European honey bees to Central and South America in the nineteenth century. English colonists introduced their native honeybee to Australia and New Zealand during the nineteenth century.

Honey, humanity's historic sweetener, was highly prized; in the Bible, the Promised Land is described several times as "a land flowing with milk and honey," and thus abundant in good things. It is noticeable how bees and honey feature in religions and folklore worldwide (see p. 54). Honey was regarded as a gift from the gods and appreciated for its therapeutic

HONEY CAKE

Makes one 8-inch cake
Preparation 15 minutes
Cooking 45 minutes

In many cultures, honey cakes—symbolic of sweetness and prosperity—are served to celebrate special festivals. This light-textured, fragrant cake is very much a treat, ideal for serving with a cup of tea or coffee.

4 eggs, separated

⅔ cup superfine sugar

1 stick salted butter, softened, plus extra for greasing

1 tsp cinnamon powder

½ tsp nutmeg powder

3 heaping tbsp honey

2 tbsp orange juice

Grated zest of 1 orange

1½ cups self-rising flour, sifted

1   Preheat the oven to 320°F. Grease and line an 8-inch, loose-based cake pan.

2   Whisk the egg whites until soft peaks form. Gradually whisk in 2 ounces of the sugar until stiff peaks form. Set aside.

3   Use a wooden spoon to cream together the butter and the remaining sugar. Beat in the egg yolks, one at a time. Mix in the cinnamon and nutmeg. Mix in the honey thoroughly, then the orange juice and zest.

4   Use a metal spoon to gently fold in the flour, then fold in the whisked egg whites. Transfer the cake batter to the prepared cake pan.

5   Bake for 45 minutes until risen and golden brown. Check that the cake is cooked through by inserting a skewer or toothpick; if it comes out clean, then the cake is ready.

6   Let cool before serving.

properties (see p. 62). Humanity has a long-standing fascination with the intricate social structure of the beehive, and the worker bee often has been cited as an example of a model citizen. The ancient Roman naturalist Pliny the Elder, in his *Natural History* (77–79 CE), wrote of their organization:

> *Nature is so great that from a tiny, ghost-like creature she has made something incomparable. What sinews or muscles can we compare with the enormous efficiency and industry shown by bees?*

The English playwright William Shakespeare wrote of the obedience of honeybees in *Henry V* (1599):

> *Creatures that by a rule in nature teach*
> *The act of order to a peopled kingdom.*
> *They have a king, and officers of sorts,*
> *Where some like magistrates correct at home,*
> *Others like merchants venture trade abroad,*
> *Others like soldiers armed in their stings*
> *Make boot upon the summer's velvet buds,*
> *Which pillage they with merry march bring home*
> *To the tent-royal of their emperor,*
> *Who, busied in his majesties, surveys*
> *The singing masons building roofs of gold,*
> *The civil citizens kneading up the honey,*
> *The poor mechanic porters crowding in*
> *Their heavy burdens at his narrow gate,*
> *The sad-eyed justice with his surly hum*
> *Delivering o'er to executors pale*
> *The lazy yawning drone.*

Honey's role as a primary sweetener, however, was challenged by the rise of sugar. Initially made from the sweet juice of sugar cane, sugar in medieval times was very expensive and time-consuming to produce. By the eighteenth century, however, sugar—due to the use of slave labor on colonial plantations—had become more affordable and available. Honey is today far more expensive than sugar or other artificial sweeteners. While considered as something of a luxury rather than an essential, honey is still regarded with affection, associated with childhood, and, interestingly, it continues to be seen as an ingredient with special, health-giving properties (see p. 62).

When it comes to bees, however, we now know what a vital role honey bees play as pollinators in agriculture. Through their busy quest for nectar, honey bees carry pollen with them from flower to flower, ensuring that fertilization happens and our crops have fruitful yields. Worryingly, honey bees are in decline, facing a number of challenges. A destructive parasitic pest

called the varroa bee mite (*Varroa jacobsoni*) has spread through bee colonies around the world, with only Australia currently free from it. Its effects on bees are devastating, and it is thought it might be a factor in a syndrome called colony collapse disorder. An active concern over the decline of bees has inspired a rise in amateur beekeeping in Europe and the United States (see "Urban Beekeeping," p. 57); the honeybee, it is clear, is still important to us.

HOW HONEY IS MADE

Honey is the food that honey bees make for themselves from nectar. This simple description belies the amount of time and effort that honey bees put into creating this sweet substance, which they store for future sustenance.

Honey bees are social insects that live together in colonies in hives. The intricate social structure of a hive sees the bees working together, each with their own clearly defined roles, for the good of the hive as a whole. At the top of the pyramid—and central to the hive's existence—is the queen bee, recognizable by her large abdomen. Having mated with drones—the male bees whose purpose within the hive is solely to mate with the queen—she lays fertilized eggs, which hatch into the worker bees. These worker bees carry out a range of tasks within the hive, such as cleaning and maintaining it and feeding the larvae and young drones. The life cycle of a bee colony follows a seasonal pattern, expanding in the spring, when the queen will lay up to 2,000 eggs a day. Summer is a busy time for the hive, the period in which the bees make and store honey. Winter sees the hive colony reduce in size considerably, with the remaining bees using the stored honey to sustain themselves throughout the cold, wet months.

Honey is created from sweet, watery nectar, collected from flowers by forager bees, who each store the nectar they find in a special honey stomach and carry it back to the hive. Here, honey-making bees take the nectar from the forager and set to work transforming this thin liquid into honey, adding enzymes to it by chewing it and breaking down the complex plant sugars into simpler, more digestible sugars. The thickened nectar syrup—transformed into what we call honey—is stored in hexagonal wax honey cells, which form into honeycomb. The bees fan the freshly made honey with their wings in order to evaporate any excess water within it and add extra enzymes to it. Once the moisture content has been reduced to 18.6 percent or less, they cap the cells with a thin layer of wax to keep the honey safe inside. A worker bee will produce only one-tenth to one-twelfth of a teaspoon of honey in her life. It is estimated that bees need to visit around two million flowers in order to produce 1 pound of honey.

Beekeeping, or apiculture, is the keeping of bee colonies by human beings, usually in human-made hives, in order to harvest their honey and wax. Bees naturally build their hives in places such as hollow trees or rocky cavities, within which they build a complex structure of wax cells. Human beekeepers, however, have developed artificial hives for the bees to live in—a practice dating back to the ancient Egyptians. In Europe, there was a long tradition of keeping bees in skeps (baskets). In order to harvest the honey, the bees were killed or driven away and the skep destroyed. Over the centuries, however, innovations in hive shapes and structures were adopted by beekeepers, which allowed the honey to be harvested without destroying the colony in the process. In 1682, the English clergyman and travel writer George Wheler described and drew a beehive he had observed in Greece. This "Greek hive," an inverted skep with wooden bars placed across the top, is taken to be an early version of the modern top-bar hive, a single-story hive in which the honeycomb hangs from removable bars.

HOT TODDY

Serves 4
Preparation 5 minutes

This classic mixture of whiskey, honey, and lemon juice is often served as a remedy for coughs and colds. One thing is for sure—it is a warming, comforting drink, perfect for cold winter days.

½ cup whiskey

4 tbsp honey

Juice of 1 lemon

1¾ cups water

4 cinnamon sticks (optional)

1 Mix together the whiskey, honey, and lemon juice in a heatproof pitcher.

2 Bring the water to a simmer in a small pan. Add the hot water to the whiskey mixture, stirring well.

3 Pour the hot whiskey mixture into four heatproof mugs, garnish with the cinnamon sticks, if using, and use them to stir the drink.

In 1789, the Swiss naturalist François Huber invented the leaf hive, a fully movable frame hive in which the frames open like the pages of a book.

It was in 1851 that a major, widely adopted breakthrough in beehive design occurred. The U.S. clergyman and apiarist Lorenzo Langstroth invented an innovative top-opening beehive with fully removable frames, which he patented in 1852. Importantly, Langstroth constructed the hive so that there was a ⅜-inch space between the sides of the frames and the main structure. The reason for this precise spacing was that bees build honeycomb to fill spaces larger than ⅜ inch and use propolis (the resinous substance known as bee glue) to fill spaces smaller than ¼ inch. Langstroth's ingenious use of this gap, known as the bee space, allowed the bees to build their combs in each frame without sticking them to one another or the sides of the wall with propolis. In his seminal and influential work on beekeeping, *The Hive and the Honey Bee* (1853), Langstroth wrote of his wish to design a hive from which the honey could be harvested without killing the bees in the process: "The Huber hive had satisfied me that with proper precautions, the combs might be removed without enraging the bees, and that these insects were capable of being tamed to a surprising degree."

It was in 1851 that a major, widely adopted breakthrough in beehive design occurred. The U.S. clergyman and apiarist Lorenzo Langstroth invented an innovative top-opening beehive with fully removable frames.

Langstroth's invention of a beehive that was easily accessible to the beekeeper without unduly disturbing the bees also allowed the beekeeper to care for the bees in a way that skeps had not. "If I suspected anything was wrong with a hive, I could quickly ascertain its true condition, and apply the proper remedies," he observed.

He had discovered a practical way to keep bees without having to destroy them to harvest their honey, and one that also allowed beekeepers to care more actively for the insects because they could monitor them. It was a major breakthrough in the history of beekeeping. So influential was it that structures based on Langstroth's original remain the most widely used types of beehive to this day.

Beekeeping involves regular inspection of the hives in order to check the health of the bees, the laying pattern of the queen, and the quantity of honey that has been made. Ideally, what a beekeeper is trying to do is maintain healthy colonies of bees, which produce ample yields of honey. Several factors come into play, among them the weather. There are also a number of pests and diseases that can affect both the brood (the developing bees) and the adult insects. In times of little or no "nectar flow" (the term given to a period when at least one major nectar source is in blossom and the weather allows the bees to forage), or when honey stores within the colony are low, beekeepers may feed their bees honey syrup in order to stop them from starving. The period following a honey harvest, for example, usually sees feeding by the beekeeper taking place.

Natural factors also play a part. A prolonged period of wet weather, for example, can result in little foraging taking place, requiring extra supplies of sugar syrup. The bee hives need to be kept clean, as poor hygiene encourages pests and diseases.

Part of the work carried out by professional beekeepers is ensuring that the beehives are placed in locations that will result in a good honey harvest. In order to create monofloral honeys (see p. 64), beehives will be placed in the center of an area filled with one particular nectar source, such as in the center of a chestnut or pine forest or a grove of orange trees. While foraging bees can fly up to 5 miles in the search for nectar, the average journey is around 1 mile; otherwise they expend too much energy. The monofloral honey made by the bees must then be harvested by the beekeeper before the next nectar source comes into blossom, in order to have honey that displays the characteristics of the target flower or plant.

There is a long-established process for extracting honey from the hive. The beekeeper usually will harvest it at the end of nectar flow, when the hive is filled with cured honey that has been capped with wax. A beehive needs 20 to 30 pounds of honey to see it through the winter, but bees are capable of producing and storing much more, up to 60 pounds in a good season. It is the surplus honey that the beekeeper collects. Traditionally smoke, produced from a piece of gear called a smoker, is used to calm the bees. The scent of smoke causes the bees to go into survival mode, making them less aggressive and less likely to sting. It also masks the scent of the alarm pheromones released by the guard bees. The frames containing the honey are removed from the hive and taken away. In order to extract the honey, the wax capping must first be removed; this is done with devices ranging from a simple hand-held knife to automatic machinery. The uncapped frames are then placed in a centrifuge and spun round so that the honey is forced out, leaving the wax honeycomb structure intact within the frames. This stage is often carried out as quickly as possible after extracting the frames from the hive, so that the honey is still warm enough to flow easily. The emptied frames are then replaced within the beehive, so that the bees can set to work filling them once more.

BAKLAVA

Serves 8–10
Preparation 20 minutes
Cooking 1¼ hours

This classic Greek dish is sweetened and moistened with a fragrant honey syrup. Serve it for dessert or as an accompaniment to an espresso or coffee.

HONEY SYRUP
1½ cups granulated sugar
1¼ cups water
1 cinnamon stick
1 tbsp lemon juice
3 tbsp honey
1 tsp orange blossom or rose
   water (optional)

10 tbsp salted butter
3 cups walnuts or blanched
   almonds, roughly chopped
3 tbsp sugar
½ tsp cinnamon powder
14 sheets of phyllo pastry

1   Preheat the oven to 350°F. Grease an 11 x 7-inch cake pan.

2   Make the honey syrup. Place the sugar, water, cinnamon stick, and lemon juice in a small saucepan. Heat gently, stirring until the sugar has dissolved. Bring to a boil and cook for 5 minutes. Stir in the honey and simmer for a further 5 minutes. Remove from the stove, stir in the orange blossom or rose water (if using), and discard the cinnamon stick. Set aside to cool.

3   Gently melt the butter. Mix together the nuts, sugar, and cinnamon.

4   Take a sheet of the phyllo pastry, leaving the remainder covered with a clean dish towel to prevent it from drying out. Brush the phyllo with the melted butter and place it in the baking pan, tucking the edges up the sides of the pan. Repeat the process with half the phyllo sheets.

5   Spread the nut mixture evenly over the buttered phyllo in a layer. Top the nut mixture with the remaining phyllo, buttering each sheet as you do so. Fold the final sheet neatly over the layers and brush generously with the remaining melted butter. Chill for 15 minutes to set the baklava and make it easier to cut.

6   Use a sharp knife to cut the baklava into even-sized triangular shapes, but without cutting all the way to the base. Bake the baklava for 30 minutes. Reduce the heat to 300°F and continue cooking for a further 20–30 minutes until golden brown. Remove from the oven.

7   Pour the syrup evenly over the warm baklava, allowing it to soak into the pastry. Set aside until the syrup has been absorbed. Cut and serve the triangular baklava.

The extracted honey is first filtered in order to remove unwanted impurities such as dirt, dead bees, or wax. At this stage, the honey is ready to eat and can be transferred into containers, usually glass jars, ready for sale. Many larger producers pasteurize their honey, heating the honey to temperatures ranging from 145°F to 150°F. In the dairy world, milk is pasteurized to get rid of potentially harmful bacteria, which can live successfully in milk. Honey, however, due to its high acidity and innate antibacterial properties, does not need to be pasteurized on these grounds. Instead the pasteurizing process is carried out to inhibit the natural granulation process, which over time sees clear, liquid honey thickening and becoming opaque. Pasteurization affects the flavor of the honey, reducing its complexity. The phrase "raw honey" is used for honey that has not been heat-treated; usually this is honey produced by small-scale producers who are interested in showcasing their honey in its natural state. In addition to honey that they have extracted, beekeepers also sell pieces of honeycomb—the hexagonal-celled wax structure built by the bees—complete with honey inside the cells. Eating a piece of honeycomb is a very traditional way of enjoying honey; the wax is edible and adds texture and body to the eating experience. Pieces of honeycomb are usually eaten as they are or spread onto toast or bread.

When stored correctly—sealed and kept at room temperature in a dry atmosphere—honey has remarkable keeping properties, which allow it to be stored for years. It is important to ensure that it stays dry; even a few drops of water added to the honey may cause it to deteriorate.

MYTHS, RELIGION, AND FOLKLORE

For many centuries, both bees and honey have been associated with the divine and the magical. Folktales in Africa and Australia, as well as elsewhere, feature bees and honey. In ancient Egypt, the *Salt Papyrus* (300 BCE) contains the following passage about the creator of the world, the sun god Re: "The god Re wept and his tears fell on the ground and were turned into bees. The bees began to build and busied themselves with flowers of every kind and so wax was made and also honey out of the tears of Re."

In India's *Rigveda*, the sacred Hindu scriptures, the gods Krishna, Vishnu, and Indra are *madhava*, meaning "honey-born." Honey is seen as being sent from heaven, with bees acting as messengers from the gods, something that is also seen in other religions. In Hinduism, newborn babies are welcomed into the world with a private family ceremony called *jatakarma* that involves touching honey to the baby's mouth. The Hindu pantheon of gods includes

Bhramari, the "goddess of bees" (from the Hindi *bramari*, meaning "bees"), depicted as a four-armed woman who in a battle between the gods and the demons was aided by the bees, hornets, and wasps that clung to her body.

In Greek mythology, the nymph Melissa (whose name comes from the Greek word *meli*, for "honey") fed the god Zeus honey when he was a baby. Also in Greek mythology, one finds the minor deity Aristaios, son of the god Apollo and the nymph Kyrene, who is credited with teaching beekeeping to humankind. Pliny the Elder gave an account of the working of the beehive in *Natural History*, but wrote of honey that it "comes out of the air and is chiefly formed in the time just before dawn, at the rising of the stars." He credited bees as being bearers of portents: "They settled in the mouth of Plato when he was a young child and foretold the charm of his pleasing eloquence."

Bees and honey also occupy a special place in Norse mythology, which sets the great ash tree Yggdrasil at the center of the cosmos, with its branches covering the Earth and its roots entering the underworld. Water from the sacred spring called Uthar is sprinkled on the tree each day; the dew that falls from Yggdrasil is called "honeyfall," and bees feed on it.

HONEY-GLAZED CHICKEN

Serves 4
Preparation 10 minutes
Cooking 30–40 minutes

4 chicken legs
⅓ cup honey
2 tbsp olive oil
Juice of ½ lemon
1 garlic clove, crushed
Salt and freshly ground
   black pepper

A simple honey glaze gives a tasty lift to chicken legs. Serve with mashed potatoes, carrots, and broccoli for a delicious meal.

1 Preheat the oven to 400°F.
2 Season the chicken legs with salt and pepper. Mix together the honey, olive oil, lemon juice, and garlic.
3 Brush the chicken thoroughly with the honey mixture. Place in a roasting pan and roast for 30–40 minutes until cooked through.
4 During the roasting time, baste the chicken two times more with the honey mixture. Serve hot from the oven.

Mead, the ancient drink made from fermented honey (see p. 68), also features in Norse mythology in the tale of the wise man Kvasir, created by the gods from their own spittle. Kvasir was murdered by two dwarves named Fjalar and Galar, who then used his blood and honey to brew a special mead. Known as the Mead of Poetry, it endowed whoever drank it with wisdom and the gift of poetry. Odin, the All-Father of the Norse gods, set out to find and steal back the precious mead, which through shape-shifting and trickery, he managed to do, returning in the form of an eagle to Asgard, the gods' fortress, with the mead held inside his body.

One enduring folklore custom found in Europe and also in the United States is known as "the telling of the bees." This is the practice of informing the colony of major events within the household—births, marriages, and deaths, the latter being particularly important. The telling could be done either through speaking formally to the bees, first tapping on their hives to attract their attention, or dressing their hives appropriately. Should the bees not be informed, so the superstition goes, the bees would die, leave their hives, or cease giving honey.

URBAN BEEKEEPING

While the traditional image of beekeeping is a pastoral one—a classic image that comes to mind is of a row of beehive skeps in a peaceful apple orchard—recent decades have seen the rise of what is known as urban beekeeping, with bees kept in cities and towns. While at first this seems an unlikely combination, in fact certain factors in the urban environment work well for bees. One of these is the lack of pesticides, in contrast to rural areas, where farmers use pesticides extensively to protect their crops. One issue facing beekeepers in cities would seem to be the lack of green spaces in which the bees can forage for nectar. Many cities, however, contain a surprising amount of green spaces in the form of public parks and private gardens. Furthermore, the trees and flowers in cities are noticeably diverse, rather than a monoculture of fields filled with a single crop such as wheat or corn. Having access to a wide range of plants gives bees in cities more possibilities of finding the nectar they need for food. Today, beekeepers are found in many cities around the world, among them major metropolises such as Berlin, Chicago, London, Melbourne, New York, Paris, San Francisco, and Toronto. In 2014, it was estimated that London was home to more than 5,000 managed hives, though the figure may well be higher, as not all beekeepers register their hives.

No single city is credited with being the first to start the urban beekeeping trend. The movement is seen as a response to an awareness of the threats facing honey bees. The news in recent decades of unprecedented colony losses, or colony collapse disorder (see p. 47), and a realization that action needs to be taken to help bees have driven a rise in beekeeping. As the global bee population declines, so urban beekeeping has increased in popularity. Beekeeping associations in Britain and the United States have seen their membership grow, with novice beekeepers keen to learn about this historic area of expertise. The practice is also linked to the locavore movement, which champions locally produced food and is rethinking the potential of urban landscapes. The idea of honey produced in cities has resonated with producers, retailers, and customers alike. The practice of installing beehives on iconic buildings has taken off—witness their presence on landmarks such as Tate Britain in London, the Bundestag in Berlin, and the Whitney Museum of American Art in New York.

The urban beekeeping movement does face issues. Many cities have legislation in place banning the keeping of bees in populated areas, though recent years have also seen changes to the laws in cities such as Los Angeles, New York City, and Washington, D.C., lifting previous bans on urban beekeeping. There is a perception that bees are dangerous insects, because of their ability to deliver painful stings. Honey bees, focused on their task of collecting nectar, are often confused with more aggressive hornets and wasps. Of course, for people who are allergic to bee stings, the concern is based on a real risk. Beekeepers respond by pointing out that knowledgeable beekeeping is a responsible activity. For example, swarming—the process in which a large group of bees led by a queen bee seeks to set up a colony, which can alarm members of the public—is something that urban beekeepers seek to minimize. The issue of how many bees can be sustained in cities is increasingly discussed, as the fear is that too many bee colonies will put undue pressure on nectar sources. Many city-based beekeeping associations campaign for increased nectar-rich urban planting in parks and gardens and more green roofs in order to provide food for their bees.

HONEY AND HEALTH

Historically, honey has long been regarded not simply as an ingredient that tastes sweet and delicious, but also as one with therapeutic properties. As the Bible says, "Eat honey, my child, for it is good" (Proverbs 24:13). For several centuries, honey has been widely used in traditional medicines in

HONEY FRUIT SMOOTHIE

Serves 4

Preparation 5 minutes

2 ripe bananas

2 cups strawberries

Juice of 2 oranges

1 tbsp wheat germ

2 tbsp honey

1 cup natural yogurt

Adding honey to a fresh fruit smoothie is a simple way to give it a mellow sweetness. Serve this for breakfast as an appealing, healthy start to the day.

1   Place all the ingredients in a jug blender and process until smooth.
2   Serve at once.

many countries, both on its own and as a useful sweetener to make bitter medicines palatable. According to India's Ayurveda, a term that translates as "knowledge of life," *madhu* (honey) is an important medicine. It can be taken internally and also used externally to treat a wide range of conditions, including coughs, asthma, vomiting, insomnia, diarrhea, worms, and eye diseases and to treat wounds. The ancient Indian physician Sushruta, whose treatise on medicine is a foundational Ayurvedic text, advised using honey to coat a pierced ear. It is also used to prevent cataracts and to treat eye ailments. In Chinese traditional medicine, honey (*feng mi*) has neutral properties and is used for a variety of purposes such as to fortify the spleen and stomach, to restore *qi* (life energy), and to treat coughs and burns.

Throughout the ancient world, one finds examples of honey being used medicinally. A Sumerian tablet dating from around 2100 BCE, one of the earliest written records of honey, significantly writes of its use as a salve for wounds. The ancient Egyptians used honey to treat wounds, with the Ebers Papyrus, a medical record dating from 1550 BCE, describing a concoction containing honey, used together with lint and grease, as a dressing. Hippocrates, the fourth-century BCE Greek physician sometimes called "the father of medicine," used honey to treat wounds and burns, and also prescribed a mixture of honey and vinegar for pain. Honey features several times in the Hippocratic Corpus (c. 469–399 BCE), including the observation that "wine and honey are wonderfully adapted to man; both in health and in disease, they are administered wisely and justly according to the individual constitution." Pliny the Elder recommended honey mixed with powdered bees as a treatment to improve hearing. He wrote that bees were admired because they "collect honey: the sweetest, finest most health-promoting liquid." The second-century CE Greek physician Galen mixed honey with sea-tortoise gall to make eyedrops, also combining it with the ashes of burned bee heads as a treatment for eyes. In the Islamic world, honey has long been regarded as a healthy food. The tenth-century Persian physician Avicenna called honey "the food of foods, the drink of drinks and the drug of drugs." His herbal formulas were ground, sifted, and mixed with honey.

Today, honey continues to be valued as a therapeutic food, thought of as having beneficial, healthy properties by many people. With its pleasant, sweet flavor and soothing texture, honey has often been used domestically to treat coughs, taken either neat or mixed with warm water or a herbal tea. Raw honey—as well as bee products such as propolis (the resinous mixture made by bees to seal their hives) and royal jelly, which is produced by nurse bees to feed larvae and queen bees—is sold in health food shops. Despite honey being used in traditional medicine, there has been a lack of scientific research into honey's therapeutic potential. In 1892, the Dutch scientist Van Ketel reported that honey had antibacterial properties, but it is only in recent decades that more research has been carried out. Recent findings show that raw honey can kill more than 250 clinical strains of bacteria, including the so-called superbug MRSA.

Honey has historically been used in many cultures to dress wounds. Indeed, in the twentieth century during World War 1, the Russians used honey to prevent infection and speed up the healing process. There is a new interest within the scientific community in honey's potential in this area. Honey helps prevent infection in the wound through osmosis, which draws moisture from the wound into the honey; this discourages the growth of bacteria, as they require moisture to thrive. Honey's high acidity and hydrogen peroxide levels (which vary from honey to honey) are important aspects of its ability to prevent bacterial growth.

In recent years, one monofloral honey (see p. 64) in particular has caught the public's imagination with regards to its healthy properties. This is manuka honey, made from the nectar of the manuka or tea tree (*Leptospermum scoparium*), which grows in New Zealand and southeast Australia. It has a powerful aroma and distinctive, slightly bitter flavor.

In recent years, one monofloral honey in particular has caught the public's imagination with regards to its healthy properties. This is manuka honey, made from the nectar of the manuka or tea tree.

The main reason for the current popularity of manuka honey among researchers is the discovery that it contains high levels of an antibacterial compound called methylglyoxal (MG). Other honeys also contain MG but only at far lower levels. The MG in manuka honey is created through the conversion of dihydroxyacetone, a compound found in the nectar of manuka flowers. The higher the concentration of MG in the manuka honey, the stronger the antibacterial effect.

Customers buying manuka honey are presented with a range of information, including MG content, non-peroxide activity (NPA), and active (A) and total activity (TA), which refer to the honey's antibacterial strength. Antibacterial ratings such as 5+ or 10+ are displayed on manuka honey labels, with the higher levels reflected in the higher cost of the honey. Manuka honey can command premium prices, and such is the demand for it around the world that there are now, sadly, issues with adulteration or counterfeit manuka.

HONEY-GLAZED SHALLOTS

Serves 4
Preparation 10 minutes
Cooking 20 minutes

8 shallots, peeled
1 tbsp olive oil
1 tbsp runny honey
Salt and freshly ground
  black pepper
2 sprigs of thyme

Shallots roasted with honey make a simple but stylish vegetable side dish. Serve with roast beef or lamb or a rich beef and wine casserole.

1   Preheat the oven to 350°F.
2   Bring a pan of salted water to a boil. Add the peeled shallots and parboil for 5 minutes. Drain and pat dry.
3   Place the shallots in a roasting pan. Toss with olive oil to coat thoroughly, then toss with the honey. Season with salt and black pepper and add the thyme sprigs.
4   Roast in the oven for 15 minutes. Serve warm.

MONOFLORAL HONEYS

One of the charms of honey is its ability to be an expression of what the French call *terroir*, a term often encountered in the world of wines. Translated literally, this means "of the earth or soil," but it is used in a larger sense to mean environment, the weather, soil, and terrain. The honey created by bees reflects the flowers and trees from which they source their nectar, resulting in honeys varying considerably in color, flavor, and texture. This is apparent even when the honey is made from a mixture of nectar sources; a jar of Italian wildflower honey, for example, will taste different from a jar of U.S. wildflower honey. One finds "regional" honeys produced from landscapes as diverse as the flower meadows of the Sussex Downs in England, the Zambian rain forests, and the Italian Alps.

The differences, however, become noticeably more apparent when the honey is from nectar predominantly of one species; honeys of this type are called monofloral honeys. These are a world away from the mild-tasting, generic blended honeys that are most widely available. Sampling a range of monofloral honeys is the best way to appreciate just how diverse honey can be.

Alfafa (*Medicago sativa*): the honey from this plant (grown around the world as forage for cattle) is lightly colored, with a mild, delicate flavor.

Blue gum (*Eucalyptus globulus*): made from the blue gum eucalyptus tree, this is a popular honey in Australia. It has a pronounced flavor and a slight minty, medicinal aftertaste.

Borage or viper's bugloss (*Echium vulgare*): this is a light, delicate, noticeably sweet honey, produced in many countries.

Buckwheat (*Fagopurym esculentum*): the honey made from this plant is dark in color, with a complex, malty, earthy flavor.

Canola or rapeseed (*Brassica napus*): widely cultivated for its oil-rich seeds, the honey from this flowering member of the *Brassica* genus is white in color and creamy textured and has a mild flavor.

Chestnut (*Castanea sativa*): this darkly colored honey is made from the sweet chestnut tree and has a very distinctive aroma, along with a slightly bitter flavor.

GRILLED GOAT'S CHEESE WITH HONEY

Serves 4
Preparation 5 minutes
Cooking 3–5 minutes

While this is quick and easy to make, the contrast between sweet, flavorful honey and salty goat's cheese makes it a very satisfying dish. Serve it as an elegant first course.

4 cups arugula

8 slices of a firm goat's cheese log, each ¼–½ inch thick

4 tbsp clear honey, such as chestnut honey

4 tbsp pine nuts, lightly roasted

1   Divide the arugula among four serving plates.
2   Broil the goat's cheese for 3–5 minutes until it is lightly browned.
3   Top the arugula with the freshly grilled goat's cheese.
4   Drizzle each portion with honey at once. Sprinkle with pine nuts and serve immediately.

Clover (members of the *Trifolium* genus): a number of clover species are cultivated for fodder. The honey produced from them is pale in color, with a creamy texture and a mild, sweet flavor.

Heather (*Calluna vulgaris*): Scotland is noted for its heather honey. Caramel colored, it has a full, floral aroma and a deep, rich flavor.

Honeydew: often called forest honey, this is made not from nectar but from the sweet substance known as honeydew, which small insects produce from the sap of trees such as pines.

Lavender (*Lavandula*): the honey from this perfumed flowering plant is delicate and noticeably fragrant, like the plant itself.

Leatherwood (*Eucryphia lucida*): the honey from this tree (which grows on Australia's island state of Tasmania) has a noticeable aroma and distinctive, complex flavor, with a long finish.

Linden, basswood, or lime (trees of the genus *Tilia*): the honey from these trees is light in color but noticeably fragrant, while the flavor has a citrus quality to it, with notes of mint and eucalyptus.

Orange (*Citrus* x *sinensis*): made from the flowers of the orange tree, this honey is mild and sweet.

Rosemary (*Rosmarinus officinalis*): a golden honey with a herbal fragrance and delicate flavor.

Sunflower (Asteraceae family): ranging in color from light to dark yellow, the honey from these flowers crystallizes quickly and has a rich sweetness.

Thyme (*Thymus vulgaris*): in the ancient world, the thyme honey from Mount Hymettus, in Attica, Greece, was renowned. The honey from this herb has an intense, aromatic flavor.

Tupelo (*Nyssa ogeche*): an uncommon honey, made from the nectar of white Ogeechee tupelo trees, which grow mainly in the wetlands of Georgia and Florida; light in color, with a unique floral flavor, for which it is prized.

MEAD

One of the reasons that honey was so valued historically is that this sweet substance could be fermented and used to produce an alcoholic drink, known as mead or honey wine. It is a drink with a long history, thought to be the oldest alcoholic beverage made by man, with its origins dating back thousands of years, possibly to the African continent.

Mead is made by fermenting raw (unpasteurized) honey with water. The honey is rich with natural yeasts, whose activity is triggered by the increased water content, thus allowing fermentation to happen easily, especially in tropical countries, where the naturally hot climate speeds up fermentation processes.

The tradition of making fermented honey drinks is found around the world. A honey drink thought to be a form of mead is mentioned in the *Rigveda*, the ancient sacred Indian texts thought to date to 1500 to 1200 BCE. In Central America, the Maya drank a honey wine called *balche*, flavored with the bark of a tree. In Ethiopia, a historic honey wine called *t'ej*, traditionally made with the twigs and leaves of a plant called shiny-leaf buckthorn or gesho (*Rhamnus prinoides*), is still made today. Interestingly, the ancient Greek historian Strabo wrote of Ethiopian Troglodytae in 64 BCE: "Most of the people drink a brew of buckthorn, but the rulers drink a mixture of honey and water, pressed out of some kind of flower." Mead was known in ancient Egypt, ancient Greece, and ancient Rome. The first-century CE Roman agriculturalist Columella gave a recipe for a fermented drink made from honey and grape juice in his *De re rustica*. Mead played a key part in Norse culture, a fact reflected in the frequent mentions of drinking mead in medieval Norse sagas. In Russia and Central Europe, mead was an important alcoholic drink for centuries. Chronicles report that, for a feast in 996 CE, Vladimir the Great ordered "300 vats of mead for a feast following the victory over the Pechenegs." Today, however, other alcoholic drinks such as wine, beer, and grain-based spirits have replaced mead in popularity in many parts of the world where it was once enjoyed.

CULINARY HONEY

By its nature, honey has never been a staple food around the world. Instead, it has always been considered something of a luxury or a treat. It is a food that can simply be eaten in its natural state, with no cooking required before its consumption. It makes an excellent topping and is often enjoyed at breakfast time, served stirred into tangy, natural yogurt

HONEY ICE CREAM

Makes approx. 2 pints
Preparation 10 minutes,
  plus cooling and churning
Cooking 10 minutes

3 egg yolks
1¼ cups full-fat milk
1 tbsp vanilla bean paste
3 tbsp honey
1¼ cups heavy cream
1 tsp vanilla extract

For best results, choose a full-flavored honey, such as heather honey, for this delicious homemade ice cream. Serve it with crisp cookies such as honey cookies (see p. 72).

1   Whisk the yolks until pale and creamy in a mixing bowl.
2   Gently heat the milk, vanilla bean paste, and honey together in a saucepan, stirring well, and bring to just below the boiling point.
3   Gradually pour the hot milk into the whisked yolks, whisking constantly as you add it, until well mixed.
4   Place the yolk mixture in a clean, heavy saucepan and cook gently, stirring constantly, for around 10 minutes, until thickened, making sure that it does not overheat. To test whether the custard is ready, dip a spoon into the mixture. If the custard coats the back of a spoon, then it is ready. Set aside to cool.
5   Stir in the cream and vanilla extract, and then chill for at least 6 hours. Churn in an ice-cream maker, following the manufacturer's instructions, until thickened into ice cream. Store in a freeze-proof container and freeze until serving.

or drizzled over a stack of delicious pancakes. Popular ways to eat honey to this day include the simple favorites of warm toast and honey or bread, butter, and honey.

With classic human inventiveness, however, honey has a history of being used in varied ways in the kitchen in both savory and sweet dishes. It was a popular flavoring in the cuisine of ancient Rome. Several recipes in a collection credited to the Roman gourmet Apicius, thought to have been compiled in the first century CE, feature honey. Honey is mixed in with lentils and added to sauces for dishes such as soft-boiled eggs in pine nut sauce, roast boar, and fried veal scallopine. Interestingly, these recipes also feature honey as a way of preserving food. The recipe "To keep meats fresh without salt for any length of time" advises simply covering fresh meat with honey and suspending it in a vessel. Honey, which has a more complex sweetness than sugar, is a traditional addition to savory dishes such as North African tagines, sometimes simply stirred in at the end of the cooking time.

With its liquid texture and sticky sweetness, honey lends itself to being used as a glaze for meat or vegetables (see p. 56). *Char siu* (barbecued pork) is a classic Chinese recipe (see p. 28) in which marinated, roast pieces of pork are brushed with honey at the final stage. Honey often features as a glaze on whole baked hams (see p. 37), a splendid dish served at festive occasions such as Easter, Thanksgiving, or Christmas. Honey is also a popular glaze for barbecued pork ribs (see p. 25); as with ham, the combination of a sweet glaze with salty, savory meat is an excellent one.

It is, however, in the world of baking and desserts that honey comes into its own. In Greece, where the appreciation and use of honey date to the Classical world, there are a number of honey-centric recipes. Honey still carries a symbolic value in Greek culture to this day, with treats containing it served at weddings and parties as a symbol of wealth and fertility. In this tradition, one finds *loukmades* (honey balls) served at celebratory meals: small dainty doughnuts, made from a yeast dough, eaten freshly fried with honey poured over them and a sprinkling of fragrant cinnamon. Honey in Greek cuisine is often used in syrups, which are then poured over baked confections to soften and sweeten them; baklava (see p. 53) is a classic example of this usage. Less well known outside Greece are *melomakarona* (Christmas honey cookies), flavored with orange juice and zest, brandy, and cinnamon and baked until golden. Once cooled, they are immersed in a hot honey syrup for a couple of minutes, then served sprinkled with chopped walnuts. Another Christmas treat called *diples* consists of an egg-rich dough, cut into strips, folded into little rolls, and fried and dipped in a honey syrup.

HONEY COOKIES

Makes about 34 cookies
Preparation 15 minutes
Cooking 18–20 minutes

Using honey gives a delicious fragrance and flavor to these crisp, golden cookies. Serve them with a cup of tea or coffee or as an accompaniment to homemade ice cream (see p. 69).

4 tbsp salted butter, plus
  extra for greasing
¾ cup all-purpose flour
½ cup granulated sugar
4 tbsp honey
1 egg, beaten

1 Preheat oven to 350°F. Grease and line 3 baking sheets with parchment paper.
2 Gently melt the butter without allowing it to brown.
3 Use a wooden spoon to mix the flour, sugar, and honey together in a mixing bowl. Add the melted butter and mix well. Mix in the beaten egg to form a soft mixture.
4 Place teaspoons of the mixture on the baking sheets, spacing them well apart. Bake for 18–20 minutes until rich gold in color.
5 Remove the baking sheets from the oven and let cool for 15 minutes to allow the biscuits to harden. Use a spatula to remove the biscuits from the baking sheets, cool on wire racks, and store in an airtight container.

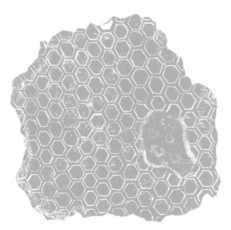

In Jewish cuisine, too, honey has symbolic associations. On Rosh Hashanah (Jewish New Year), honey cake is traditionally eaten in order to make the forthcoming year a sweet one.

That sense of honey as a special, celebratory ingredient recurs in a number of traditional baked treats. Germany's thriving *Lebkuchen* tradition traces its origins to medieval times and the custom of making honey cakes. A traditional Christmas treat, *Lebkuchen* come in a range of shapes, flavors, and textures, but honey and spices remain key ingredients to this day. The Bavarian city of Nuremberg is particularly associated with *Lebkuchen*, a fact linked to its purchase in 1427 of the surrounding Reichswald, a forest otherwise known as "the Empire's bee garden," thus ensuring an ample supply of honey for the city's bakers and the specialty for which they became renowned.

In Italy, the Christmas cake *panforte*, a specialty of Siena, Tuscany, is reputed to trace its origins back to the thirteenth century. Its medieval ancestry is evident in its combination of ingredients: nuts, spices, candied citrus peel, and honey. A flat, round cake, *panforte* has a dense, chewy texture and a rich, distinctive flavor.

Honey is a key ingredient in nougat, a historic European confection classically made from honey, nuts, and egg whites but available in different versions. French nougat is said to have been first made in Marseilles in the sixteenth century and included walnuts. In the eighteenth century, however, the custom of combining almonds with Provençal honey saw the creation of *nougat de Montélimar*, for which the town became famous.

In Italy, *torrone* (the Italian name for nougat) is traditionally associated with the town of Cremona, Lombardy, and is considered a classic Christmas sweet. Each year, the town hosts the Festa del Torrone in November.

In Spain, nougat is called *turrón* and remains very popular, again eaten especially during the Christmas period. The origins of *turrón* in Spain are thought to date to the time of the Moorish occupation. As in France and Italy, certain towns in Spain have long been associated with *turrón*, notably Jijona and Alicante, both in the south of Spain. Each champions a particular style of *turrón*, with Jijona's being soft and chewy, while Alicante's is firm and crunchy. While *turrón* is widely produced today in factories in Spain, convents such as Hermanas Clarisas de Salvatierra in Álava, in the Basque country of northern Spain, have kept the time-consuming tradition of making *turrón* by hand alive, finding a receptive market for this artisan version of a honey-based treat.

SALT

Salt (sodium chloride) is a truly fundamental ingredient.
Our bodies contain salt, and it is essential for life. Historically,
it was a very valuable ingredient, a source of social status,
wealth, and power. Today, while salt is widely available and
affordable, it continues to play a major part in our lives.

So important is salt to human beings that it has shaped language, society,
and landscape. Biologically speaking, our bodies are hardwired to recognize
salt. Receptors on our tongues recognize five basic tastes: salty, sweet, sour,
bitter, and umami. These receptors are part of a gustatory system that allows
human beings to distinguish between foods that are safe to eat and those
that are harmful. Bitterness and sourness, for example, are associated with
foods that may be poisonous or tainted. Sweetness, umami, and saltiness
(up to a certain point) trigger pleasurable sensations. Saltiness, therefore,
is a taste that humans enjoy, and salt has a special status as a widely used
seasoning, routinely placed on tables so that diners can add more salt to
their food if desired. For centuries, this vital flavoring was also essential
for preserving (see p. 99), a fact that added hugely to its historic value.
Salt acquired a cultural value as well as a monetary one, used in religious
rites and featuring in superstitions, with the spilling of salt seen as unlucky.
There are numerous references to salt in the Bible, with the phrase "salt
of the earth" (Matthew 5:13) used to express the idea of goodness.

It was salt's preserving properties that made it especially valued
by the ancient Egyptians, who used it both for keeping food and for
mummification—the embalming of dead bodies. It is thought that
the Egyptians began mummifying the dead in around 2600 BCE, with the
practice developing and used into the Roman Period (c. 30 BCE–364 CE).
A key part of the mummification process involved the embalmers removing
all moisture from the body. This was done by coating it with natron—a
naturally occurring type of salt with powerful dehydrating properties—and
also placing natron within the corpse. Using natron in this way dried out the

body, after which it was wrapped in linen. Natron, called "the divine salt," was harvested from deposits found in the beds of dried lakes in the Wadi el Natrun valley. Ancient Egyptian religious texts, known as the Pyramid Texts, describe the use of natron in funerary rites for pharaohs. Those who were poorer used ordinary salt for mummification.

Salt has been sourced both from the land and from the sea since ancient times. Over the years, much human ingenuity and hard labor have gone into the production of this essential ingredient. One striking example of this inventiveness comes from the state of Shu (known today as Sichuan Province) in China in 250 BCE. The governor of the region, Li Bing, was a notable engineer; among his achievements, he created a pioneering river irrigation system at Dujiangyan. Salt had long been made in Shu. In 252 BCE, having realized that the natural brine from which it was produced seeped up to the surface from underground, Li Bing ordered the drilling of the world's first brine wells. This innovative project saw the Chinese develop drilling technology, which enabled them to drill deep into the earth. Bamboo tubes were used to transport the brine to the surface, where it was piped to boiling houses and processed into salt.

Salt was very important in ancient Rome, widely used in its cuisine for both seasoning and for preserving food, and also valued for its healthy properties. The word "salad" comes from the Latin word *salata*, meaning "salted," and originates in the Roman practice of salting green vegetables. A sense of salt's financial worth remains with us in the word "salary," which describes the wages paid to an employer. The word's linguistic origins are traced to the Latin *salarium*, denoting a Roman soldier's allowance to buy salt, from the Latin word *sal*, for "salt." Having access to salt was of strategic importance to the Romans. Ancus Marcius, the fourth king of Rome, who ruled from 640 to 614 BCE, conquered Ostia and established saltworks there. The expansion of the Roman Empire saw the Romans acquiring existing saltworks, Celtic, Phoenician, Greek, Carthaginian, and Middle Eastern ones among them. They also spread the practice of salt making, introducing new saltworks in the countries they conquered. In Britain, Middlewich in Cheshire, established on the site of a prehistoric brine spring, was named Salinae by the Romans and was a major source of salt production. The Romans used shallow lead pans to heat the brine over open fires in order to create the highly prized salt crystals. Salt was such an essential part of life for the Romans that the government manipulated salt prices, often ensuring that salt remained affordable to the general citizenry, called the plebeians. Salt taxes, however, were raised during the Punic Wars (264–146 BCE) in order to

SALT-CRUSTED SEA BASS

Serves 2
Preparation 10 minutes
Cooking 30 minutes

There is a distinctly theatrical element to this striking French dish, which consists of a whole fish covered in a mound of glittering white salt and baked. The flavor and texture live up to the promise of the appearance, with the fish inside moist and tender from cooking in its own juices and well seasoned but not overly salty. Be sure to buy a fish with its scales still on, as these are needed to prevent undue saltiness.

3 lb 5 oz coarse sea salt crystals
1½-lb sea bass, gutted and
   cleaned but not scaled

1 Preheat the oven to 425°F.

2 Into a shallow ovenproof dish large enough to hold the sea bass, pour enough salt to form an even layer just under ½ inch deep.

3 Rinse the sea bass and pat dry. Place the sea bass on the salt layer.

4 Pour over more salt until the sea bass is totally covered by the salt crystals. Bake for 30 minutes.

5 Remove from the oven. Carefully lift off the salt crust. Peel off the skin from the fish and serve the white, cooked flesh inside.

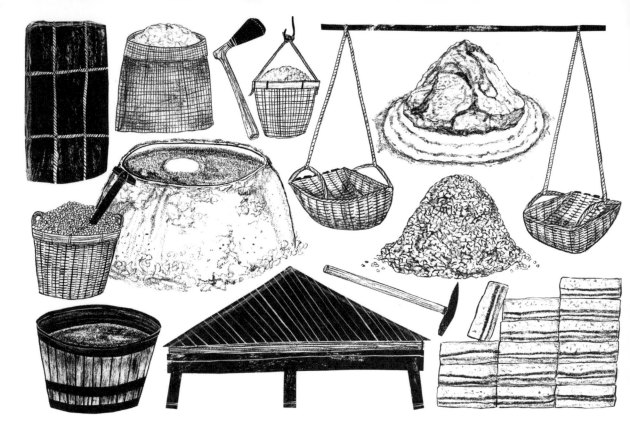

generate revenue for the Roman army. During this period, a Roman consul named Marcus Livius came up with a tax system on salt in the Roman Empire and accordingly became known as the salinator.

For many centuries, salt was a precious commodity, traded both within and between countries. The existence of ancient "salt roads"—prehistoric and historic trading routes linked to the commercial trafficking of salt—testifies to its importance in trade. In Italy, the name of an historic Roman road, the Via Salaria, reflects its use as an ancient trading route for salt. The same route was used by the Sabines to transport salt from the marshes at the mouth of the River Tiber. One ancient salt route is found in the form of a steep, perilous track in the Himalayan mountains of Nepal and Tibet, where yaks were used to transport the precious saline cargo. In northern Germany, the Alte Salzstrasse (Old Salt Road) was a road connecting the town of Lüneburg, where salt was produced from brine springs, with the port of Lübeck.

Seas, rivers, and waterways—not just roads—were also used to transport salt. Trade in salt played a major part in the creation of the historic Italian port of Venice. Salt produced in the shallow waters of the Venetian Lagoon was used for bartering by the early dwellers who had settled on the islands in the lagoon. As Venice developed into a maritime and trading power, salt produced in a number of saltworks in the lagoon was a prime source of revenue. Not content with producing salt, the Venetians shrewdly focused their entrepreneurial energies on controlling the trade in salt and creating a monopoly. In 932 CE, Venice destroyed the nearby saltworks at Comacchio, ensuring the dominance of their own saltworks at Chioggia. In 1281, the Venetian government offered a subsidy to salt landed at Venice in order to give merchants an incentive to ship salt there. This salt was then sold at high prices within the Venetian states, other regions of Italy, and, as Venice's network enlarged, foreign countries. Large, reinforced warehouses known as *saloni* were constructed in Venice during the fourteenth century specifically to store salt. It was trade in this valuable commodity that allowed Venice to achieve its dominant position, allowing the Venetians to create the beautiful and magnificent buildings for which La Serenissima is admired.

While salt today is no longer expensive, it remains useful. One of the striking aspects of salt is the variety of uses it has been put to, including tanning, making ice cream, and medical purposes. Today, salt continues to be used in a variety of ways: in agriculture, for deicing roads, and in water conditioning, for example. Primarily, however, salt is used by the chemical industry. Over 50 percent of chemical products depend on salt during their manufacture. Salt is also used in the manufacturing of commodities such as glass, paper, rubber, and textiles. In 2016, around 309 million tons of salt were produced in the world. Today the world's major producers of salt are China and the United States. Despite salt's importance as an ingredient, only 6 percent of the salt produced in the world today is used for food purposes.

HOW SALT IS PRODUCED

Salt is found either in the sea, since sea water is naturally salty, or in the ground, in deposits created millions of years ago through the evaporation of ancient seas. Humans have long exploited both resources in order to extract this valuable commodity. Pliny the Elder, writing in his *Natural History*, observed: "Salt both occurs naturally and is manufactured. Each type is formed in several ways, but there are two main agents involved: condensation and evaporation."

One ancient way of creating salt was a natural method using the power of the sun. Sea water, lying in shallow pools created by rising and falling tides, was evaporated through the natural, powerful heat of the sun and the

drying effects of the wind, which drew off the water, leaving salty residues behind. It is thought that human beings observed this natural phenomenon on the shores of seas and lakes and set about replicating it and using it for salt production. Salt made using solar evaporation is still produced in a number of countries, including Australia, France (see p. 93), Italy, Peru, and Portugal. Making salt through natural solar evaporation, while historically possible in sunny climates, was not, however, a reliable option in colder, wetter climates. Boiling sea water over fire to extract its salt, however, is possible regardless of climate and has long been a technique for producing salt. Archaeological evidence—including the discovery of fragments of coarse ceramic vessels used in salt evaporation, known as *briquetage*—suggests salt was produced this way in Europe during the Bronze Age. A written record dating from 800 BCE in China describes a traditional way of making salt through boiling sea water in clay pots.

Pliny the Elder wrote that, as well as the powdery salt produced by evaporation of sea water, "there are also mountains of natural salt such as at Oromenus in India, where it is cut out like blocks of stone from a quarry." Human beings have quarried rock salt from the ground since prehistoric times. There is evidence of mining activity at the Hallstatt salt mines in Austria from around 1500 BCE. A wooden staircase in one of the mine shafts, made from spruce and fir, has been dated to 1344 BCE, making it the oldest-known staircase in Europe. Digging salt from the ground was historically difficult, laborious, and dangerous; hence the phrase "back to the salt mine" is associated even today with hard, unrewarding work. Nowadays, rock salt is removed from the earth through two methods. The first involves the use of large, powerful mechanical diggers, rather than human labor, which physically dig out rock salt from mines. Salt extracted this way is used to salt our roads in cold weather. The second method is a process known as hydraulic mining or solution mining. Water is pumped into underground salt deposits, transforming them into brine, with the brine then pumped up to the surface and evaporated to make salt.

Today, most salt is produced through the vacuum evaporation method, which uses pressure in the process to ensure an efficient use of energy. This system involves pumping brine (either in the form of natural sea water or rock salt brine) through tubes into a series of three, four, or five closed vessels, each containing steam chambers. Brine boils in the first vessel at a temperature set by the inlet steam pressure, causing salt crystals to grow and the water to evaporate. The resulting brine, thick with salt crystals, is fed into the second chamber, where more moisture is evaporated. As the brine

FRUIT CHAAT MASALA

Serves 4
Preparation 20 minutes, plus
15 minutes macerating

In Pakistani and Indian cuisine, mineral-rich Himalayan black salt is used as a spice, most classically in a flavoring called *chaat masala*. This take on a traditional recipe combines fresh fruit and chickpeas with the aromatic, pungent spice mixture to refreshing effect.

CHAAT MASALA

1 tbsp *kala namak*
   (Himalayan black salt)
2 tbsp cumin powder
1½ tbsp *amchoor* (dried
   mango powder)
1 tsp chile powder
1 tsp freshly ground
   black pepper
1 clove, finely ground
Seeds from 3 green cardamom
   pods, finely ground

FRUIT AND CHICKPEA
MIXTURE

1 apple
Juice of 1 lemon
1 banana
1 cup grapes
2 cups diced fresh mango
1 cup canned chickpeas, rinsed
Mint leaves, to garnish

1 First, make the *chaat masala* by mixing together all the spices well.

2 Quarter, core, and finely slice the apple, tossing with a little of the lemon juice to prevent discoloring. Slice the banana, then toss it with the remaining lemon juice to prevent discoloring.

3 Toss together the apple, banana, grapes, mango, and chickpeas with 2–3 tablespoons of the *chaat masala* (reserving the remainder in an airtight jar for future use). Set aside for 10 minutes to let the flavors develop. Garnish with mint leaves and serve.

progresses through the vessels, the pressure becomes lower, with the final ones operating under vacuum. This means that the brine can be boiled at far lower temperatures than at normal air pressure, so the process requires far less energy, making it economically viable. In order to create salt for the food industry, the moist salt is then cooled, sieved, and graded. Brine can also be processed in a long, open pan called a grainer, heated by steam pipes. The heating process causes salt flakes to form on the surface, where they grow until they sink to the bottom of the pan, from which they are collected and dried. Salt made this way consists of small flakes rather than cubes.

SALT MINES

The quest to extract salt from the ground has driven the excavation of extraordinary salt mines. Where large underground deposits of salt have been found, huge complexes have been carved out deep underneath the surface of the earth in the process of extracting this valuable mineral.

The second-largest salt mines in the world are the ones at Khewra in Pakistan. Legend has it that when Alexander the Great, the Macedonian king and redoubtable military commander, was making his way across Asia, he and his army halted for a rest in Khewra. Alexander's horse began licking the stones, as did his soldiers' horses, and the soldiers realized that the rocks were salty, and so Khewra's salt deposits were discovered. The salt in these mines is particularly striking, as the presence of mineral deposits, including iron ore, naturally tints it pink and red. Most rose-colored Himalayan salt comes from Khewra's mines. Within its tunnels, miners built a small mosque called the Badshahi mosque from colored salt blocks. Today, the mines are a popular tourist destination, with features including a replica of the Great Wall of China and a post office built of salt.

The quest to extract salt from the ground has driven the excavation of extraordinary salt mines. Where large underground deposits of salt have been found, huge complexes have been carved out deep underneath the surface of the earth.

In southern Poland, one finds the historic Wieliczka Salt Mines, established in the thirteenth century and worked continually until the twentieth century. Over this time they grew substantially, becoming a huge complex of passageways, caverns, underground lakes, and carvings, and attracted many visitors who came to see what had been created in the depths of the earth. With an official guest book kept since 1774, records reveal that celebrities visiting the mine included the Holy Roman Emperor Joseph II, the German poet Johann Wolfgang von Goethe, and the Polish composer Frédéric Chopin. Among the highlights of the Wieliczka mines is the Chapel of St. Kinga, built by devout miners, featuring sparkling chandeliers carved out of the crystalline rock salt. In 1978, UNESCO recognized the mines as a World Heritage site, and the mines, while no longer in working use, remain a popular tourist attraction.

ESSENTIAL SALT

In chemical terms, salt consists of sodium chloride, an ionic compound often called simply sodium. The human body requires salt in order to function properly, so salt is vital for life. Within the body, sodium is found in extracellular fluid through which oxygen and nutrients reach cells. Sodium plays an important role in regulating bodily functions and maintaining our overall fluid balance. This is because sodium is an electrolyte, a mineral that carries an electric charge when dissolved in liquid. Sodium, potassium, chloride, and bicarbonate are known as blood electrolytes. Half of a human body's weight consists of water, contained within what are called fluid compartments. Electrolytes help the body maintain normal fluid levels within these compartments, because the fluid varies with the concentration of electrolytes within a compartment. If the electrolyte concentration is high, fluid will flow into that compartment through a process called osmosis. If there is a low level of electrolytes, then fluid moves out of that compartment. Electrolyte balance, therefore, helps maintain fluid balance within the body.

While sodium is an essential nutrient, the body cannot produce it, so it has to be consumed. The biological need for salt and other minerals is why certain animals seek out what are called salt licks—naturally occurring deposits of salt in the ground—that the animals lick in order to get these important nutrients. Excreted body fluids—blood, sweat, and tears—all contain sodium, which is why they taste salty. In 1684, the Anglo-Irish pioneer of chemistry Robert Boyle demonstrated scientifically that this salty taste is indeed caused by the presence of salt in our bodies.

Sodium levels within the body need to be correctly balanced. Low levels of sodium can result in a condition known as hyponatremia, which causes cramps, muscle spasms, headaches, and fatigue. Loss of sodium from excessive sweating due to heat or high levels of physical activity can also result in hyponatremia. On the other hand, too much sodium results in lethargy or restlessness—a condition known as hypernatremia. Our contemporary diet is high in salt, which is present in processed foods.

GRAVLAX

Serves 6

Preparation 20 minutes (including turning the gravlax)

Curing 48 hours

A classic of Scandinavian cuisine, gravlax—also known as gravadlax—demonstrates the curing capacity of salt in an elegant and delicious way. Making gravlax is simple, though be sure to find two pieces of sushi-grade salmon fillet that match each other in shape and thickness to ensure even curing. Serve the gravlax with a dill and mustard sauce, accompanied by rye bread or new potatoes.

3½ oz kosher salt

3½ oz granulated sugar

2 tsp peppercorns, roughly crushed

1 tsp juniper berries, roughly crushed

1 small bunch of dill, finely chopped

2 evenly sized pieces of sushi-grade salmon fillet, skin on, each weighing 1 lb 2 oz

1 tbsp gin (optional)

1 Mix the salt, sugar, peppercorns, juniper berries, and dill together in a small bowl.

2 Rinse the salmon fillets and pat dry. Place one of the fillets on a large sheet of plastic wrap, skin side down. Spread the dill mixture evenly over the salmon. Sprinkle over the gin, if using. Top with the other salmon fillet, placing it flesh side down.

3 Wrap the salmon tightly in the plastic wrap, forming a parcel. Place in a deep-sided dish and top with a small board or slightly smaller dish, adding weights (such as cans of food) to help press down the board or dish.

4 Chill in the refrigerator for 48 hours, turning the salmon parcel over every 12 hours. As it cures, a briny liquid forms in the dish, which is part of the curing process.

5 At the end of the curing period, unwrap the salmon fillets and pat dry. Slice across each fillet, making long, thin pieces, pulling the flesh away from the skin, until only the skin is left behind. Dispose of the skin.

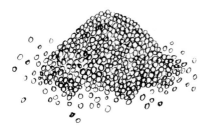

SALT CELLARS

Salt was historically so costly and important in Europe that its consumption was linked to social status. In the medieval world, with its rigid hierarchy, the way in which people dined and the food that they ate reflected their position in society. Royalty and nobility sat at the high table, positioned on a dais, while their social inferiors ate at lower tables below them. Among the privileges granted to the elite was access to salt, placed in a container on the high table. This clear expression of social divide is reflected in the phrases "above the salt," referring to someone of high rank, and "below the salt," which means someone of lower rank or less socially acceptable.

Reflecting the value of salt, the containers that held the salt for dining, known as salt cellars or simply as salt, were special pieces of tableware. The use of salt cellars has been traced back to ancient Rome, and it is thought that the ancient Greeks, too, may have used them. During the Middle Ages, salt cellars became increasingly grand centerpieces, often made from silver. As salt was created by boiling sea water to extract it, salt was seen as a gift of the sea, and so salt cellars usually had a maritime theme.

The most famous salt cellar is the one made between 1540 and 1543 by Benvenuto Cellini, the renowned Italian Renaissance sculptor and goldsmith. Known as the *Saliera* or the Cellini Salt Cellar, it is an elaborate piece of craftsmanship. Made from gold, enamel, and ebony, it depicts Neptune, the god of the sea, and Tellus, the Roman goddess of the earth, with the salt held in a small boat next to Neptune. The work was commissioned by King Francis 1 of France. According to Cellini's autobiography, the king exclaimed on seeing the model of the proposed salt cellar: "This is a hundred times more divine a thing than I had ever dreamed of." He commissioned it to be made from costly gold. Today, this exquisite work is on display at the Kunsthistorisches Museum in Vienna, Austria.

SALT AND TAXES

Historically, salt's importance to people meant that governments around the world found raising duty on it to be a useful source of revenue. Rulers in China established a state monopoly on it in the seventh century BCE. The Venetian explorer Marco Polo, writing in 1300, describing the salt trade in China, observed that it was a source "of revenue to the Great Khan."

One of the strands in the story of salt is of popular resistance to unpopular salt taxes. In France, the *gabelle* was a deeply unpopular tax on salt imposed from the mid-fourteenth century onward; the nobility, the clergy, and other privileged members of society were exempt from this high tax. The resentment caused by the *gabelle*, perceived by ordinary citizens as extortionate and unjust, was one of the factors that led to the French Revolution of 1789. In 1790, the French National Assembly abolished this salt tax, although Napoleon Bonaparte reimposed it in 1806.

Salt continued to be politically potent during the twentieth century. The colonial British authorities in India had passed Salt Acts, prohibiting Indians from collecting or selling salt. Instead, salt had to be bought from the British, who imposed heavy taxes, collecting substantial revenues from the mineral's sale in India. The impact of this British monopoly adversely affected all Indians, particularly the poor, who struggled to afford this basic necessity. Mahatma Gandhi, the Indian lawyer campaigning for Indian independence from the British, saw scope for an act of *satyagraha* (nonviolent resistance). On March 12, 1930, accompanied by a small band of followers, Gandhi set off from his ashram to walk 240 miles to Dandi, a coastal town on the Arabian Sea. There he planned to defy the British Salt Acts by harvesting sea salt himself, an illegal act under British rule. When Gandhi reached Dandi in early April, he went to the beach to collect sea salt. The British, attempting to forestall him, had crushed the salt into the mud. Gandhi, however, picked up a small lump of salt, a symbolic act of defiance, and was duly imprisoned by the British. Gandhi's Salt March garnered enormous support for the independence movement both within and outside India.

SALT AND HEALTH

Salt has long been esteemed for its purifying, auspicious, health-giving properties. The ancient Egyptians used salt medicinally to dry out and disinfect wounds and in laxatives. In ancient Greece, salt was similarly valued. The ancient Greek physician Hippocrates recommended the use of salt for various ailments, including using steam from salt water to treat respiratory conditions. In ancient Rome, too, salt was valued for its healing capacity. The name of the Roman goddess of health and welfare, Salus, has its roots in the Latin for "salt."

For thousands of years, bathing in salt water has been thought to be beneficial to health, with the salt used to treat wounds, cuts, or sores. There is a long history of people seeking out saline or mineral springs to bathe in, a tradition that led to the rise of spa resorts and towns around these special waters. Many historic spas are still in use, such as Spa Bad Ischl, Austria's oldest saline spa, where salt baths were first built in the town's salt mine.

SALTED CARAMEL SAUCE

Makes 1 cup
Preparation 5 minutes
Cooking 4–5 minutes

4 tbsp unsalted butter
2 oz soft light brown sugar
2 oz superfine sugar
½ cup heavy cream
½–1 tsp sea salt

Adding salt to a classic caramel sauce rounds out the sweetness in a pleasing way. Taste the sauce before adding the salt and taste it again afterward to see the effect salt has on sweetness.

1 Place the butter, light brown sugar, superfine sugar, and cream in a small, heavy saucepan.
2 Heat gently, stirring, until the butter has melted and the sugar has dissolved.
3 Bring to a boil and let bubble for 1 minute. Remove from direct heat and stir in ½ teaspoon sea salt. Taste and add a further ½ teaspoon if required.

When it comes to salt in our diet, there is concern that the contemporary diet contains an excess. So widely used is salt in food processing that it is a hidden ingredient, consumed in far larger quantities than is often realized. High sodium intake is connected with increased risk of cardiovascular disease and strokes. The World Health Organization recommends that adults consume just under a teaspoon of salt per day and reports that most people consume around twice that.

TYPES OF SALT

Salt for culinary use exists in a variety of forms, including flavored types such as celery salt, made by the addition of ground spices and dried herbs.

GRANULATED TABLE SALT

Widely available, this everyday salt is mined from underground salt deposits, treated to remove mineral deposits, and comes in the form of tiny, white, cubic crystals. Usually, table salt includes anticaking ingredients such as magnesium carbonate or sodium aluminosilicate, which are added in order to stop the salt crystals from sticking together and thus enabling them to be easily poured or shaken.

IODIZED SALT

A type of fortified salt, iodized salt is table salt to which tiny amounts of iodine have been added. Iodine is a micronutrient that our bodies need in order to produce thyroid hormones. Our bodies do not make iodine and so it must be consumed. Iodine deficiency can lead to goiter (a swelling of the thyroid gland), hypothyroidism, and mental retardation in babies whose mothers were iodine deficient. In an attempt to address the issue of iodine deficiency in the United States, the 1920s saw the introduction of iodized table salt as a simple, practical way to increase consumption of iodine. Salt was regarded as a useful vehicle for this public health initiative, as it is widely consumed, affordable, and long lasting. Since this initiative, a number of other countries have followed suit in making it a legal requirement to add iodine to salt for human consumption.

KOSHER SALT

In the United States, *kosher salt* is the term used to describe a particular coarse-flaked salt, free of iodine. The larger surface area of the crystals allows them to absorb more moisture than cubic salt crystals, so kosher salt

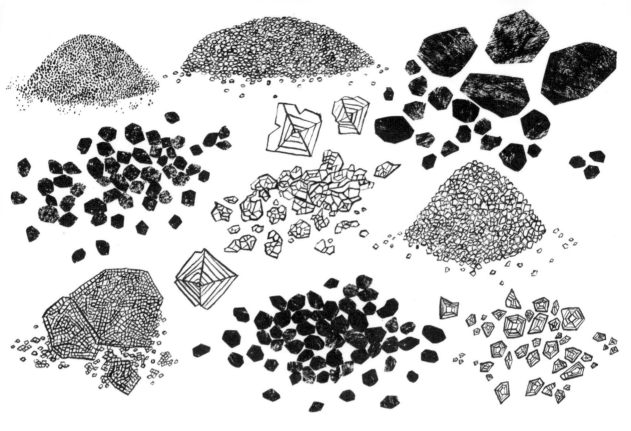

is associated with preservation techniques such as meat curing, canning, and pickling. The salt's name comes from its use in koshering meat, a process that uses salt to draw out blood from meat through osmosis. Kosher-certified salt is salt produced following kosher guidelines, certified by kosher certification agencies, and suitable for consumption by those following a kosher diet.

PICKLING SALT

Designed specifically for use in making pickles, this is really just pure sodium chloride, without the addition of iodine, which can cause pickles to turn dark, or anticaking agents, which can cause cloudiness in the pickling solution. Furthermore, its grains are very small, so it dissolves quickly in water to create brine.

CURING SALTS

These are salt products created specifically for curing meat in order to make products such as bacon or salt beef. They usually consist of table salt with the addition of sodium nitrate and are colored pink in order to distinguish them from ordinary salt.

BRINED AND FRIED CHICKEN

Serves 4

Preparation 20 minutes,
  plus overnight brining

Cooking 25 minutes

⅔ cup salt

2 quarts water

8 chicken drumsticks, skin on

1½ cups all-purpose flour

1 tsp garlic powder

1 tsp cayenne pepper

Salt and freshly ground
  black pepper

Sunflower or vegetable oil, for
  deep-frying

Brining chicken is an excellent way of ensuring
that the meat is moist when cooked. Deep-fried
chicken is always popular with all the family.
Serve with a green salad, coleslaw, and potato
salad for a satisfying meal.

1 First, make the brine. Place the salt and water in a large
pan and gently heat together, stirring until the salt has
dissolved. Remove from the heat and let cool.

2 Place the chicken drumsticks in the cooled brine,
making sure they are submerged. Cover and chill in the
refrigerator for 24 hours.

3 Mix the flour, garlic powder, and cayenne together and
season the mixture well with salt and black pepper. Tip
the flour mixture into a large plastic bag.

4 Place the oil for deep-frying in a deep-fat fryer or
a large, deep saucepan, filled two-thirds with oil.
Heat the oil to 350°F.

5 Add the chicken to the flour mixture in the bag and
shake well until thoroughly coated. Fry the chicken in
two batches in the hot oil until cooked through and
golden brown. Drain on paper towels and serve at once.

SALT

SEA SALT

This is produced from sea water through evaporation processes (see p. 79). Unrefined sea salt contains trace minerals, which can give it a more complex flavor. Its color, too, may be affected by traces of sediment; Guérande coarse sea salt, for example, is gray from its contact with clay. In France, unrefined sea salt is called *sel gris*, meaning gray salt. Sea salts are often sold in flake form, as their distinctive, crunchy texture is considered part of their appeal. Finely ground sea salt, resembling granulated table salt, is also produced commercially.

HAWAIIAN SALT

On the islands of Hawaii, sea salt has long been harvested using solar evaporation. Traditionally, it was mixed with red *alaea* clay, from the Waimea mountains, giving the salt a reddish hue. The use of this clay is believed to give the salt special powers, and it is used in purifying and blessing ceremonies.

HIMALAYAN SALT

A rock salt, formed by an inland sea millions of years ago, naturally tinted a delicate pink by the presence of trace minerals such as potassium, magnesium, and calcium.

KALA NAMAK (BLACK SALT)

An Indian salt, historically made from rock salt deposits found in the Himalayas and fired with charcoal and spices to create black crystals. When ground, however, it takes on a pinkish color and has a noticeably sulfurous smell and flavor.

FLEUR DE SEL

In the world of culinary salt, what is known as *fleur de sel* in French—a poetic name that translates as "flower of the salt"—carries a particular cachet. Noticeably more expensive than everyday salt, it is highly esteemed by chefs and home cooks for both its flavor and its texture. It is a salt that historically was naturally created through the interaction of the sea with a particular terrain and climate. In his *Natural History*, Pliny the Elder wrote of a type of salt created by the sea: "Another kind of salt spontaneously produced from sea-water is foam left on the edge of the shore and on the rocks by the sea." He was describing a simple, natural form of *fleur de sel*. Over the centuries, however, as humans developed their salt-harvesting techniques, the creation of *fleur de sel* involved both the natural movement of the sea and human ingenuity and input in using the salt water. It is important to understand that *fleur de sel* is not simply sea salt or salt obtained by evaporating sea water. It is the crust of salt crystals that forms on the surface of the water as sea water in a shallow pool evaporates due to the actions of wind and sun.

One country in particular is associated with *fleur de sel*, and that is, of course, France. Guérande in Brittany, the Île de Ré, and the Camargue are all areas where this specialty is produced. Of the three places, it is the town of Guérande, located on a peninsula, that has a long tradition of harvesting salt from the large local marshes known as *pays blanc* (white country) because of the color of the salt in the shallow waters. Salt is thought to have been gathered here since the Iron Age, and saltworks dating to the third century, following the arrival of the Romans, have been found on the marshes. The current production technique used in the Guérande marshes dates to the ninth century CE—there are saltworks still in use at Batz-sur-Mer that date to this period. The salt workers in this region are called *paludiers*, a word derived from *palud*, a French dialect word for "marsh." Over the centuries, the saltworks in the marshes were built up and expanded, with the last constructed around 1800, and the salt trade is still an important source of income for the town.

The saltworks function by gravity, using high tide to fill the reservoirs and low tide to empty them. The production of salt is an annual process, which begins with the high spring tides of April and ends around early September. Not only is the period of time for harvesting a relatively short one, but the weather conditions need to be right for harvesting to be successful; heat from the sun, wind, and the absence of rain are required. At high tide, sea water flows through *étiers* (canals) into an intricate system of constructed ponds, through which the *paludiers* make their way along narrow dikes. These ponds are the saltworks, formed in the marshes from the local clay, which has the advantage of being malleable, waterproof (in order to retain water), and cool enough to create the ideal conditions for the best crystallization. The movement of the sea water involves both the tides and the use of sluice gates and pipes to guide the water as required.

The *vasière* (primary pond) acts as a large water reserve, while the *corbiers* (expansion ponds) are designed to increase the concentration of salt to a high enough level to remove unwanted algae and crustaceans. Next come the smaller *fares* (evaporation ponds), designed to be as flat as possible and to allow for a shallow flow of water, less than ½ inch deep; here the sea water is concentrated still further through natural evaporation, which

removes the water, leaving the salt within the sea brine behind. The *adernes* are reserve ponds used to store sea water, which is then used to top up the final set of ponds, known as *oeillets*. These rectangular ponds, the water's final destination, measure around 23 by 33 feet and are constructed in order to allow harvesting by hand to take place. Overall, *oeillets* form around just 10 percent of the saltworks, which demonstrates how concentrated the sea water has become during its slow journey through the marshes. The preparation and maintenance of the *oeillets* are very important, with flatness in the middle part vital, while a shallow trough runs around the edge. They must not be allowed to dry out, so water from the *adernes* is fed into them.

Each day, late in the morning, as the sea water reacts to the actions of wind and sun, the salt contained within the brine in the *oeillets* begins to crystallize, floating on the surface of the water. It is this delicate layer, which does not touch the clay, that is *fleur de sel*. At the clay base of the *oeillets*, where the water is colder, crystallization also takes place, forming what is called coarse salt, a different product from *fleur de sel*, naturally tinted gray through its contact with the clay on which it forms. Both the coarse salt and the *fleur de sel* are harvested by hand, daily during the summer, as they have been for centuries. The harvesting technique used in the Guérande salt marshes is thought to have been developed by Benedictine monks at the priory at Batz-sur-Mer, founded in 945 CE.

Fleur de sel, which forms in far smaller amounts than the coarse salt, is collected as late in the day as possible to ensure that the crystals have formed properly and to maximize the day's harvest. This fragile layer of salt is carefully skimmed from the surface of the still sea water using a *lousse*, a special type of rake. This task, which requires a delicate touch but not too much strength, was historically carried out by women. Each *oeillet* yields only around 4½ pounds of *fleur de sel* a day. Once the *fleur de sel* has been harvested and set to drain in the sun, then the coarse salt lying underneath the surface is collected. This process is an intricate and laborious one. First, fresh water from the *adernes* is gently fed into the *oeillets* to replenish the water in order to create salt for the following day's harvest. Next, the coarse salt crystals are moved using a long-handled tool called a *lasse* toward a *ladure*, a central platform in the *oeillet*. The salt is then pulled out of the water onto this platform, forming a pile of salt crystals known as a *ladurée*. Here it drains before being moved to form larger piles on the edge of the saltworks, where it is then collected and stored in silos. The yield of coarse salt is considerably larger than that of *fleur de sel*, around 110 to 154 pounds a day per *oeillet*. Just as with farmers and their crops, the correct weather

ROSEMARY AND
SEA SALT FOCACCIA

Makes 1 loaf

Preparation 20 minutes, plus
1½ hours rising

Cooking 20 minutes

4 cups bread flour, plus extra
  for dusting

1 tsp quick yeast

1 tsp table salt

1 tsp granulated sugar

1¼ cups hand-hot water

6 tbsp extra-virgin olive oil

2 large sprigs of rosemary

3 tsp sea salt flakes

This classic Italian bread is simple to make—the results look impressive and taste good, too. Serve it plain or with a selection of cheeses, cured meats, and cherry tomatoes.

1   In a large mixing bowl, mix together the flour, yeast, salt, and sugar. Gradually add the water and 2 tablespoons of the olive oil, mixing together to form a sticky dough.

2   Transfer the dough to a lightly floured work surface and knead until smooth and supple. Place the dough in a clean, lightly oiled bowl, cover with a clean kitchen cloth, and set aside in a warm, sheltered spot to rise for 1 hour.

3   Break down the risen dough and shape it into a rough, large oval on a greased baking sheet. Push a finger firmly into the dough a number of times to form several indents in its surface. Tear the rosemary into small sprigs and place in the indents. Spoon over 2 tablespoons of the olive oil so that it fills the indents and coats the surface. Set aside for 30 minutes.

4   Preheat the oven to 500°F. Sprinkle 2 teaspoons of the sea salt flakes over the surface of the focaccia. Bake for 20 minutes until golden brown. Remove from the oven. Spoon the remaining olive oil over the focaccia, sprinkle with the remaining sea salt, and serve warm from the oven or at room temperature.

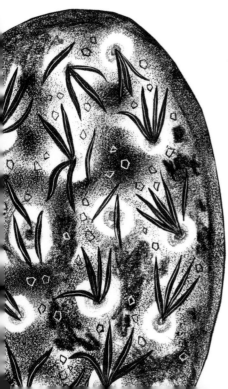

SALT COD CROQUETTES

Makes 24 croquettes

Preparation 30 minutes, plus 24 hours soaking and cooling

Cooking 25 minutes

These small, tasty croquettes are a popular Portuguese dish. When cooking with salt cod, bear in mind the time required for soaking the fish beforehand. This softens the salt cod and also removes excess salt.

1 lb 5 oz salt cod

1 lb 5 oz floury potatoes, peeled and chopped

2 eggs, lightly beaten

½ onion, very finely chopped

2 tbsp freshly chopped parsley

Sunflower or vegetable oil, for deep-frying

1   Soak the salt cod for 24 hours in cold water, changing the water three times during the soaking period.
2   Place the soaked salt cod in a saucepan, cover generously with fresh water, bring to a boil, and simmer until the salt cod has softened, around 20 minutes; drain.
3   Meanwhile, cook the potatoes in boiling, salted water until tender; drain and mash thoroughly.
4   Once the salt cod is cool enough to handle, use your hands to go through it, picking out and discarding any skin and bones. Flake the remaining salt cod.
5   In a large bowl, thoroughly mix together the mashed potatoes, flaked salt cod, eggs, onion, and parsley. Using 2 tablespoons, shape the mixture into 24 even-sized croquettes and set aside to cool.
6   Place the oil for deep-frying in a deep-fat fryer or a large, deep saucepan, filled two-thirds with oil. Heat the oil to 350°F. Fry the croquettes in batches in the hot oil, turning them over during cooking so that they brown evenly. Once golden brown on all sides, remove and drain on paper towels.
7   Serve the croquettes warm or at room temperature.

conditions are vital to ensure a good harvest for the *paludiers* from the Guérande saltworks. If the weather remains too hot over a sustained period of weeks, the sought-after crystallization fails to happen, with the salt instead forming a powder at the base of the *oeillets*.

Given the time and effort that go into forming Guérande's *fleur de sel*—and the small quantities that can be harvested—it is unsurprising that its price is higher than that of industrially produced table salt. Guérande's *fleur de sel* has long been appreciated for its quality and, sold in upmarket food shops, it finds an appreciative audience of keen cooks around the world. Its flavor has a particular minerality and a sweet finish. It is, however, valued especially for its distinctive texture, created by the delicate crystals, which vary in shape and size. Consequently, it is best used as a finishing salt, with a pinch of it sprinkled over dishes such as grilled steaks or fish or tomato salad just before serving.

The twentieth century saw a decline in demand for Guérande's salt. In recent decades, however, there has been a revival in the area's salt economy, with a new appreciation of quality sea salt and *fleur de sel.* The surviving local salt workers came together in 1988 to form a cooperative, ensuring the quality of what is being produced. In 2012, Guérande's *fleur de sel* was granted Protected Geographical Indicator status, a way of protecting the traditional product. Today, around 300 salt workers carry on the skillful tradition of farming salt in the marshes of Guérande.

Given the time and effort that go into forming Guérande's fleur de sel—*and the small quantities that can be harvested—it is unsurprising that its price is higher than that of industrially produced table salt.*

SALT IN PRESERVING

One of the reasons that salt has long been perceived as an essential ingredient is the important role it plays in preserving food. Salting food is an ancient, widely practiced form of preserving, still used today. As a means of preserving perishable foods such as meat or fish, it was very important in the days before refrigeration. The way in which salt helps to preserve food is through osmosis. Sprinkle salt onto a raw ingredient such as a piece of meat or sliced onion, and soon little droplets of water appear on its surface. Their appearance is caused by the action of the salt as it seeks to reach equilibrium with the salt content of the food and so draws out the moisture from the ingredient, seeking to replace the water molecules within the food with salt molecules. The process of salting causes dehydration, and it is the lack of water that inhibits microbial growth. Bacteria require water in order to thrive, and adding salt creates an environment without water that is, therefore, hostile to microbes.

Furthermore, salt, by changing the electrical balance, also prevents decay caused by enzymes in food. Many preserved foods involve the addition of salt: cheeses, cured meats such as hams, salamis (see "Charcuterie," p. 29), and pickles, among them. Salt also plays an important role in the creation of fermented foods such as sauerkraut and kimchi. These use a traditional process of lacto-fermentation, which begins with the liberal addition of salt to the raw ingredient. The salt creates an alkaline environment in which *Lactobacillus*, a particular strain of bacteria, can grow. These bacteria convert lactose or other sugars into lactic acid, creating an environment that is hostile to harmful bacteria.

In preserving, salting takes two forms: dry salting and brining, also known as wet salting. The process of dry salting, for example, a loin of pork to turn it into bacon starts with directly rubbing the meat all over with salt, then setting it aside in a cool place to rest for 24 hours. The resulting leached salty liquid is drained from the meat and fresh salt is rubbed in. This dry salting process is repeated for five days, after which the bacon can be eaten or smoked. Salt plays an important part in cheesemaking, in which highly perishable milk is transformed into a food with longer keeping qualities. Having curdled the milk by adding a coagulant such as rennet, many cheese recipes involve adding dry salt to the curds. Using salt in this way not only flavors the cheese, but also shrinks and dries out the curds, thus controlling moisture levels and lessening the risk of pathogens developing in the cheese.

Brining begins by adding salt to water, bringing it to a boil to dissolve it, then cooling. The food being cured is then submerged in this brine, an advantage being that the salty solution totally covers the food and so allows for efficient penetration. The ratio of salt to water in brine solutions and the contact time between food and brine depend on the ingredient being preserved. Salt pork, historically an important food for armies and navies, was made by salting pork flesh and immersing it in a strong brine solution in barrels, which allowed it to be safely kept for long periods of time. Another salted meat is corned beef, made by immersing beef brisket in a brine solution flavored with spices for a number of days, then draining, rinsing, and cooking it until tender. Brining is also used in cheesemaking, with certain types of hard cheeses immersed in brine for flavor and also in order to kill off harmful bacteria and aid successful rind development.

ROASTED SEA-SALTED ALMONDS

Makes 8 oz

Preparation 3 minutes

Cooking 12–18 minutes

Salted nuts are a popular snack for good reason. Served as an accompaniment to a classic martini, gin and tonic, or a glass of wine, their texture and savoriness contrast well with drinks. Making freshly roasted nuts at home is simple, and the results are irresistible. This recipe uses almonds, but following the same technique, you could also roast cashews, hazelnuts, or a mixture of nuts.

8 oz blanched almonds

2 tsp olive oil

1 tsp coarse sea salt

½ tsp fine sea salt

1   Preheat the oven to 350°F.

2   Spread the almonds out on a roasting pan. Roast for 10–15 minutes until golden brown, turning the nuts over every now and then.

3   Add the olive oil and sea salts to the nuts, mixing well. Roast for a further 2–3 minutes. Remove, cool, and store in an airtight container.

Despite the development of technology such as canning, refrigeration, and freezing, which successfully extend the period of time for which foods can be safely consumed, salt continues to play an important part in food preservation, as it has done for centuries.

SALT COD

Among the many foods preserved through the use of salt was fish. Applying salt to fresh fish transformed this perishable ingredient into a food that could be safely kept and eaten for several days, rather than eaten fresh. For fishermen going out to sea in boats, the ability to preserve their catch in this way made it economically viable. Salted fish was an essential food in medieval Europe, where religion played a key part in creating a demand for it. The injunction to abstain from meat on fast days led to fish being eaten instead. In an age of slow transport and without refrigeration, obtaining fresh fish was challenging, so salted fish that kept well was a useful alternative.

Cod fish, a large fish that is low in fat, lent itself well to being salted and dried, and was able to outlast salted oily fish such as herring. It became the salted fish of choice in many countries. Cod is a coldwater fish, found in coastal waters in the North Atlantic. The tradition of preserving it was an old one; the Vikings had transformed the cod fish they caught into stockfish by simply wind-drying it in the cold air, without the use of salt. Salt cod, created by gutting, splitting, and heavily salting fresh cod and allowing it to dry, was appreciated not only for its durability but also for its flavor and texture, once rehydrated through soaking. Such was the demand for salted cod in medieval Europe that cod fish were a valuable, sought-after resource. In May 1497, the Italian navigator and explorer Giovanni Caboto, also known as John Cabot, sailed west from Bristol. In June he sighted land, encountering what he mistakenly thought was Asia but which was, in fact, what is now called Newfoundland. He returned to England, and among his reports was one on the abundance of fish found in the sea off the coast of this newly discovered land. Reporting on Cabot's voyage, the Milanese ambassador to England wrote:

> *They assert that the sea there is swarming with fish which can be taken not only with the net but in baskets, let down with a stone so it sinks in the water.*

In an age of slow transport and without refrigeration, obtaining fresh fish was challenging, so salted fish that kept well was a useful alternative. Cod fish, a large fish that is low in fat, lent itself well to being salted and dried.

I have heard this Messer Zoane [Cabot] state so much. These same English, his companions, say that they could bring so many fish that this kingdom would have no further need of Iceland, from which place there comes a very great quantity of the fish called stockfish.

In 1534, the French explorer Jacques Cartier "discovered" the mouth of the St. Lawrence River, where he found a large fleet of Basque vessels. For centuries, it turned out, the Basque had been exploiting the cod-rich seas off what is now the Canadian coast, conducting a lucrative trade in salt cod. The discovery by fishermen of the Grand Banks off the Newfoundland coast was a significant one for the salt cod market. Fish, including cod, were found in abundant numbers in the plankton-rich waters of these underwater plateaux, part of the North American continental shelf. Salt cod offered an affordable, transportable food and was adopted as a basic ingredient in many parts of the world. The use of salt cod by the Europeans as a cheap food to feed to slaves on plantations in the Americas meant that salt cod became an ingredient widely eaten in the Caribbean and Central and South America. Salt cod is enjoyed in a number of European countries, including France, Italy, and Spain. It is, however, especially beloved in Portugal, where it is nicknamed *fiel amigo* (faithful friend) and used in many dishes. In 1992, the Canadian government declared a moratorium on the Northern Cod

PEANUT BUTTER COOKIES

Makes about 46 cookies

Preparation 20 minutes, plus
  1 hour chilling

Cooking 15–30 minutes

1 stick softened butter

2 oz dark brown sugar

4 oz granulated sugar

1 egg, beaten

½ tsp vanilla extract

1 cup smooth or crunchy
  peanut butter

5 oz all-purpose flour

½ tsp baking soda

These much-loved cookies are a perfect example of how well the salty-sweet flavor combination works. Easy and satisfying to make, the small golden-brown cookies are a real treat and are perfect with a cup of coffee.

1 In a mixing bowl, use a wooden spoon to mix together the butter, dark brown sugar, and granulated sugar until well combined.

2 Gradually mix in the beaten egg and vanilla extract until incorporated. Mix in the peanut butter.

3 Sift in the flour and baking soda and mix together, forming a soft, sticky dough. Cover and chill in the refrigerator for 1 hour.

4 Preheat the oven to 350°F. Shape the chilled dough into small, even-sized balls. Place the dough balls on greased baking sheets, spaced well apart, pressing down with a fork to flatten them and also to create a characteristic lined appearance.

5 Bake in one or two batches, depending on your oven's efficiency. Bake each batch for 15 minutes until a deep golden color. Let cool on a wire rack and store in an airtight container.

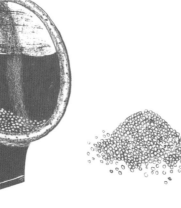

fishery, which had played such a prominent part in sustaining the market for salt cod. Overfishing had caused a collapse of cod stocks in that area. Nowadays, salt cod is no longer a widely available, cheap food; instead it is a costly luxury, enjoyed for its particular flavor and texture.

CULINARY SALT

The fact that saltiness is one of the five basic tastes our tongues detect means that all around the world salt is used in food production and cooking, adding what is widely regarded as an essential flavor. Staple ingredients such as rice, pasta, or potatoes are usually cooked with a pinch of salt to enhance them. Furthermore, salt is placed on the table—contained in salt shakers, salt grinders, or small receptacles—to allow diners to season their food with salt to their taste. Salt is so powerful that cooks are advised to use it judiciously, as adding an excessive amount will spoil a dish. When cooking, a piece of good advice is to add a little salt first, taste the dish, and then add more salt if required, as once too much has been added, it is hard to rectify it. Another thing to bear in mind when seasoning with salt is the saltiness of other ingredients in the dish; additions such as bacon, soy sauce, and Parmesan cheese will increase the dish's salty flavor.

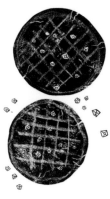

So beloved is saltiness, however, that it characterizes a number of key condiments. In ancient Greece, Byzantium, and Rome, *garum*, the liquid drawn off from salted and fermented fish, was an important flavoring. *Garum* features extensively in the Apicius cookbook, compiled in the first century CE. Southeast Asia's fish sauce, known as *nam pla* in Thailand, is made by fermenting fish in brine; used widely to this day, it is characterized by its salty, fishy flavor. China's essential condiment soy sauce, made from fermented soybeans and brine, is famously salty, often used in place of salt in dishes such as stir-fries, braises, and roast meats. Soy sauce, rather than salt, is the seasoning placed on Chinese tables.

Salt's usefulness in preserving foods (see p. 99) means that it plays a key role in many much-loved foodstuffs, lending its flavor to them in the process. It is striking that a number of highly prized fish-based delicacies are noticeably salty. *Caviar* is the word traditionally used to describe the salt-cured roe of various species of sturgeon, although the term is also applied to the roe of other fish species. Historically, caviar was produced using wild fish from the Caspian Sea and the Black Sea. The roe extracted from the female fish is salt cured; hence its characteristically salty flavor. Another salted fish roe delicacy is Italian *bottarga*, made by salting and drying gray mullet roe. Traditionally, *bottarga* is served either finely sliced and dressed with olive oil and lemon juice or grated and tossed with spaghetti. More affordably, preserved anchovies, cured in brine and packed in salt or stored in oil, are a popular Mediterranean ingredient. They add a distinctive salty umami note to dishes such as pizzas, stews, dips, and roast meats. The traditional Venetian dish of *bigoli in salsa* combines a type of thick spaghetti with slow-fried onions and anchovy fillets, cooked until they melt into the onion. It is a simple but effective dish, as the sweetness of the onions and the saltiness of the anchovies make it remarkably flavorful.

Salt's capacity to draw out moisture through osmosis means that there is a tradition of salting certain ingredients before cooking them. Traditionally, eggplants were sliced and salted for 20 to 30 minutes to draw out their bitter juices, then rinsed and patted dry before frying. Salting chopped onions before deep-frying them is a useful step, as this draws out their moisture, enabling them to be fried to a deep brown color more quickly. Similarly, when pounding garlic to a paste, adding a pinch of salt helps break it down. In Peruvian ceviche, a little salt is sprinkled on raw fish or seafood to help open up its pores before adding the marinade. Salting is an important stage in pickling vegetables such as cucumbers or zucchini, helping to firm them up and remove excess moisture. In North Africa, pickled lemons are made by salting fresh lemons, transforming them into a long-lasting condiment used to flavor aromatic meat, poultry, and fish tagines.

One striking use of salt is to encrust an ingredient in it, coating it thoroughly in a large quantity of salt (often mixed with egg white), and baking it. In the Mediterranean region, this is a classic way of cooking whole fish such as sea bass or bream (see p. 77). The hard salt crust is then cracked open, revealing moist, tender fish. In Chinese cuisine, one finds salt-baked chicken, in which a whole young bird is seasoned, covered in salt, and cooked. This way of cooking has been enjoying a new wave of popularity, used for whole root vegetables such as celery root, beet, and parsnips.

The cooking of salt cod, an iconic salted preserved food (see p. 98), begins with first soaking the hard, dried fish in order both to soften it and to make it less salty. In France, a famous dish made using salt cod is *brandade de morue*, a specialty of Languedoc and Provence, with the first written recipe for it dating from 1830. The name comes from the Provençal verb *brandar*, meaning "to stir." It is made by poaching the salt cod, then vigorously beating in olive oil and milk to form a thick puree. There are numerous French recipes for *morue* (salt cod), ranging from using it in hot dishes such as gratins and soufflés to poaching it and eating it cold in vinaigrette. It is, however, in Portuguese cuisine that one finds the widest range of *bacalhau* (salt cod) recipes; indeed, it is popularly said that the Portuguese have a different *bacalhau* recipe for every day of the year. *Pasteis de bacalhau* (salt cod fritters), made from poached salt cod mixed with mashed potato, eggs, and parsley, are a hugely popular snack throughout Portugal (see p. 98). Other dishes include *bacalhau a Bras* (salt cod in the style of Bras), a combination of sautéed salt cod, potatoes, and beaten eggs; *bacalhau com todos* (which translates as "salt cod with everything"), a Christmas Eve dish of salt cod, freshly boiled potatoes, cabbage, and hardcooked eggs; and *arroz de bacalhau* (salt cod rice). It is indeed a versatile ingredient.

Recent years have seen the rise of salt—often in the form of prestigious sea salt flakes—as a fashionable flavoring. It is added in larger quantities than was traditional to baked goods such as cookies, desserts, and confectionary.

An iconic salted food in the United States is corned beef, also known as salt beef, a salt-cured beef made by curing brisket in brine seasoned with spices, a process that gives the meat a particular flavor and texture. It is a popular item in New York's Jewish delicatessens such as Katz's, and it is famously used in the Reuben sandwich, in which the salt beef is layered with sauerkraut, Swiss cheese, and Russian dressing between slices of rye bread, grilled, and served hot.

Intriguingly, salt is often used to enhance sweet dishes. Small amounts of salt are added to sweet confections such as cookies, cakes, chocolate puddings, meringues, or sauces to heighten the sweetness. Salt has the capacity to enhance the sweetness and umami qualities and to suppress bitterness in food. A historic candy in the United States that uses this salty sweetness is saltwater taffy, originating from Atlantic City and produced since the late nineteenth century from a syrup of sugar, corn syrup, salted water, and butter.

Recent years have seen the rise of salt—often in the form of prestigious sea salt flakes—as a fashionable flavoring. It is added in larger quantities than was traditional to baked goods such as cookies, desserts, and confectionary, such as milk chocolate bars. In Brittany, France, an area noted both for its rich dairy tradition and its sea salt (see p. 94), one finds salted butter caramels, a clever combination of local ingredients. Nowadays, salted caramel is exceedingly fashionable in the West, found in numerous contemporary recipes ranging from cakes, brownies, and tarts to puddings served with salted caramel sauce. Our fascination with salt, it seems, continues into the twenty-first century.

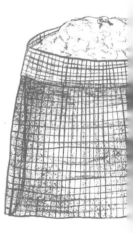

CHILE

Originating in South America, the chile is a globally successful food, widely grown and eaten around the world. Our culinary fascination with chiles has to do with the unique fiery sensations that eating hot chiles creates in our mouths—a pleasurable pain that humans enjoy and which has spurred us to use chiles in the kitchen in numerous inventive ways.

Chile peppers, which belong to the genus *Capsicum*, are thought to trace their origins to Bolivia in South America, where wild chile plants continue to grow to this very day. From there, the wild chile pepper plant was introduced to other countries in South America, Mesoamerica, and the Caribbean, possibly spread simply by birds excreting chile seeds that passed through their systems. There is considerable uncertainty as to when and where this shrubby perennial plant was first domesticated by humans. Among the earliest evidence of humans using chiles is plant material excavated from the Coxcatlan Cave in Mexico. While seeds from the cave's older layers are thought to be wild, it is believed that those dating from around 3000 to 2000 BCE were from domesticated plants.

The first encounter between Europeans and the chile peppers of the New World came with the arrival of Christopher Columbus in 1492 on the island of Hispaniola (now the Dominican Republic and Republic of Haiti). Treated with great hospitality by the Taíno, the indigenous islanders, the Genoese explorer returned to Spain with a new spice called *aji* in the Taíno language, but which Columbus called *pimiento*, as its fiery heat reminded him of the valuable spice he sought, namely *pimienta* (black pepper). Although the plants are unrelated, the term "pepper" for the fruit of the chile plant continues to be used to this day. It was the Spanish conquistadors, through their encounter and subsequent conquering of the Aztec kingdom in Mexico in the sixteenth century, who began to use the word "chile," based on the Nahuatl word for this fiery fruit. In Nahuatl, *chil* means both the chile plant and the color red. On his return from his first voyage to the New World in 1493, Columbus offered his patrons, King Ferdinand and Queen Isabella, a tasting of exotic and novel foodstuffs he had brought back with him from the other side of the world. This intriguing meal was described by the secretary of the Spanish conquistador Hernán Cortés: "They tried *aji* [chile peppers], a spice of the Indians which burned their tongues, and *batatas* [sweet potatoes], which are sweet roots, and *gallipavos* [turkeys], which are better than peacocks and hens."

In his encyclopedic sixteenth-century record of Aztec life, now known as the Florentine Codex, based on his experience of living in Mexico, the Franciscan friar Bernardino de Sahagún includes a fascinating description of an array of chiles being sold at the vast market at Tlatelolco. He describes how the chile dealer sells "yellow chile, cuilachilli, tenpichilli, and chichioachilli. He sells water chiles, conchilli, smoked chiles, very tiny chiles, tree chiles, slender chiles, those that look like beetles. He sells hot chiles, those sown in March, those with a hollow base. He sells green chiles, pointed red chiles, a later variety, those from Atzitziucan, Tochmilco, Huaxtepec, Michoacán, Anahuac, the Huaasteca, the Chichimecca." A number of the chile peppers Sahagún describes are now impossible to identify, but his words vividly evoke the richness of Aztec chile culture. In his great work, Sahagún records how the Aztecs used chiles medicinally, to treat toothaches and coughs. In their culinary life, the Aztecs used chiles to add relish to their food, foregoing the pleasures of chiles during their religious fasts.

In his great work, Sahagún records how the Aztecs used chiles medicinally, to treat toothaches and coughs. In their culinary life, the Aztecs used chiles to add relish to their food, foregoing the pleasures of chiles during their religious fasts.

The Spanish also encountered chiles with their conquest of the Incas in Peru. Here, despite it being a more temperate climate than Mexico, the chile pepper was cultivated and widely eaten. An account of Inca life by El Inca Garcilaso de la Vega (who was the son of an Inca princess and a Spanish soldier), published in 1609, describes chile peppers as hugely popular among the Incas: "the seasoning put in everything that they eat—whether stews, boiled or roasted, there is not eating anything without it." So beloved were chile peppers by the Incas that they chose to go without them during periods of fasting. De la Vega's account includes a description of different chiles eaten by the Incas, among them the rocoto, enjoyed to this day in Peruvian cuisine.

Of the five domesticated *Capsicum* species, three in particular—*Capsicum annuum*, *Capsicum chinense*, and *Capsicum frutescens*—have spread around the globe. The distribution of chiles in the sixteenth century is linked to European imperialism and trade. It was the Spanish and Portuguese who introduced chiles to countries outside the New World. The Portuguese explorer Vasco da Gama voyaged by sea to India in 1498, while in 1500 his fellow countryman Pedro Álvares Cabral reached Brazil, claiming it for King Manuel 1 of Portugal. Portuguese traders following these routes took with them the abundant, easily stored seeds of the chile plant. The passage of slave ships from the New World to the slave coast of West Africa is thought to have played its part in introducing chiles to Africa. Chiles quickly became important to African cuisine and are grown in every country on that continent.

What is striking is the speed with which chiles were adopted by some countries. Sadly, there are very few records documenting the introduction of chile to India by the Portuguese. What is known, however, is that within thirty years of Vasco da Gama's arrival in India, three varieties of chile peppers were being grown and traded along the Malabar coast. India, of course, was familiar with the heat caused by its own black pepper (*Piper nigrum*) spice and took to chile peppers with enthusiasm. Like garlic, wherever they were introduced, chile peppers must have been valued by the poor for their transformative effect on food, the way in which they gave zest to the dullest of ingredients.

MARINATED CHICKEN ADOBO

Serves 4
Preparation 15 minutes,
  plus 30 minutes soaking, plus
  overnight marinating
Cooking 30 minutes

1 ancho chile
1 guajillo chile
2 garlic cloves, peeled and
  crushed
1 tsp cumin powder
1 tsp dried oregano
8 skin-on chicken drumsticks
Salt
2 tbsp olive oil
1 onion, peeled and chopped
Juice of 1 orange

Dried Mexican ancho and guajillo chiles, with their distinctive fruity, earthy flavors, are first toasted to enhance their flavor, then soaked and turned into a marinade for chicken, with piquant, tasty results. Serve with warm tortillas, guacamole, and sour cream.

1 Pull off the stems from the ancho and guajillo chiles, slice them open, and deseed them.
2 Now, toast the chiles to bring out their flavor. Heat a heavy skillet until hot. Place the ancho and guajillo chiles in the pan, pressing them against the surface with a spatula for a few seconds, then turning and repeating the process, taking care not to burn them.
3 Place the toasted chiles in a heatproof bowl, cover with warm water, and set aside to soak for about 30 minutes until softened.
4 Drain the chiles and blitz them into a paste in a food processor. Mix together the chile paste, garlic, cumin, and oregano.
5 Place the chicken drumsticks in a large bowl and season well with salt. Add the chile paste and olive oil and mix together, coating the chicken well. Add the onion and orange juice and mix well. Cover and marinate in the fridge for at least 4 hours, preferably overnight.
6 Preheat the oven to 400°F. Place the chicken drumsticks in a roasting pan and roast for 30 minutes until cooked through, turning over halfway through roasting. Serve at once.

The Portuguese also played a major part in introducing chiles to Southeast Asia. In 1511, Afonso de Albuquerque conquered the strategic port of Malacca in Malaysia, which controlled access to the Straits of Malacca and so seagoing trade with China and India. In the same year, the Portuguese first visited the Siamese kingdom of Ayutthaya, in what is now Thailand. Chiles became a key flavoring in Southeast Asian cuisine, with the Thais cultivating their own chiles, including the tiny, formidably hot *prik ki nuu*, also known as bird chile. The Japanese were also introduced to chiles by the Portuguese but remained largely indifferent to the plant's charms. It is the Japanese, however, who introduced the chile to Korea, a country that adopted it with relish. It is not known how chile peppers reached China, but in Sichuan Province, the chile pepper was taken up with enthusiasm (see p. 126, "Culinary Chiles").

In Europe, the chile pepper was initially cultivated in Spain by the monasteries, which enjoyed royal favor and so were granted access to seeds and cuttings from Spain's colonies in the New World. In Europe, it was regarded as a novelty, a curiosity grown by gardeners. Sometimes the routes it took to Europe were long and circuitous. In 1597, English botanist and herbalist John Gerard wrote in his *Herball* of chile peppers being "brought from foreign countries as Ginnie [Guinea, West Africa], India and those parts, into Spain and Italy, from whence we have received seed for our English gardens." The arrival of chiles in Turkey was followed by their spread throughout the Ottoman Empire. Chiles were introduced into Hungary in the second half of the sixteenth century, thought to have been brought by Bulgarians, who had, in turn, been introduced to chiles by the Turks.

Today, chiles enjoy an extraordinary cosmopolitan popularity and are widely cultivated around the world. It is estimated that a quarter of the planet's human population eat chiles in some form every day.

CHILE HEAT

The "heat"—characterized by burning sensations upon contact with the mouth—that many chile peppers produce when eaten is their best-known and distinguishing characteristic. This effect is created within the chile pepper pods by what are called capsaicinoids, a group of compounds created only in capsicums and no other plants. Basically, these capsaicinoids are a powerful, defensive botanical chemical weapon, created to deter mammal predators—through the irritation that they cause—from eating the plant's precious seed-bearing chiles.

The five principal capsaicinoids are capsaicin (the one that is found in the largest quantities), dihydrocapsaicin, nordihydrocapsaicin, homodihydrocapsaicin, and homocapsaicin. Each of these contributes to the complex sensations one feels on eating a chile pepper. Three of them create what are called "rapid bite" sensations at the back of the palate and throat, while the other two cause a long, low-intensity sensation on the tongue and the middle palate. These compounds are found in differing levels, which is why different chile "burns" vary in how they feel.

On the whole, capsaicinoids in chiles are found inside what is called the placental tissue—the internal, pulpy part of the chile pod that holds and nourishes the seeds. Scientists, however, have discovered that in some hot cultivars, the capsaicinioids are found throughout the chile, present even in the pericarp (fleshy outer structure) that is normally free of capsaicinoids. The amount of capsaicinoids in chiles varies and is affected by the chile cultivar, the age of the fruit, and how the plant has grown, with conditions such as altitude, drought, and excess rain all being factors. Even on the same plant, the amount of capsaicinoids within the individual chiles will vary.

When a mammal eats a hot chile, the capsaicinoids produce particular effects on the body. To begin with, they create a feeling of heat, which is why it is common to begin sweating upon eating a hot chile, and increase the metabolic rate. A pain receptor in human bodies, called TRPVI, is triggered

KASHMIRI POTATO CURRY

Serves 4
Preparation 15 minutes
Cooking 40 minutes

Kashmiri chile powder adds a characteristic bright red color and a moderate, but not overpowering, heat to this traditional, hearty potato dish. Serve it as a vegetable side dish as part of an Indian meal or eat with naan bread for a vegetarian meal.

1 lb small, even-sized potatoes
¼ cup sunflower or
  vegetable oil
½ lb onions, peeled and finely
  chopped
1 cinnamon stick
4 cloves
4 cardamom pods
2 garlic cloves, peeled
  and chopped
1-inch slice of ginger root,
  peeled and finely chopped
½ cup full-fat natural yogurt,
  whisked
½ cup canned chopped
  tomatoes
1 tsp coriander powder
1 tsp fennel powder
½ tsp turmeric powder
1 tsp Kashmiri chile powder
Salt
½ cup hot water
Chopped cilantro, to
  garnish (optional)

1   Boil the potatoes in their skins in salted water until just tender, around 10 minutes. Drain, peel, and quarter.

2   Heat the oil in a deep skillet and fry the potatoes until golden on all sides, around 10 minutes. Remove with a slotted spoon, leaving the oil in the pan, and drain on paper towels.

3   Heat the skillet once again over medium heat, add the onion, cinnamon stick, cloves, and cardamom pods. Fry for about 5 minutes, stirring often, until the onion is lightly browned. Add the garlic and ginger and fry for 1 minute until fragrant.

4   Mix in the whisked yogurt and cook, stirring, for an additional minute.

5   Add the chopped tomatoes, coriander, fennel, turmeric, and chile powders, mixing together well. Season with salt. Add the hot water, mix together, and bring to a boil.

6   Add the potatoes to the spicy sauce, mixing to coat well. Reduce the heat and simmer for 10 minutes, stirring now and then, until the potatoes are heated through. Serve at once, garnished with cilantro if liked.

SPAGHETTI AL AGLIO, OLIO, E PEPERONCINO

Serves 4
Preparation 5 minutes
Cooking 10 minutes

This flavorful spaghetti dish originates from the south of Italy, where they have a penchant for chile heat. It uses the dried Italian chiles, properly called *peperoncini picante* but usually known simply as *peperoncini*, which are a popular pantry spice in southern Italian kitchens. In classic Italian fashion, this dish frugally combines a few simple ingredients—spaghetti, olive oil, garlic, and dried chile peppers—to excellent effect.

Salt
1 lb spaghetti
½ cup extra-virgin olive oil
4 garlic cloves, peeled
  and sliced
4 *peperoncini* (small, dried
  Italian chile peppers)
Finely chopped parsley,
  to garnish

1 Bring a large saucepan of generously salted water to a boil. Add the spaghetti and cook until al dente.

2 Toward the end of the spaghetti's cooking time, heat the olive oil in a small skillet over medium-low heat. Add the garlic and fry until golden brown, stirring often. Crumble in the *peperoncini* (taking care to wash your hands with soap and hot water afterward) and fry briefly, mixing well.

3 Drain the cooked spaghetti, return to the saucepan, and toss at once with the piquant garlicky olive oil mixture, mixing thoroughly. Sprinkle with parsley and serve at once.

by capsaicinoids, causing the sense of fiery pain that one gets when eating a hot chile. These pain receptors are found throughout the body, including in the nerves that control the diaphragm, which may be why hiccups, which are caused by an involuntary contraction of the diaphragm, can be triggered by eating chiles. On the beneficial side, capsaicinoids stimulate the appetite. They also increase saliva and gastric juice production within the stomach, thus helping with the digestion of food.

The instinctive reaction to pain caused by consuming a hot chile is to reach for a glass of water. Capsaicin, however, does not dissolve in water, and drinking it will not relieve the pain triggered. It is recommended that you consume a dairy product, such as a glass of milk or a spoonful of yogurt. Capsaicin dissolves in the fat in these dairy foods, and so they have a soothing and counteracting effect.

The powerful effects of capsaicinoids have also seen them used in nonculinary ways. Capsaicin is the active ingredient in pepper spray, which causes pain, tears, and temporary blindness when sprayed in the eyes and is used as a deterrent weapon by police forces seeking to control crowds. In agriculture, pepper spray is used as a biochemical pesticide to repel and kill insects. Scientists are also exploring the potential of capsaicinoids, using them and our mammalian sensitivity to help with analgesia (pain relief). Research shows that repeated exposure to capsaicinoids can desensitize TRPV1 and dull the experience of pain, as the pain receptors become exhausted and fail to pass along the message of pain.

The instinctive reaction to pain caused by consuming a hot chile is to reach for a glass of water. Capsaicin, however, does not dissolve in water, and drinking it will not relieve the pain triggered.

The complexity of the burning sensations caused by chile peppers are among the areas being studied by the Chile Pepper Institute at New Mexico State University in the United States. Dr. Paul Bosland, the university's Regents professor of horticulture, has devised a heat profile in order to help accurately chart the development of the heat sensations felt when consuming a particular chile pepper. There are five stages to the heat profile:

1. Development *(how quickly is the heat experienced?)*
2. Duration *(how long does the heat last?)*
3. Location *(where in the mouth is the heat sensation?)*
4. Feeling *(sharp, like a pinprick, or more widespread?)*
5. Intensity *(classify as mild, medium, or hot)*

The structure of the heat profile gives us particularly useful insight into just how varied the experience of eating a chile pepper can be and the levels of chile heat one can expect.

In what seems a rather perverse way, humans, rather than being repelled by the sensations caused by capsaicinoids, derive enjoyment from them, hence the widespread success of the chile plant around the world. The idea of "benign masochism" is cited by psychologists in this context. Despite their painful effects, eating hot chiles does not harm the body in any way, and, furthermore, the pain subsides. So, just as human beings choose to go on scary fairground rides for the thrill and terror these rides offer, the idea is that we enjoy the temporary "danger" offered to our palate by eating capsaicinoids. One theory for the human fascination with chiles is the idea that, in response to the pain caused by eating chiles, the body releases endorphins. These are neurotransmitters that the body produces and uses as an internal painkiller and which create a sensation of happiness; thus the endorphin rush after exposure to chiles creates a feeling of well-being. Our fascination with chile heat continues unabated, as the rise of super-hot chiles and the amount of events focused on chile heat demonstrate.

THE SCOVILLE SCALE

The hotness of chiles is usually measured in what are called Scoville Heat Units (SHU). This scale for measuring chile heat is named after Wilbur Scoville, a U.S. pharmacist, who devised the Scoville Organoleptic Test as a way of measuring heat in chiles in 1912 while seeking to make a heat-producing ointment. In Scoville's original test, a precise weight of dried chile peppers was dissolved in alcohol to extract the capsaicinoids (the heat-containing elements of the chiles). This extract was then diluted in a sugar water solution. A panel of five human tasters were given decreasing concentrations of the solution until a majority of the panel could no longer detect the heat in what they were tasting. The heat level was based on the level of dilution and measured in Scoville Heat Units. The disadvantage of the Scoville Organoleptic Test was that it relied on human tasters to assess the levels, with very real issues of palate fatigue and desensitization to capsaicinoid levels due to the repeated tasting required, as well as the subjectivity of the individual response, leading to very inconsistent results.

These days, laboratories no longer rely on human palates to assess levels of chile heat. Instead, an analytical chemical technique known as high-performance liquid chromatography is used to detect the exact amount of heat-creating capsaicinoids within chile peppers. Each amount of capsaicinoid is weighted according to its ability to create the sensation of heat. This result is measured in American Spice Trade Association (ASTA) pungency units. In order to get a measurement in Scoville Heat Units, the number of ASTA pungency units is multiplied by fifteen, so Scoville's historic way of measuring chile heat is still in use to this day. As an example of how this works, a bell pepper (which is a member of the *Capsicum* family) would score zero on the Scoville scale, as it contains no capsaicinoids. A jalapeño pepper would score between 3,500 and 10,000 SHU. A hotter habanero chile pepper scores between 100,000 and 350,000 SHU.

The ability to measure the heat contained within chile peppers in SHU has played a part in the rise of a competitive chile heat culture, with the heat, rather than flavor, achieving cult status. The awarding of the Guinness World Record for the World's Hottest Chile has spurred chile growers around the world to seek to secure the fame and financial rewards that achieving this record can bring. As a result, recent years have seen the rise of "superhot" chiles. Between 1994 and 2006, the Guinness World Record for the Hottest Chile went to the Red Savina Habanero, measuring 577,000 SHU. In 2007, the Bhut Jolokia, measuring over one million SHU, took over the record spot. Its position was, however, superseded first by the Trinidad Scorpion "Butch T" pepper in 2011, measuring 1,463,700 SHU, and then by the Trinidad Moruga Scorpion, with individual chiles measuring two million SHU. The current holder of the Guinness World Record is the Carolina Reaper (originally known, less picturesquely, as HP22B), cultivated in the state of South Carolina by a commercial chile grower known as "Smokin'" Ed Currie of the Puckerbutt Pepper Company. It is a chile that Currie spent ten years developing by crossing Sweet Habanero and Naga Viper chiles, then stabilizing and testing to ensure its heat-creating capabilities. A gnarled, blistered red chile pepper with a distinctive pointed tail, the Carolina Reaper achieved 2.2 million SHU for one of its individual peppers, while the average score for a batch was 1,569,300. As well as awards for growing the hottest chile pepper, there are now Guinness World Record awards for the rapid consumption of these ferociously hot chiles. In 2016, an American named Wayne Algenio ate twenty-two Carolina Reaper chiles in under 60 seconds, and so achieved the World Record.

The ability to measure the heat contained within chile peppers in SHU has played a part in the rise of a competitive chile heat culture, with the heat—rather than flavor—achieving cult status.

CHILE SAMBAL

Serves 6 as a condiment
Preparation 10 minutes
Cooking 2–3 minutes

In Malaysia and Singapore, a *chile sambal* is regarded as an essential condiment, used to give a bracing jolt of chile heat to many dishes. This recipe uses another classic Southeast Asian ingredient, namely *blachan* (dried shrimp paste), which gives the condiment its characteristic salty depth of flavor. *Blachan* can be bought online or in specialist Asian food stores and, when stored in an airtight container in a cool, dark place, keeps well. Making *chile sambal* from fresh chiles is quick and easy, and the results are addictively tasty.

6 fresh red chiles

1 tsp *blachan* (dried
  shrimp paste)

2 tsp lime or lemon juice

1   Trim the stalks from the chiles. If you wish to reduce the level of chile heat, slice the chiles open using a sharp knife and carefully remove the seeds and the membrane. Chop the chiles into short pieces.

2   Wrap the *blachan* in foil to prevent it from burning. Place the *blachan* in a small, dry skillet and cook over low heat for 2–3 minutes, turning now and then, to cook through and bring out its flavor.

3   Place the chiles and the *blachan* in a small food processor and blend until well mixed. Mix in the lime or lemon juice.

VARIATION: If you are making *chile sambal* the traditional way, in a pestle and mortar, pound the chopped chiles into a paste with a pinch of salt. Add the roasted *blachan* and pound until well mixed. Stir in the lime or lemon juice.

One popular way of enjoying chile heat is in the form of hot sauce or chile sauce. Recipes for these vary, but chiles are always the key ingredient, blended with water, vinegar, sugar, garlic, spices, and herbs. The resulting thickened sauce is then bottled and used as a condiment to add a piquant hit to dishes. The first advertisement for a bottled hot sauce in the United States appeared in Massachusetts in 1807, promoting a cayenne sauce. Today, there are thousands of brands of hot sauces produced in the United States, and the market for them continues to expand. Tabasco is a famous and historic hot sauce brand, first produced in 1868 by Edmund McIlhenny. Made from tabasco peppers, initially grown on Avery Island in Louisiana, a dash of Tabasco sauce is a traditional addition used to pep up Bloody Mary cocktails. A more recent hot sauce enjoying cult appeal is sriracha, based on a traditional Thai sauce. It is made to a secret recipe from jalapeño peppers in the United States by Huy Fong Foods, founded in Los Angeles in 1980 by a Vietnamese refugee named David Tran. Such is the popularity of Huy Fong's "Rooster Sauce" as a condiment that it is used to enliven everything from noodles and sushi to hot dogs and popcorn. Among chile heat aficionados, there is also demand for hot sauces made from superhot chiles, such as Carolina Reaper Killer Hot Sauce and Trinidad Scorpion Hot Sauce.

HANDLING CHILES

When it comes to handling chiles, fresh or dried, it is advisable to treat them with a cautious respect. The capsaicinoids contained within them, as described above, create sensations of pain in sensitive parts of the human body, such as the eyes and the mouth. After handling or chopping chiles, it is advisable to thoroughly wash one's hands, as well as the knife and chopping board, in hot soapy water so as to help get rid of most traces of them; otherwise inadvertent contact, such as touching your eye, may have painful consequences. Wearing latex gloves and protective goggles for the eyes is a practical precaution taken by those working extensively with hot chiles.

When it comes to handling chiles, fresh or dried, it is advisable to treat them with a cautious respect. The capsaicinoids contained within them create sensations of pain in sensitive parts of the human body.

In most chiles, other than a few superhot varieties, the capsaicinoids are contained within the seed-carrying placenta. Recipes that use chiles often stipulate deseeding the chile in order to reduce the heat of a dish. This is done by slicing open the chile pepper with a small, sharp knife and carefully scraping out the seeds within and also (importantly) the membrane to which they are attached. Removing this part of the chile reduces its heat and is an effective way of including chiles in a dish while making the dish much milder.

Another way of minimizing heat in recipes when cooking with hot chiles is to use them whole in the dish, rather than chopping them and thus maximizing the effects of the capsaicinoids. In Caribbean recipes, for example, you are often instructed to add a whole Scotch bonnet pepper to a soup such as callaloo, simmer it, and then remove it. This approach adds in the fragrance and flavor of the chile pepper, as well as some of the chile's formidable heat, but not so much that it overpowers the dish.

DIVERSITY OF CHILES

While overall there are around thirty *Capsicum* species, there are just five domesticated species: *Capsicum annuum*, *Capsicum baccatum*, *Capsicum chinense*, *Capsicum frutescens*, and *Capsicum pubescens*. But from these five species, numerous cultivars have been created. It is thought that there are thousands of cultivars today, with new cultivars appearing all the time. Within these cultivars one finds chiles ranging from the mild to the hot, from small to large, chiles that are colored red, green, purple, and yellow,

STIR-FRIED EGGPLANTS WITH GOCHUJANG

Serves 4
Preparation 10 minutes
Cooking 15 minutes

Gochujang, a chile-flavored soybean paste, is an essential seasoning in the Korean kitchen, adding an umami-rich, mellow piquancy to numerous dishes. In this simple stir-fried dish, it is used to glaze eggplants to tasty effect. Enjoy it simply with steamed rice as a light meal or serve as a vegetable side dish.

2 tbsp sunflower or vegetable oil

1 garlic clove, peeled and chopped

1-inch piece of ginger root, peeled and chopped

2 eggplants, cubed

1 tbsp rice wine (optional)

1 heaped tbsp *gochujang* (Korean chile paste)

2 tbsp soy sauce

1 tsp granulated sugar

1 scallion, finely chopped

1 tbsp sesame seeds

1 Heat the oil in a wok or large skillet over high heat. Add the garlic and ginger and stir-fry until fragrant.

2 Add the eggplants, mix well to coat in the fragrant oil, and stir-fry for 5 minutes. Add the rice wine, if using, and cook, stirring, for 2 minutes until the wine has largely cooked off.

3 Add the *gochujang*, soy sauce, and sugar and mix well so as to coat the eggplant evenly. Stir-fry for 5 minutes until the eggplant has softened and glazed. Sprinkle with scallion and sesame seeds and serve at once.

and chiles in an assortment of shapes. It is worth remembering that chile heat is not related to size; a small chile might pack a fiery kick, but so, too, can a large one. The heat level depends on the variety, the stage of maturity at which the fruit has been harvested, and how it has been grown.

Capsicum annuum is the most widely cultivated of the domesticated species. It encompasses a great range of physical diversity in its peppers, which vary in their shape, size, and color. Furthermore, the capsaicinoid content of its peppers varies from zero to very high, depending on the cultivar; the mild bell pepper is a *Capsicum annuum* cultivar. It is a versatile species, found growing in a wide range of climates and habitats. A number of popular chile cultivars are found within this species, including the jalapeño, the cayenne, the poblano, and the Kashmir.

The name *Capsicum baccatum* comes from the Latin word *baca*, which means berry; some of its cultivars do indeed have small, rounded fruit that resemble berries. As a species that thrives in areas close to the equator, it grows particularly well in South American countries, including Bolivia, Chile, Ecuador, and Peru. Indeed, its cultivars, such as the bright yellow *aji amarillo*, are central to Peruvian cuisine, lending their particular flavor to dishes such as ceviche. The *Capsicum chinense* species is noted for its aromatic qualities, complex depth of flavor, and capacity for serious heat. Many of the superhot chiles, such as the Dorset Naga, the Bhut Jolokia, and the Carolina Reaper, belong to this species. Less ferocious chiles found within the same family include the Apricot, a mild, flavorful habanero, and Bellaforma, known as a "seasoning pepper."

Capsicum frutescens is a species containing a few cultivars; botanically speaking, it is regarded as the least interesting of the five species, due to its lack of diversity. All of its cultivars produce similar small chiles, which, while delivering a hot kick, lack the flavorful, fragrant qualities found in the other species. In North America, however, *Capsicum frutescens* tabasco is very well known, as this is the pepper from which Tabasco sauce, the popular hot sauce, is made. Thought to have originated in Mexico, the cultivar is named after the Mexican state of Tabasco. In Thailand, tiny, slender bird chiles, a cultivar of *Capsicum frutescens*, are widely used in cooking, adding a fiery touch to dishes in the form of salad dressings and condiments. In Africa, the piri-piri chile, much loved for the heat it brings, is also a *frutescens*.

While *Capsicum pubescens* is a familiar species within the Andes, where it grows in high mountain valleys, it is little known in the wider world. Among the species' distinguishing traits are the presence of a fuzzy down on its leaves and the dark black or purple seeds contained within its fruits.

Its cultivars include the *rocoto*, or *locoto*, which is native to the Andes. With its rounded shape and thick, fleshy skin, it is eaten fresh, not dried, often stuffed with meat or cheese.

While chiles are often written about in generic terms, certain varieties are valued in their own right. In Caribbean cooking, for example, the Scotch bonnet pepper is appreciated for its fruity flavor and is used to make chile sauces and jerk chicken marinades. In New Mexico, the Hatch chile, a large, long green chile grown in Hatch Valley, has acquired a cult following across the Southwest and is usually roasted to enhance its flavor.

CULINARY CHILES

The sheer variety of chiles—the numerous cultivars offering different levels of heat, their assorted sizes, their range of flavors, the fact that they can be used at different stages of ripeness and, importantly, either fresh or dried—makes them a truly versatile culinary flavoring. The potency of chiles is another reason for their usefulness in the kitchen. Adding just one or two chiles or a teaspoon of chile powder can transform a dish. Chiles are a handy ingredient, easy to keep, and, in dried form, a very affordable, effective spice. What is striking when one considers the culinary chile is the important part it plays in different cuisines around the world and how creatively it is used within them.

Chiles are a handy ingredient, easy to keep, and, in dried form, a very affordable, effective spice. What is striking when one considers the culinary chile is the important part it plays in different cuisines around the world.

The cuisine most famously associated with chiles is Indian—and indeed, an extensive use of a range of chiles (fresh, dried, and ground) characterizes Indian cuisine. India is a notable producer, consumer, and exporter of chiles and a country that has embraced the chile pepper with enthusiasm for centuries. In the Ayurvedic tradition, chiles are valued for their digestive properties and are also seen as a stimulant to appetite.

As a general rule, green chiles, high in vitamin C, are used fresh in Indian cookery, while red chiles are usually used in their dried form. Fresh green chiles are used in piquant relishes, such as cilantro chutney and refreshing, crisp-textured kachumber salads. Fresh chiles are also used in curries, with Indian cooks using them whole, slit (in order to impart more pungency), or chopped, as in *aloo gosht* (lamb with potatoes), in order to adjust the amount of heat they will give to a dish.

In Indonesia, Malaysia, and Thailand, both fresh and dried chiles are widely used. In Malaysia and Indonesia, what are called *chile sambals* (see p. 121)—pastes made from chiles—are popularly used to enliven dishes. There are numerous recipes for *chile sambals*. A classic version is made simply from pounded fresh red chiles mixed with toasted dried shrimp paste (*blachan*), lime juice or shredded kaffir lime leaves, and a pinch of salt and served as a condiment. There are also fried *sambal* dishes, in which ingredients such as raw prawns, fish fillets, or vegetables such as *kang kong* (water spinach) are stir-fried in a chile paste, often made from both fresh and dried red chiles. In Thailand, fresh green chiles play a central part in creating one of the country's best-known dishes, Thai green curry. To make it, a paste made from fresh green chiles and aromatic flavorings such as lemongrass and kaffir lime zest is fried and used to flavor a coconut milk curry. The resulting curry takes on a green hue, as well as a notable chile kick. Also in Thailand, dried red chiles are deseeded, soaked, and pounded into a paste with aromatic flavorings such as galangal, lemongrass, shallot, garlic, and dried shrimp paste. This paste is then fried in coconut cream until fragrant and used to make red curries with poultry, beef, or prawns.

Drying chiles has long been a simple, practical way of extending their usefulness, enabling them to be stored successfully for several months. Mexican cuisine is marked by its extensive and sophisticated use of a range of dried chiles. Such is their importance as ingredients in their own right that the dried versions of chiles are given different names from the fresh. Dark reddish-brown in color, the ancho is a dried poblano, characterized by a distinctive smoky, earthy, raisiny flavor. It is a particularly prized dried chile in Mexico and Central America, used in a variety of ways. When soaked, the chile turns a dark red, adding a richness of color and flavor to dishes. Soaked, softened anchos are stuffed with ingredients such as chorizo and potato and baked. Toasted dried ancho chiles are soaked in water and then ground into a paste as part of the complex flavorings composing Mexico's famous *mole poblano*, served as a celebratory feast dish. Chipotle peppers, made from smoke-dried jalapeño, have a smoky flavor. They are usually toasted, soaked, or simmered and turned into a paste used to flavor soups and adobo sauce. Guajillo, the dried version of the mirasol pepper, is used in stews and spice blends, to which it adds a tangy flavor.

Mexican cuisine is marked by its extensive and sophisticated use of a range of dried chiles. Such is their importance as ingredients in their own right that the dried versions of chiles are given different names from the fresh.

ZHOUG

Makes 1¼ cups
Preparation 10 minutes

Originally from Yemen, where chiles are highly prized for their health-giving properties by the Jewish community, *zhoug* is now a popular chile-hot condiment throughout the Middle East. It is served with a wide array of dishes, such as hummus and falafel, fried eggplants, and lamb shawarma. It is quick and easy to make, and the quantity of chiles can be adjusted to taste.

6–10 fresh green chiles, stemmed and chopped

3 garlic cloves, peeled and chopped

3 cups chopped fresh cilantro

1 tsp salt

Pinch of granulated sugar

2 tsp cumin powder

½ cup vegetable oil

1 Place the green chiles, garlic, cilantro, salt, sugar, and cumin in a food processor and blend into a smooth paste.

2 Add the oil and blend to mix together well.

3 Cover and chill until serving.

JERK CHICKEN

Serves 4

Preparation 10 minutes, plus 3 hours to overnight marinating

Cooking 40 minutes

Jerk is Jamaica's beloved national dish, made by marinating pork or chicken in a spicy marinade. A key flavoring in the marinade is the Scotch bonnet pepper, *Capsicum chinense*, which is prized not only for its formidable heat but also its particular aromatic and fruity flavor. Historically, jerk dishes are cooked over charcoal, which adds a smoky note. Traditionally, jerk chicken is served with Rice 'n' Peas (see p. 153), another Jamaican classic, made from rice cooked in coconut milk with beans—an excellent accompaniment to the fiery jerk chicken.

8 chicken thighs, skin on

2 scallions, chopped

2 garlic cloves, peeled

1-inch piece of ginger root, peeled and chopped

1 red Scotch bonnet pepper, deseeded and chopped

Juice of 1 lime

1 tsp salt

2 tbsp fresh thyme leaves or 1 tbsp dried thyme leaves

1 tsp allspice powder

1 tbsp freshly ground black pepper

1   Cut slashes into the tops of the chicken thighs to help the marinade penetrate.

2   Make the jerk marinade by blending the scallions, garlic, ginger, Scotch bonnet pepper, lime juice, salt, thyme leaves, allspice, and black pepper into a paste in a food processor.

3   Spread the marinade over the chicken pieces, rubbing it well into each chicken thigh. Cover and marinate in the fridge for at least 3 hours, ideally overnight.

4   Preheat the oven to 400°F. Place the chicken thighs in a roasting pan and roast for 40 minutes, turning the thighs halfway through cooking, until the chicken is cooked through and crispy golden brown all over.

In Korea, *gochugaru*—dried red chile, in either coarsely ground flake form or finely ground powder form—is a very important ingredient. Nowadays, dried chile (in its flaked form) is a key flavoring in Korea's famous traditional dish kimchi (a term given to an array of fermented vegetables), served as a popular accompaniment. Kimchi itself is an ancient food with a long history of being made in Korea; there is a written reference to Koreans making fermented foods in the third century CE. The use of chile to flavor kimchi is far more recent (first recorded in 1614), but nowadays it is regarded as essential, adding a scarlet color and heat. Powdered *gochugaru* is used to make *gochujang* (see p. 124), an important condiment in Korea. It is an umami-rich mixture of fermented soybean paste, chile powder, and glutinous rice powder, formed into a thick paste, with varying levels of heat. *Gochujang* is served as a condiment with dishes such as *bibimbap* (see p. 167), as an ingredient in dipping sauces, including *ssamjang*, in marinades, and to add chile piquancy to soups and stews.

One part of China is particularly known for its penchant for chile heat, namely Sichuan Province in southeast China. Admired throughout China for the flavorful quality of its food, Sichuanese cooking is characterized by its use of Sichuan pepper and also dried chiles, which add a ruby-red richness of color as well as heat to a variety of dishes. Sun-dried Sichuanese chiles include the fragrant "facing heaven" (*chao tian jiao*) chile and the seven-star (*qi xing jiao*) chile. These are used in stir-fried dishes such as spicy cucumber salad, where the oil is aromatized with dried chiles and Sichuan peppercorns; and a Congqing specialty, chicken with chiles, in which marinated chicken pieces are stir-fried with a generous quantity of deseeded dried chiles. Coarsely ground chile powder is also important in Sichuan; it is used to make chile oil, an important ingredient for dressing cold dishes such as *bang bang* chicken, and also in cooking and dips. Chile bean paste, made from long, mild "two golden strips" chiles and broad beans, is another key flavoring in Sichuanese cooking. It is a specialty of Pixian County, where, so the story goes, the sauce was discovered by accident in the seventeenth century by a traveler called Mr. Chen. When his only supply of food, a few broad beans, got wet in the rain and became mildewed, rather than wasting them, he ate them with fresh chile. The flavor was so good that he went on to make chile bean paste, with his descendants setting up a workshop to produce it on a larger scale in 1804. The chile bean paste adds its distinctive rich taste to classic Sichuanese dishes such as fish braised in chile bean sauce.

TOM YAM GUNG

Serves 4
Preparation 15 minutes
Cooking 25 minutes

Chiles play a central part in Thai cuisine and are used to give heat and flavor to dishes from condiments to curries. Here Thailand's favorite bird chiles are simmered whole in a classic Thai prawn soup, to which they add an appealingly piquant kick. Using kaffir lime leaves, with their particular citrus flavor, and salty fish sauce also delivers an authentic taste of Thailand. Serve this as an elegant first course to start a Thai meal or on its own as a light meal.

12 raw prawns
2 lemongrass stalks
1 tbsp vegetable oil
4½ cups chicken or
   prawn stock
4 kaffir lime leaves
3 red bird chiles or small
   red chiles
Salt
2–3 tbsp fish sauce
Juice of ½ lime
Handful of fresh cilantro
   leaves, to garnish

1   Peel and devein the prawns, leaving the tail tips on. Peel off the tough outer casing from the lemongrass stalks. Finely slice the lower bulbous white part of each stalk.

2   Heat the oil in a saucepan. Add the lemongrass and fry, stirring for 1 minute, until fragrant. Add the stock, lime leaves, and whole red chiles, and season with salt. Bring to a boil. Add the fish sauce and lime juice and simmer gently for 20 minutes.

3   Add the prawns and simmer gently for about 2 minutes, until they turn pink and opaque. Serve the soup at once, garnished with cilantro leaves.

In Indian cooking, whole dried chiles are generally cooked using the *tarka* method—fried briefly in ghee or oil to bring out their flavor, with the flavored oil either used as a frying medium or poured over dishes such as dhals to add piquancy. Dried red Kashmiri chiles are valued for both their bright red color and the mildness of their heat, which allows them to be used liberally in curries (see p. 115) such as *rogan josh*. A curry legacy of Portugal's influence on Indian cuisine is Goan pork vindaloo, based on a marinated Portuguese meat dish, *carne de vinha d'alhos*, using vinegar and large amounts of dried red chiles. In Indian restaurants in postwar Britain, the vindaloo became a generic term for a ferociously hot curry, with which diners could test their capacity to withstand chile heat.

Dried chiles are also found in European cuisines. In southern Italy, small, dried chile peppers called *peperoncini* are fried with garlic in olive oil and tossed with spaghetti as a simple but tasty meal (see p. 116). A mild, dried chile pepper called *nora* is used in Spanish cooking to flavor *salsa romesco*, a nut-based sauce served as an accompaniment to fish, meat, or vegetables.

It is in their dried, ground form, known as chile powder, that chiles are most widely available and used around the world. The powder is an effective way of delivering chile heat, whether used on its own or combined with other spices to make mixtures such as curry powders. In Ethiopia, the aromatic spice paste called *berbere* is made from numerous spices, chile powder, onions, garlic, and ginger and is used as a base for the country's characteristic fragrant stews, called *wot*. Chile powder is a key ingredient in North America's chili, a hearty, slow-cooked dish made by simmering meat in a chile-flavored sauce. The origins of this popular dish are in the Southwest, and it is associated with the region's Mexican community. Chili was a popular frontier food, eaten by cowboys and soldiers, and has long been linked with the state of Texas. By the late nineteenth century, San Antonio was known for its "Chili Queens," Mexican women who set up stalls selling bowls of the spicy meat dish. The U.S. writer Stephen Crane, who visited the city in 1895, described how, in one of its plazas, "Mexican vendors with open-air stands sell food that tastes exactly like pounded fire-brick from Hades—chili con carne, tamales, enchiladas, chili verde, frijoles." Chili has played such a part in Texan history that in 1977 the dish was declared to be its state food. It was not only in Texas, however, that chili became popular in the United States. Such was its popularity nationally during the twentieth century that casual, affordable chili parlors were found across the country. There are numerous regional variations: the Texan "bowl of red," usually without beans;

Chile powder is a key ingredient in North America's chili, a hearty, slow-cooked dish made by simmering meat in a chile-flavored sauce. The origins of this popular dish are in the Southwest.

Cincinnati chili, featuring combinations of spaghetti, chile, onions, beans, and cheese; Springfield chili, made from beef and turkey in some versions and topped with oyster crackers; and fiery Cajun chili, laced with hot sauce.

Paprika, a ground powder made from large, sweet chile peppers, is a spice that is central to Hungarian cuisine, adding flavor and an orange-red hue to classic dishes such as goulash. In Hungary, paprika is found in a range of nuanced heats, from sweet, mild *különleges* through the most commonly used, slightly hot *édesnemes* to the hottest, which is called *erös*. In Spain, there is *pimentón*, a type of paprika pepper. As with Hungarian paprika, there are different heat levels to Spanish *pimentón*, ranging from *dulce* (sweet) to *agridulce* (bitter-sweet) to *picante* (hot). A regional specialty is *pimentón de la Vera*, produced in the La Vera valley in Extremadura, made with peppers that are dried slowly for days with oak smoke, then finely ground. The resulting powder has a distinctive smoky flavor and is most famously used to flavor chorizo, the much-loved Spanish sausage. The chile's capacity to insinuate itself into cuisines in an array of forms is impressive.

CRISPY CHILE BEEF

Serves 4
Preparation 20 minutes
Cooking 15 minutes

Crispy chile beef is a Chinese restaurant favorite. It offers an appealing combination of crisp-coated beefsteak strips and a hot and sweet chile sauce glaze. Making it at home is very easy and well worth a go. Serve it with steamed rice and blanched greens, such as bok choy, *gai lan* (Chinese broccoli), or spinach.

1 lb sirloin steak, cut into short, fine strips

3 tbsp cornstarch

Oil for deep-frying

Salt

Pinch of Chinese five-spice powder

1 garlic clove, peeled and chopped

4 dried red chiles (ideally Sichuanese)

4 scallions, chopped into 1-inch pieces, separated into white and green parts

1 tbsp Chinese rice wine

2 tbsp soy sauce

1 tbsp Chinese rice vinegar

3 tbsp sweet chile sauce

1 fresh red chile, deseeded and finely sliced

1 Toss the steak strips with the cornstarch until they are all evenly coated.

2 Pour the oil for deep-frying into a wok. Heat the oil to 350°F. Add the steak strips in two batches and fry for 5 minutes per batch until browned and crispy. Remove with a slotted spoon and drain on paper towels. Season with salt and a pinch of Chinese five-spice powder.

3 Carefully pour out the hot oil from the wok, leaving around 1 tablespoon in the wok.

4 Heat the oil again. Add the garlic, dried chiles, and white scallions. Stir-fry for 1 minute until fragrant. Add the rice wine and allow to sizzle briefly. Add the soy sauce, vinegar, and chile sauce and mix well. Return the beef strips to the pan and stir-fry, coating in the glaze, for 2 minutes. Serve at once, garnished with the green scallions and sliced red chile.

CHILE

135

RICE

Rice is one of our major foodstuffs, sustaining over half of the world's population. It is a staple food and an important source of calories for over three and a half billion people. Domesticated from wild varieties thousands of years ago, it now grows on every continent of the world, except Antarctica. It is in Asia that rice has historically played a particularly important role, with its labor-intensive cultivation shaping society.

Rice, one of our primary food crops, is a cereal. It is a member of a genus containing twenty wild species and two cultivated species, Asian rice (*Oryza sativa*) and African rice (*Oryza glaberrima*). It is the seed of these two cultivated species, descended from wild species, that we eat as rice. Where rice originated is not known. One theory is that these different species share an ancient common ancestor that grew on the supercontinent Pangea before it broke apart into separate continents about 200 million years ago. Where rice was first cultivated is also the subject of much debate, with cases made for both India and China. Recent archaeological evidence discovered in China at the site of Shangshan, near the Yangtze River, suggests that semiwild rice was being grown by inhabitants of prehistoric villages there, dating these early signs of cultivation to around 9,400 years ago. It is thought that both in Africa, where *Oryza glaberrima* was cultivated, and in Asia, home to *Oryza sativa*, prehistoric people living as hunter-gatherers collected and ate wild rice grains from which, over millennia, the two cultivated species were derived. One of the traits distinguishing cultivated rice is that, whereas wild seed heads break in order to disperse their seed, cultivated rice retains its seed, making it easier to harvest.

Of the two cultivated species, it is Asian rice (*Oryza sativa*) and its subspecies that have spread around the world. It is primarily humans who transported it, carrying the small, light, portable grains with them to use as a food source and for trading purposes. From India and China, rice was introduced to Japan and Korea and Southeast Asian countries. It is thought

that rice reached the Middle East from India around 1000 BCE and then was introduced into Europe from the Middle East, with the Arabs bringing rice to Spain. *Arroz*, the Spanish word for rice, comes from the Arabic word *roz*. The Portuguese and Spanish, through their colonies and trade routes, are thought to have introduced rice to the Caribbean and to Central and South America. *Oryza sativa* was also introduced to Africa in the sixteenth century, probably by the Portuguese, largely replacing the indigenous *Oryza glaberrima* as a crop due to its higher yields.

Rice was introduced to North America in the seventeenth century (see "Carolina Gold Rice," p. 152) and was first cultivated in the swampy lowlands of South Carolina. One of the Founding Fathers of the United States, Thomas Jefferson—who believed that the newly established republic should be an agrarian society—was excited by the potential offered by rice cultivation. While serving as minister to France in 1787, he smuggled Italian rice out of Europe to the United States. The reason for Jefferson's interest in Italian rice was that it was a grain that could grow in dry, upland conditions, with his laudable aim being "to save the lives of thousands, and health of tens of thousands annually" lost to malaria, which endangered those growing rice in wet conditions in South Carolina. From a commercial point of view, dry rice did not compete with the "wet rice" being grown in the United States. Jefferson, however, was proud of his attempts to pioneer it. In his personal tally of his achievements in public service, he listed the encouragement of "upland rice" alongside the Declaration of Independence, writing, "The greatest service which can be rendered any country is to add a useful plant to it's [*sic*] culture."

> *As rice spread around the world, different cultivars were bred, making it a versatile crop that can be successfully grown in a range of climates and environments.*

As rice spread around the world, different cultivars were bred, making it a versatile crop that can be successfully grown in a range of climates and environments. Rice grown in shallow, slow-moving water gives good yields, and many societies developed systems of water irrigation for growing rice, undertakings that required a high level of social cooperation and industriousness (see "Rice in China," p. 146, and "Rice in Bali," p. 148). Rice assumed a particular importance as a staple food in Asia, which accounts for nearly 90 percent of global rice consumption. It is a grain that has long been an important source of calories for the poor in many parts of the world.

RISOTTO ALLA MILANESE

Serves 4
Preparation 5 minutes
Cooking 30–35 minutes

A classic Italian risotto, this elegant Milanese dish is given a yellow color and aromatic flavor through the use of saffron. It is traditionally served with *ossobuco alla milanese* (braised veal shank), also from the same part of northern Italy, but it can be enjoyed simply on its own.

4 cups good-quality beef or
    chicken stock
½ onion, finely chopped
3¾ tbsp butter
1½ cups risotto rice
½ cup dry white wine
½ tsp saffron strands, finely
    ground
⅔ cup freshly grated Parmesan
    cheese, plus extra to serve
Salt and freshly ground
    black pepper

1   Bring the stock to a simmer in a saucepan.

2   In a separate heavy pan, fry the onion in 2 tablespoons of the butter until it has softened. Add the rice and fry it, stirring, for 2 minutes, coating it well in the butter.

3   Add the white wine and cook, stirring now and then, until largely reduced. Sprinkle in the ground saffron, mixing well, and season with salt, bearing in mind that you will be adding salty Parmesan. Add 2 ladles of the simmering stock and cook the rice over medium heat, stirring all the time, until absorbed.

4   Repeat the process, gradually adding the hot stock, for around 20–25 minutes, until the rice is cooked through but retains texture. Stir in the remaining butter and the Parmesan cheese. Taste and season with salt, if required, and freshly ground pepper. Serve at once.

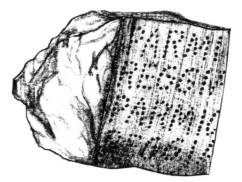

What is striking about rice is the central role it has assumed in those countries where it is a staple. In these nations, it is also a culturally significant ingredient, one with a large number of origin myths, folklore rituals, and superstitions attached to it. In China, with its venerable history of growing rice to feed its large population, the cultivation of rice was at the heart of an annual cycle that patterned the year. Key stages in the growing of rice, such as rice planting and the all-important harvest, are still marked in several countries with special festivals. In parts of Asia, including China, it is considered unlucky when eating a meal to leave even a few grains of rice uneaten. Rice is an ancient symbol of plenty and fertility; hence the custom of throwing rice over the bride and groom at a wedding.

In developing countries, the growing of rice continues to be carried out largely in the traditional way, on small plots of land, requiring the input of much labor. There has, however, also been innovation in how rice is cultivated. In 1960, the International Rice Research Institute (IRRI) was founded, with its headquarters in the Philippines. Among its goals in this period was to increase rice productivity through rice breeding, due to fears that Asia, being dependent on rice, was vulnerable to famine because of its increasing population. A seminal moment in the history of rice happened in 1966 with IRRI's release of a new rice cultivar called IR8, a rice created from a tall strain of Indonesian rice (*peta*) crossbred with a dwarf variety from China (DGWG). Nicknamed a "miracle rice" because of its high yields—ranging from twice to five times as much as traditional cultivars—IR8 played an important part in what is called the Green Revolution in tropical rice growing and is credited with averting famines in Asia. Critics of IR8, however, point out that it needs expensive inputs of not just fertilizers but also herbicides, requirements that have had social and environmental consequences. Rice growing continues to be an innovative area. In California today, for example, it is increasingly sophisticated, using GPS or laser-guided equipment to accurately level the ground in which the rice is grown and state-of-the-art harvesters to collect the crop. Water shortage and droughts are a major issue for farmers in California. Technology such as sensor networks (measuring humidity and temperature), data analytic systems, and management software is being used in order to minimize water usage while ensuring good yields.

The appetite for rice in Asia continues to be high. In many Asian countries, consumption exceeds 220 pounds per capita, ensuring it continues to be a staple food. Demand for rice is increasing in many other parts of the world, including sub-Saharan Africa, Latin America, the Caribbean, and the Middle East. Rises in rice prices, due to increased demand, take a toll upon the low-income groups who depend on this staple grain. Given its long-held role as a fundamental food and the growth in the world's population, ensuring that rice can be grown successfully and sustainably is vital. Understandably, IRRI and other organizations continue to carry out research into this important grain.

GROWING, HARVESTING, AND PROCESSING

Rice has historically been a labor-intensive crop, both to grow and to harvest—one that has required a high level of collective enterprise. As a semiaquatic plant, it is the only cereal crop able to withstand water submergence. While growing, the plant is very sensitive to water shortages. In order, therefore, to ensure that the valuable crop received adequate water, the practice of growing rice in flooded paddy fields, surrounded with low walls to keep the water in, was developed many centuries ago. In general, rice farmers look to maintain a level of between 2 and 4 inches of water flooding their fields. Landscapes were shaped to provide terraces and ponding in which to grow rice, with the accompanying need for efficiently organizing irrigation and crop calendars requiring social cooperation. A famous example of rice terracing is the Banaue rice terraces, carved out of the side of mountains on the island of Luzon in the Philippines. Created by indigenous people around 2,000 years ago, and fed by an ancient irrigation system from the rain forests above, these striking terraces are called "the eighth wonder of the world." Irrigated lowland rice is the major way of cultivating rice, producing around 75 percent of the world's rice. It is not only in Asia that rice is grown in this way. Italy is the main rice-producing country in Europe; here risotto rice is grown in *risale* (paddy fields), using the irrigation method, in the Po Valley, Lombardy, and Piedmont. The growing of rice in Italy is dated back to the fifteenth century, with the fertile, swampy land around the Po River lending itself to this crop. The nineteenth-century Italian statesman Cavour promoted the improvement of irrigation systems for Italian rice growers, and in 1866 the Canal Cavour was constructed to transport water effectively from rivers and lakes to the paddy fields. Rice grown with irrigation can offer up to two or three crops a year, and this way of cultivating it has been shown to ensure an effective nutrient cycle, conserving organic matter and receiving nitrogen.

> *A famous example of rice terracing is the Banaue rice terraces, carved our of the side of mountains on the island of Luzon in the Philippines… these striking terraces are called "the eighth wonder of the world."*

There are also other ways of cultivating rice. For instance, rice is grown in areas such as river deltas or coastal areas, in fields that flood with rainwater for part of the year. This is a more precarious way of growing rice, affected by natural events such as droughts and flash flooding. High salinity levels, which stress the rice plants, are another issue. This way of growing rice is found today largely in Africa, South Asia, and parts of Southeast Asia. What is known as "deepwater rice" is found in areas prone to severe monsoon flooding, with tall rice plants able to grow in water levels of over 20 inches. While this flooding cultivation method accounts for around 20 percent of world rice production, and is an important subsistence crop for over 100 million people in South and Southeast Asia, yields are characteristically substantially lower than irrigated rice yields.

It is also possible to grow rice on dry land rather than in flooded fields; this is known as "upland rice." Rice grown in this way is found in Asia and Africa and is an important food crop for impoverished rural communities.

EGG-FRIED RICE

Serves 4
Preparation 15 minutes,
  plus 20 minutes cooling
Cooking 25 minutes

This simple Chinese stir-fried dish is a much-loved staple, enjoyed both in people's homes and in Chinese restaurants. Serve this vegetarian version as part of a Chinese meal, alongside dishes such as *char siu* (see p. 28) and blanched bok choy or *gai lan* tossed with oyster sauce.

1¾ cup jasmine rice

Scant 2 cups water

Salt

2 tbsp peanut or
  sunflower oil

3 scallions, chopped, separated
  into white and green parts

3 oz baby sweet corn, chopped
  into ½-inch pieces

2 oz roasted cashews, chopped

2 oz frozen peas, cooked
  and drained

2 eggs, beaten

1 tsp sesame oil

1   Rinse the jasmine rice to remove excess starch. Place it in a heavy saucepan with the water and add a pinch of salt. Bring to a boil, reduce the heat, cover, and simmer for 15 minutes, until the water has been absorbed and the rice is tender. Spread the rice out on a baking sheet and set aside to cool for 20 minutes. Stir with a fork to break it up before stir-frying.

2   Heat a wok over high heat and add the peanut or sunflower oil. Add the white scallion pieces and stir-fry for 1 minute until fragrant. Add the baby sweet corn and stir-fry for around 2 minutes.

3   Add the rice, cashews, and peas, mixing together well. Stir-fry for 4 minutes.

4   Add the eggs and stir-fry for 2 minutes, mixing the egg through the rice. Sprinkle over the sesame oil and stir-fry for 1 minute. Garnish with the chopped green scallions and serve at once.

In order to grow rice, rice seed is first either collected or purchased. The land is prepared for planting by ploughing the soil, using either draft animals, such as water buffalo, or machinery, and harrowing it to break up the dirt. In systems using flooding, the earth is then leveled to allow for even depths of water, which help with crop management and good yields. Rice plants are grown either through transplanting or direct seeding into the prepared ground. In Asia, transplanting pregerminated seedlings is the most popular method. Although labor intensive, it requires less seed and less weed control.

Once the rice crop has reached maturity, around 105 to 150 days after planting, it requires harvesting. In Asia, this continues to be predominantly a manual process, with harvesters using hand tools such as sickles. The process that sees the crop transformed into an edible ingredient is a long and laborious one. The harvested rice must next be threshed in order to separate the edible grains from the stalks; this is done by human labor or using machinery. This threshed, unhulled rice is known as "paddy rice." Next, the paddy rice must be thoroughly dried, a process that is usually done simply in the sun. This is an important stage that, if not done properly, will affect the quality and quantity of the final product. The dried rice is now ready for hulling. This is a process of pounding the grains in order to remove their hulls or husks—the hard protective coating formed of silica and lignin, which cannot be digested by humans—and it is generally carried out at a mill. The kernel that remains after hulling is brown rice, which is edible. The layer of bran that gives brown rice its distinctive color contains useful nutrients but also an oil, which causes brown rice to spoil far faster than white; in the tropics, this spoiling can happen in just two weeks. Usually, therefore, rice is milled further to remove the outer bran layer and polished, creating white rice in the process. Traditionally, this process was done by hand in rural communities, using

The layer of bran that gives brown rice its distinctive color contains useful nutrients but also an oil, which causes brown rice to spoil far faster than white; in the tropics, this spoiling can happen in just two weeks.

a pestle and mortar to pound the grains to remove the hulls and bran. Next, the rice was skillfully winnowed, using bamboo trays to separate the grains from their husks. Rice mills vary considerably in sophistication. Among the most basic are simple single-pass mills, usually found in villages, with an unfortunate by-product being a large percentage of broken grains. At the other end of the spectrum are commercial rice mills, designed to reduce the impact and heat of the milling process in order to minimize grain breakage and produce uniformly polished whole grains that are free of husks and stones. In these commercial mills, once the rice has been milled, it is graded, separated, then mixed to provide varying ratios of head rice (whole kernels) and broken kernels, depending on the grade and country standards. Next, the rice is mist polished, a process that adds a fine water mist to the dust retained on the rice and whitens it further. Finally, it is bagged and sold.

RICE IN CHINA

Rice is central to China in many ways: it is not only as an essential foodstuff with which to sustain a large population but also is woven into its legends, history, society, and culture. In Chinese mythology, it is Shennong, a legendary ruler whose name means "Divine Farmer," who taught his people about agriculture and how to cultivate five grains, including rice. Rice has long had a special place as an esteemed food in China, eaten by aristocrats and the social elite as well as the rural poor. Inscriptions on bronze storage vessels from the Zhou dynasty (1100–256 BCE) demonstrate the long importance of rice in China.

In China, predominantly an agricultural society for much of its history, rice was at the center of the national way of life. Rice is a labor-intensive crop and, in order to grow it successfully, social cooperation is required. Ideals such as filial piety within the family and the importance of maintaining social order are linked to rice cultivation in China; the term "rice culture" is often used to describe traditional Chinese society.

The Chinese character for rice is *mi*, based on a representation of rice grains separated by leaves. The term for cooked rice is *mi fan*, which means "rice food," giving a sense of rice's fundamentality as a source of sustenance. Rice is appreciated at a spiritual level in Chinese culture, too. *Qi* (also written as *ch'i*), meaning "vital energy," is an important concept in Daoist philosophy and is used in *feng shui* and Chinese traditional medicine. For thousands of years, until the 1980s, the character for *qi* included the rice character and was derived from the steam that rises from boiled rice.

Rice also features in traditional Chinese festivals, which continue to be celebrated to this day. Cakes made from glutinous rice flour are among the auspicious foods eaten at a dinner on the eve of Chinese New Year to bring advancement in the forthcoming year. Rice cakes are eaten during the Double Ninth Festival, while a special congee (rice porridge) is eaten for the Laba Festival, celebrating the founder of Buddhism, Siddharta Guatama, and his attainment of Buddhahood in the fourth or fifth century BCE.

MEJADRA

Serves 6–8
**Preparation 10 minutes, plus
 20 minutes salting**
Cooking 1 hour 10–15 minutes

This earthy combination of rice and lentils
is popular across the Middle East. While the
ingredients are simple and homely, the depth of
flavor and combination of textures make it a deeply
satisfying dish. Serve it with marinated roast or
grilled lamb and a tomato salad for a main meal.

2 onions, 1 finely sliced
 and 1 chopped
Salt
1 cup brown lentils
Vegetable oil, for deep-frying
4 tbsp olive oil
1 cup basmati rice
1 tsp allspice powder
1 tsp cinnamon powder
½ tsp sugar
1⅔ cups water

1 Sprinkle the finely sliced onion with salt and set aside
   for 20 minutes.
2 Place the lentils in a strainer and rinse well. Transfer the
   lentils to a saucepan, cover generously with cold water,
   and bring to a boil. Reduce the heat and cook slowly for
   20 minutes until tender; drain.
3 Pour vegetable oil into a small, deep skillet or saucepan
   to a depth of around ½ inch and heat until very hot.
   Pat the salted onion dry and fry in batches in the hot oil
   until it crisps up and turns deep brown in color. Drain
   on paper towels.
4 Heat the olive oil in a heavy saucepan. Fry the chopped
   onion until softened. Add the basmati rice and mix,
   coating with the oil. Add the allspice, cinnamon, sugar,
   and a good pinch of salt, mixing together well. Stir in the
   lentils and add the water.
5 Bring to a boil, cover, reduce the heat, and cook over a
   low heat for 20–25 minutes until all the water has been
   absorbed and the rice is tender. Mix in the deep-fried
   onions and serve at once.

RICE IN BALI

Rice also plays a central part in the landscape, religion, social structure, and culture of the Indonesian island of Bali. The island's rich volcanic soil and tropical climate, with its heavy rainfall, make it suitable for growing rice, a crop that requires a lot of water. In Indonesia, as in other parts of the world, rice is grown in paddy fields, parcels of arable land that are flooded through irrigation systems. The word "paddy" comes from the Malay word *padi*, which means "rice plant." The rice fields are flooded, as semiaquatic rice grown in these conditions yields a higher crop; furthermore, the flooding keeps down weeds, which would compete with the young rice seedlings, and destructive pests, such as rats. Farmers in Bali have farmed in the flat valleys and also carved rice terraces—an iconic part of the island's landscape—out of the rugged sides of Bali's volcanoes. The rivers and streams that flowed down these sacred mountains were used in an ingenious irrigation system to allow access to this vital resource, which allowed the Balinese to become among the most prolific of the rice farmers in the Indonesian archipelago.

Irrigating rice in this way requires a communal approach, with the farmers working together. In order to use the water efficiently, farmers plant at different agreed-upon times in a rotating regional system. The cooperative social system that regulates water management of the rice paddies is called *subak*, a Balinese word that first appeared in an inscription dating from 1072. There are around 1,200 water collectives in Bali managing the irrigation system. Underlying the *subak* system is the philosophical concept of *Tri Hita Karana*, a term that means "the three causes of happiness and well-being." Within this philosophy one finds the following key concepts:

Parahyangan
The harmonious relationship between human beings and God.

Palemahan
The harmonious relationship between humanity and nature.

Pawongan
The harmonious relationship between human beings; people should treat one another with respect, as to hurt another human is to hurt oneself.

There is a profound religious aspect to the way in which rice is grown in Bali. Rice is seen as a gift from the gods, and the *subak* system is intertwined with the water temple network on the island. These water temples vary in size and importance, some marking the spring (the source of the water) and others having the water pass through their grounds before it irrigates the land. One of the most prominent of these is Pura Taman Ayun, a large, majestic temple built in 1634 and surrounded by a moat and gardens.

Bali is a predominantly Hindu island, but among the pantheon of its native gods is Dewi Sri, the island's goddess of fertility, also often called the goddess of rice, about whose origins there are many legends. She is depicted as a beautiful young woman and regarded as a protector of those who work in rice fields. Shrines in her honor are found in Balinese rice paddies. Offerings to the gods are a daily part of Balinese life and are woven into the fabric of society. These offerings are many and varied, including colorful, fragrant flowers and different types of rice: raw, cooked, sticky, white, black, and red.

The religious, moral, and social aspects of *subak* allowed for an intricate system to be constructed and followed. Members of the *subak* system are categorized according to their level of participation. The members form groups with responsibilities for different aspects of rice production: preparing the land, organizing the water treatment, monitoring the water and pests, planting seedlings, weeding, harvesting, and transporting the rice. These clearly defined roles allow members to ensure that water distribution is carried out fairly and that problems can be discussed and resolved by the whole community. In 2012, the importance of *subak* was recognized by UNESCO with the granting of World Heritage Cultural Landscape status to this unique Balinese rice-centric system.

TYPES OF RICE

One of the reasons that rice is successful as a crop is that it exists in thousands of cultivars, enabling it to be grown in a range of climates and environments. These cultivars have been created over centuries through a process of both natural and human selection. The International Rice Genebank, maintained by IRRI, is the biggest collection of rice genetic diversity in the world and holds over 127,916 rice accessions and 4,647 wild relatives. It is worth noting here that what is usually meant by "wild rice" is, in fact, grasses belonging to *Zizania*, a different genus from rice.

Within *Oryza sativa*, the major rice species grown around the world, there are two major subspecies to be found: *japonica* or *sinica*, which are short-grained and sticky, and *indica*, which is long-grained and nonsticky.

From a culinary point of view, rice is usually divided into broad groups based on both the shape of the grains and their starch content. Starch is made up of amylose and amylopectin, and different types of rice contain varying amounts of these components, which affect their texture when cooked. High levels of amylopectin result in rice that is sticky when cooked. These culinary rice groups are:

Long-grain rice: slender grains, high in amylose, that separate when cooked. India's basmati rice (see p. 151) belongs in this family and is valued for the length of its grains.

Medium-grain rice: shorter and stubbier than long-grain rice, with less amylose, this has a soft texture when cooked. Italian risotto rice and Spanish paella rice both belong to this group.

Short-grain rice: slightly longer than it is wide, with a tender texture and slight stickiness when cooked due to its amylopectin levels. In this group, one finds Japan's sushi rice.

Sticky rice: also known as glutinous rice; a particular type of short-grain rice, very high in amylopectin. As its popular names suggest, this group is characterized by its stickiness when cooked, which allows it to be shaped and molded.

Another distinction is made between brown rice and white rice. Brown rice consists of rice grains that have been dehusked but still possess their natural bran coating. In contrast, white rice has been milled to remove this bran layer and polished to maximize the white color of the grains. Brown rice contains more fiber, vitamins, and minerals than white rice but does take longer to cook due to its bran layer.

Rice can also be found in naturally occurring pigmented versions, usually red or purple-black in color. This is due to the presence of anthocyanin pigments in the bran layer, which give a distinctive hue. These pigmented types of rice tend to be eaten with their bran layer intact. Black and purple rice cultivars are usually *japonica*, so short-grained and sticky. An example of this is the black rice found in Southeast Asia, used in desserts such as Malaysia's *bubur pulot hitam* (black rice pudding), where it is cooked with a pandan leaf for fragrance and served with coconut milk. Red rice are usually *indica*, so long-grained and not sticky. As they retain their bran

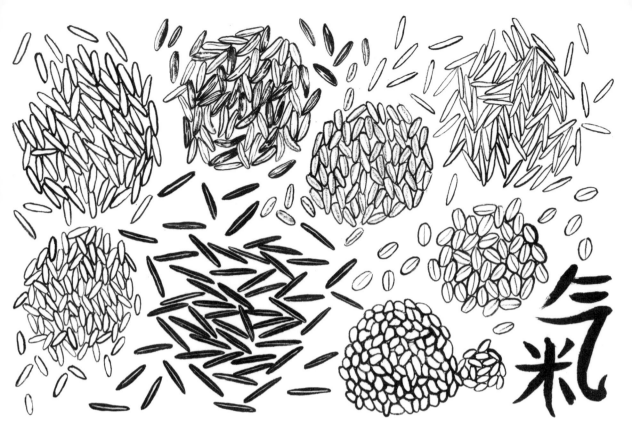

layer, these pigmented types of rice are characterized by a nutty flavor and are rich in fiber and minerals such as iron and zinc, while the anthocyanin pigments are known to have free-radical scavenging capacities.

Another rice category is what is known as aromatic rice. These consist generally of long-grain and medium-grain rice cultivars that are high in a particular volatile compound. The best-known of these are basmati rice (see below) and jasmine rice, named after the jasmine flower, both because of its fragrance and its bright whiteness. Freshly harvested jasmine rice, known as "new crop jasmine rice," is especially valued for its aroma and texture.

BASMATI RICE

One type of rice that is particularly prized is basmati rice, often known as "the king of rice." This slender, long-grained variety of rice is valued for a number of reasons: its delicate, fluffy texture, its long grains, which elongate to twice their length on cooking, and particularly for its distinctive aroma, noticeable in both its raw and cooked states. In fact, its name comes from the Hindi word for "fragrant." True basmati rice is grown in the foothills of the Himalayas, on both sides of the Gangetic plain, in India and in Pakistan. It has long been esteemed in Indian culture. An early mention of basmati rice is in the acclaimed epic poem "Heer Ranjha," written in 1766 by the Punjabi poet Waris Shah. Through historic trade routes, this rice was introduced by Indian traders into the Middle East, where it is also much appreciated.

The fragrance for which basmati is noted and valued is due to the presence of a particular aroma compound called 2-acetyl-1-pyrroline (2AP). This compound, which is also found in pandan leaves, is found in high levels in basmati rice.

Basmati is an expensive rice, for which customers are prepared to pay a high price, and this makes it a very important crop for India, which is the leading exporter of basmati rice to the rest of the world, followed by Pakistan. Within India, basmati rice production is found within Haryana, Punjab, Himachal Pradesh, Uttarakhand, and western Uttar Pradesh. In Pakistan, basmati rice is grown within the province of Punjab. In Indian cuisine, aged basmati (harvested and stored in controlled conditions for a number of years) is particularly esteemed. The ageing process enhances the flavor and also dries out the rice thoroughly, ensuring light-textured, separate grains when cooked.

Traditionally, basmati rice was always a luxury, enjoyed by India's royalty and aristocrats. It is a rice used on special occasions, for celebratory feasts at weddings and religious festivals. A dish particularly associated with basmati is the biriyani, a luxurious recipe that originated in the royal kitchens of the Moghul Empire.

CAROLINA GOLD RICE

The United States, too, has its own rice heritage, as the tale of Carolina Gold rice demonstrates. During the colonial era, South Carolina became a major producer of rice in North America.

Henry Woodward of Charleston, South Carolina, was a pioneer of rice cultivation in the United States. In 1685, he obtained African rice (*Oryza glaberrima*) seed from Captain John Thurber, who had brought a packet of rice seed back with him from the island of Madagascar and had put into Charleston harbor for repairs. Woodward grew rice from the seed, either in his garden at Charleston or on his property at Abbapoola Creek. Rice

RICE 'N' PEAS

Serves 4
Preparation 10 minutes
Cooking 30 minutes

1⅓ cups long-grain rice

1 tbsp sunflower or
  vegetable oil

1 onion, finely chopped

1 garlic clove, peeled

½ tsp allspice berries (optional)

1 Scotch bonnet pepper or
  red chile

2 sprigs of thyme

14 fl oz canned coconut milk

3½ fl oz water

1⅓ cans kidney beans or
  black beans in water,
  drained and rinsed

Salt

This much-loved rice dish is a Jamaican staple. The "peas" are actually beans, which can be black beans or kidney beans.

1 Rinse the rice in cold water to wash out excess starch.
2 Heat the oil in a heavy saucepan and fry the onion gently until softened. Mix in the rice and add the whole garlic clove, allspice berries, Scotch bonnet pepper or red chile, and thyme. Pour in the coconut milk and water and mix in the beans. Season with salt.
3 Bring to a boil, cover, and cook over a very low heat for around 20 minutes, until all the liquid has been absorbed and the rice is tender. Discard the garlic, chile, and thyme and serve at once.

CUCUMBER SUSHI ROLLS

Makes 12 pieces of sushi roll

Preparation 15 minutes,
   plus soaking, standing,
   and cooling

Cooking 15 minutes

These sushi rolls are a classic of Japanese cuisine. Making them requires using Japanese ingredients, including sticky sushi rice, nori sheets, Japanese rice vinegar, and wasabi paste, plus a small bamboo sushi mat. The filling here is a traditional one, but once you've learned how to make rolled sushi, you can experiment with fillings.

½ cup sushi rice

Scant 1 cup water

2 tbsp Japanese rice vinegar

1 tbsp granulated sugar

1 tsp salt

2 sheets of nori

Wasabi paste, to taste

1 tsp sesame seeds

¼ cucumber, deseeded and
   cut into long, thin strips

TO SERVE

Pickled sushi ginger

Light soy sauce

1   Rinse the rice several times in cold water to wash off any excess starch. Cover in cold water and set aside for 15 minutes.

2   Drain the rice, place in a small, heavy pan, and add the water. Bring to a boil, cover the pan tightly, reduce the heat, and cook over very low heat for around 15 minutes, until all the water has been absorbed. Set aside and leave covered for 15 minutes.

3   Meanwhile, mix together the rice vinegar, sugar, and salt, stirring until dissolved. Spread the warm rice out on a large plate or tray, sprinkle with the rice vinegar mixture, and fold in. Set aside to cool to room temperature.

4   To make the sushi rolls, take a sheet of nori and place it on a sushi mat. Spread half the rice evenly over the nori, leaving a ½-inch strip along the top uncovered. Spread a little wasabi paste in a line in the middle and sprinkle some sesame seeds over the top of the wasabi. Neatly arrange cucumber strips over the sesame seeds.

5   Use the bamboo mat to fold the nori sheet up and over the cucumber strips. Lightly brush the uncovered part of the nori sheet with water. Working quickly, use the bamboo mat to firmly roll up the nori over the filling, using the wet part of the sheet to seal the roll together.

6   Repeat the process. Use a sharp knife with a wetted blade to slice each roll into six even-sized pieces. Serve the sushi roll pieces with pickled sushi ginger, wasabi, and light soy sauce on the side.

was a valuable commodity, and South Carolina's subtropical climate and its landscape of marshes, rivers, streams, and tidal basins lent itself to its cultivation in the state.

African slaves from the rice-growing regions of West Africa, known as the Rice Coast, were transported to Charleston (a major port used in the transit of slaves) and set to work to grow this new, labor-intensive crop, one that required the land to be cleared and canals and dikes to be built for irrigation systems, as well as planting, hoeing, and harvesting the rice.

The knowledge of rice growing that the African slaves possessed played a vital part in its successful cultivation in the United States' colonial period. Rice became an important part of the South Carolina economy, a major export, alongside tobacco, which raised revenue for the state, with Carolina's rice noted for its quality in countries such as England.

In 1714, the colony adopted a system of weights for rice, including one specifying the size of the barrel used to ship rice. It is this measurement that is the origin of the barrel (weighing 162 pounds), still used for measuring rice yields in southwest Louisiana, where rice is grown commercially today. The name Carolina Gold is said to come from the appearance of the fields of the golden-hued grain.

Despite being valued for its flavor, one issue in processing Carolina Gold rice was that its grains were fragile and broke easily, with around 30 percent broken during milling. While the valuable whole grains were exported, the broken grains, traditionally known as middlins and nowadays called rice grits, were kept for home consumption and enjoyed for their particular texture, with their use becoming a characteristic of South Carolina's cuisine.

The name Carolina Gold is said to come from the appearance of the fields of the golden-hued grain.

By 1820, more than 98,000 acres of land in South Carolina were turned over to the growing of Carolina Gold rice. However, following the Civil War and the abolition of slavery, the lack of a cheap labor source made farming rice in South Carolina uneconomical, and rice production in the state declined considerably, with rice growing shifting to other states, including Louisiana. Two destructive hurricanes in the early part of the twentieth century and the Great Depression compounded the difficulties commercial rice growers were experiencing in the state, and Carolina Gold rice, an uncommercial rice to farm using modern techniques, became virtually extinct.

FRAGRANT VEGETABLE PULAU

Serves 4
Preparation 10 minutes
Cooking 20–25 minutes

½ tsp saffron strands,
   finely ground
1½ cups basmati rice
2 tbsp butter
1 cinnamon stick
6 cardamom pods
½ onion, finely chopped
4 oz frozen peas
2 carrots, peeled and finely
   diced
2 oz French beans, chopped
   into 1-inch lengths
2 cups chicken stock
Salt

In many countries, rice is cooked in stock to give it extra flavor. This Indian-inspired recipe uses fragrant basmati rice, fried in butter for richness and cooked with aromatic spices. Serve it as a side dish or enjoy it as a meal in its own right.

1   Soak the saffron in 1 tablespoon hot water and set aside. Thoroughly rinse the rice in cold water to wash out any excess starch.

2   Heat the butter in a medium, heavy saucepan. Add the cinnamon stick, cardamom, and onion. Fry gently, stirring often, until the onion has softened.

3   Add the rice, peas, carrots, and French beans. Add the stock and saffron water and season with salt. Bring to a boil, reduce the heat, cover tightly, and simmer for around 15–20 minutes, until all the stock has been absorbed and the rice is tender. Serve.

This situation, however, was to change. During the 1980s, a Savannah eye surgeon named Richard Schulze began growing rice on his Turnbridge plantation in Hardeville, South Carolina, in order to attract ducks to it for hunting purposes. He decided that he would like to grow the original rice of the area and tracked down and obtained 14 pounds of Carolina Gold rice seed from the United States Department of Agriculture seed bank in Texas. He planted it on his plantation in 1986, thus restoring the rice to its historic location in Carolina's coastal wetlands. Having planted this now rare rice, long esteemed for its flavor and texture, Schulze also wanted to eat the rice himself. This required milling the rice, and so Schulze's next step was to restore an old, derelict rice mill in Ridgeland. In 1988, following a productive harvest that yielded 10,000 pounds, Schulze held a special "reintroduction banquet" at which he was able to offer his guests a chance to eat this now legendary local rice. He and his guests were impressed by the quality of the Carolina Gold rice, which lived up to its reputation of offering excellent eating.

Interest grew in reviving Carolina Gold rice. Glenn Roberts, founder of Anson Mills, became fascinated by heritage seeds and began researching the growing of Carolina Gold rice in 1998, pursuing the dream of making it a viable southern crop once more. By 2000, he had a commercial harvest, and today Anson Mills grows and sells organic Carolina Gold rice. Among the land it grows on is Prospect Hill field, near Charleston, which is one of the oldest tidal trunk and dike rice fields in the United States. A specialty that Anson Mills offers is "new crop rice," Carolina Gold that is milled within two months of harvest, characterized by a delicacy of flavor and a particular texture, as the rice has not been thoroughly dried. The Carolina Gold Rice Foundation was established in 1998 by Roberts and David Shields, a specialist in the southern state's heritage foods. It is a nonprofit organization that works to sustainably restore and promote Carolina Gold rice and other historic grains. Scientists Merle Shepard of Clemson University, Gurdev Khush, and Anna McClung began working on creating a hardier, more disease-resistant variety of Carolina Gold rice. The result of their work is an aromatic rice called Charleston Gold, which is now being commercially grown and sold.

This work in reintroducing the southern state's heritage foods, which had largely vanished, has been reflected by a locavore movement among chefs and restaurateurs across the country. A key figure in promoting this rich food heritage is the acclaimed chef Sean Brock, whose restaurants Husk and McCrady's in Charleston celebrate ingredients and dishes of the southern states. Brock is a keen advocate of Carolina Gold rice, which he uses in traditional recipes such as hoppin' John. The so-called renaissance of Carolina Gold continues, with South Carolina today home to 150 acres producing 140,000 pounds of the pure heirloom rice each year.

RICE WINE

In many countries, rice has been valued not just as a food but as an important source of alcohol. Rice wine, an alcoholic beverage made from the grain, is widely found in countries where rice is eaten as a staple, among them China, India, Japan, Korea, and nations in Southeast Asia. It is created in a process akin to brewing beer, in which the starch in cooked rice is fermented to produce alcohol. Alcohol has been brewed in China for thousands of years, made from grains including millet and sorghum as well as rice. Rice wine is a drink with an important role in Chinese culture, used for temple offerings, served at weddings, and featuring in classic Chinese poetry, mentioned, for example, in the *Shijing* (The Book of Songs), a collection of poems dating from the eleventh to the seventh centuries BCE.

BAKED VANILLA
RICE PUDDING

Serves 4
Preparation 5 minutes
Cooking 3 hours

Rice pudding is a gentle, old-fashioned English dessert, often bringing back nostalgic memories to those who ate it in their childhoods. It is very simple indeed to make and requires little input from the cook as it bakes slowly in the oven. It is a comforting, creamy-textured dish, ideal for cold winter nights. Usually it is served with strawberry or raspberry jelly, but it would also go well with a compote of dried fruits.

3 tbsp short-grain rice

1 tbsp vanilla sugar

2½ cups whole milk

Pinch of salt

1 tsp vanilla extract

Strawberry jelly, to serve

1 Preheat the oven to 300°F.
2 Place the rice and sugar in an ovenproof dish and pour over the milk, making sure all the grains are covered. Stir in the salt and vanilla extract.
3 Bake the rice pudding in the oven for 3 hours, stirring it once or twice during the first hour. By the end of cooking, the rice should have softened and swollen, absorbing most of the milk. Serve it hot from the oven, with strawberry jelly on the side.

Of the many rice wines, it is probably Japan's sake that is best known outside its country of origin. Within Japan, it is considered a national drink, enjoyed on social occasions in homes, bars, and restaurants and also served to celebrate formal occasions, festivals, and holidays. Traditional sake is made from steamed rice, a portion of which is inoculated with *koji* mold, a fermentation culture. The resulting *koji* rice is mixed with the remaining rice, spring water, and yeast to make a seed mash. After a period of time, this is mixed with more spring water and fermented. At a certain stage, distilled alcohol is often added, both to halt the fermentation process and to act as a preservative. There are two overall types of sake: *futsu-shu* (everyday sake) and *tokutei meisho-shu* (special designation sake), available in a range of grades. Sake is served chilled, at room temperature, or warm, depending on the season, the type of sake, and the drinker's preference. It is served in special ceramic sake flasks called *tokkuri* and drunk from small ceramic cups known as *sakazuki*, *guinomi*, or *choko*, depending on their type. Fine sakes are appreciated by connoisseurs for the quality of their aroma, delicate color, and flavors, which range from the elegantly floral or fruity to umami-rich.

CULINARY RICE

Just as rice is an adaptable plant that can be grown in a variety of conditions, so rice in the kitchen is a very flexible ingredient. Its delicate, unobtrusive taste makes it an excellent foundation for meals: a basic palette on which dishes such as spicy curries, textured savory stir-fries, or rich stews are enjoyed. It is also an ingredient enjoyed in its own right, taking center stage in a number of recipes.

Rice requires cooking in order to transform its small, hard seeds into a food that humans can easily eat and digest. Rice can be simply boiled in water until tender, drained, and eaten. What is striking, however, in cultures where rice plays a central part in the diet, is the care taken to cook it. In India, one classic way of cooking long-grain rice sees the rice first washed and soaked to get rid of excess starch, then cooked in a covered saucepan using the absorption method and a precise ratio of rice to water. By the end of the cooking time, this results in tender grains, with all the water absorbed. A similar method is used in Chinese cooking for long-grain rice. In Iraq (formerly part of Persia), where rice was historically hugely esteemed as a luxury, the traditional method of preparing long-grain rice requires that it be washed, soaked in salted water, parboiled, drained, and finally steamed, with the result being light-textured, dry rice.

In Italy, rice is cooked in a very different way, classically used to make a dish called risotto. This is made using what is known as risotto rice, short- to medium-grain Italian rice such as Arborio or *carnaroli*, which has a high amylopectin content. To make a risotto, the rice is first sautéed in butter, usually with onion; then hot, simmering stock is gradually added to the pan over a period of around 15 to 18 minutes, while the rice is stirred frequently to ensure even cooking. As the grains cook, they release their starch, giving a characteristic creamy texture to the finished dish. Ideally, the individual grains, while cooked through, should retain some resistance. Often risotto is enriched at the end with the addition of butter and grated Parmesan cheese. It is a versatile dish, which exists in many regional and seasonal variations, made with ingredients such as asparagus, black squid ink, zucchini, seafood, Italian sausages, or dried porcini mushrooms.

In Spain, medium-grain rice, such as *bomba*, is used to make paella, which has a special place in Spanish affections and is regarded as a national dish. Paella originated from the rice fields near the Albufera lagoon in Valencia. The word *paella* means "frying pan" in the Valencian dialect, and the dish is traditionally cooked in a large, shallow pan. The making of a paella in Spain is often a sociable affair, cooked for family and friends outdoors over a fire in huge pans, large enough to feed several people. For a paella, the rice is cooked with flavorings and ingredients, with the liquid element consisting of wine and hot stock. Unlike a risotto, the stock is added to the rice all in one go, with the rice then gently cooked, uncovered, without stirring, for around 20 minutes until it has absorbed the stock and become tender.

Traditional additions to paella vary from region to region and area to area: snails, eels, rabbit, seasonal vegetables, chicken, and sausage are all classic ingredients. Of the variations, seafood paella is particularly eye-catching.

Traditional additions to paella vary from region to region and area to area: snails, eels, rabbit, seasonal vegetables, chicken, and sausage are all classic ingredients. Of the variations, seafood paella is particularly eye-catching. Historically made in coastal regions but now eaten all over Spain, it is flavored with saffron, which gives the rice a rich yellow color, and topped with seafood such as shrimp, mussels, and clams.

One also finds rice cooked until soft in large quantities of water to create a rice porridge, naturally thickened by the starch present in the grains. In China, this type of dish is called congee and is often eaten as a simple, sustaining, digestible breakfast with deep-fried Chinese doughsticks.

NASI GORENG

Serves 4
Preparation 10 minutes
Cooking 17–18 minutes

Indonesian-style fried rice is a very tasty dish indeed that is eaten as a meal on its own. Red chiles give it a distinct kick, while the use of *blachan*, a Southeast Asian shrimp paste, adds a salty umami richness.

2 eggs

Salt and freshly ground
  black pepper

4 tbsp sunflower oil

2 red chiles

½ onion, chopped

2 garlic cloves, chopped

½ tsp *blachan* (shrimp paste)

9 oz chicken thigh fillet,
  cut into short strips

6 oz raw peeled prawns

2 cups cold cooked rice

1 tbsp *kecap manis*
  (Indonesian soy sauce)

2 tbsp crispy fried shallots

1 Beat the eggs together in a small bowl and season with salt and pepper. Heat ¼ tablespoon of the oil in a skillet. Pour in half the beaten egg, tilting the pan to spread it around evenly, and fry until set. Repeat the process with the remaining egg. Roll the two thin omelets up, slice into fine shreds, and reserve.

2 Blend together the chiles, onion, garlic, and *blachan* into a paste in a food processor.

3 Heat the remaining oil in a wok. Add the chile paste and fry, stirring constantly, for 2–3 minutes until fragrant. Add the chicken strips and stir-fry for 2 minutes. Add the prawns and stir-fry until they turn opaque and pink.

4 Add the rice and *kecap manis*, mixing it thoroughly and breaking up any lumps. Stir-fry for 5 minutes until heated through.

5 Sprinkle with the shredded omelet and crispy shallots and serve at once.

It is a basic, affordable dish, and there are numerous regional variations of congee found in China, including the addition of assorted ingredients such as fish balls, marinated chicken, seafood, or preserved salted or "century" eggs. Variations on this rice gruel are found in countries where rice is eaten as a staple, among them India, Indonesia, Japan, Korea, the Philippines, and Sri Lanka.

Contrasting with congee both in terms of texture and luxury is the biriyani, a festive rice-based delicacy from the Indian subcontinent, a specialty of Moghul cuisine. Its name is thought to have Persian origins, coming from either *birinj* (Persian for "rice") or *biryan* (Persian for "to fry"). It is made by layering partially cooked long-grain rice, such as basmati, with cooked, spiced meat, fish, or vegetables, covering it, and baking it in a sealed pot, traditionally sealed with dough, until the rice has cooked in its own steam. Costly aromatic spices such as saffron, black and green cardamom pods, cinnamon sticks, and ground mace are often used in biriyanis. The result is a rich, fragrant dish served for special occasions, in which the lightness and separateness of the cooked rice grains are seen as an important way of assessing how well it has been cooked. In Persian cooking, one also finds celebratory rice dishes, such as *morasa polow* or "jeweled rice." Often served at weddings, this is a splendid creation of golden-colored saffron rice decorated with candied carrot slivers, strips of orange peel, dried barberries, pistachios, almonds, and crystallized sugar "diamonds."

Costly aromatic spices such as saffron, black and green cardamom pods, cinnamon sticks, and ground mace are often used in biriyanis. The result is a rich, fragrant dish served for special occasions.

For more everyday eating, one finds variations around the world of pilaf rice recipes. In these, rice is cooked in stock to give it more flavor, and sometimes meat, fish, or vegetables are added. Other extra touches, in order to enhance and enrich, include first frying chopped onion in butter, then adding the rice and coating it well; the use of aromatic herbs such as bay leaves or spices like cinnamon sticks; and the addition of nuts and dried fruits. Jambalaya, a Louisiana dish of Spanish and French origins, is an example of this approach to cooking rice. There are numerous recipes for jambalaya, but classic elements include andouille sausage, pork, chicken, and crayfish. Hoppin' John, made from rice and peas, is another much-loved rice dish of the southern United States. In tropical countries, rather than stock, rice is often cooked in coconut milk, which adds a subtle sweetness and a fatty richness of texture (see p. 153). In Malaysia, *nasi lemak* is popular, consisting of coconut rice served with other foods, such as fried, salted fish and peanuts, a piquant chile relish called *sambal*, and pickled vegetables, all of which contrast both in texture and flavor with the mildness of the rice.

Frying cooked rice is another popular technique that is found around the world. In rice-eating countries, it has long been an effective way of using up leftover rice. In China, stir-fried rice, cooked briskly in a wok over high heat, is a popular dish (see p. 143). Often it is made simply with spring onion and egg, but there are more elaborate versions, using additions such as strips of marinated beef, slivers of salted fish, barbecued pork, or seafood.

A visually striking culinary use of rice is sushi, Japan's best-known rice dish (see p. 154). Indeed, this quintessentially Japanese specialty is now widely known and made in countries around the world. The dish was invented as a way of preserving fish, with salted fish placed inside boiled rice, where it fermented. During the Edo Period (1603–1867), sushi made with raw fish, without fermentation, appeared. The nineteenth century saw the use of vinegared rice develop. The capacity of short-grained rice to clump together is central to the sushi we are familiar with today, allowing it to be shaped successfully and presented elegantly. There are four main types of sushi: *maki-zushi* (rice rolled in sheets of dried nori), *oshi-zushi* (rice in a mold, topped with cooked or cured fish), *nigiri-zushi* (fingers of rice topped with fish, seafood, or omelet), and *chirashi-zushi* (rice in a bowl, topped with slices of fish). Achieving the right texture of rice for *nigiri-zushi*—firm enough to hold together, yet soft enough to eat—is not simple. Making sushi well requires considerable experience and expertise, and master sushi chefs are hugely admired in Japan.

> *Achieving the right texture of rice for* nigiri-zushi—*firm enough to hold together, yet soft enough to eat—is not simple. Making sushi well requires experience and expertise, and master sushi chefs are hugely admired in Japan.*

Rice is not used only in savory dishes, although that tends to be how we first think of it. There is a varied tradition of using rice in puddings around the world. In India, one finds *kheer*—a rice pudding made by cooking rice slowly and gently in milk with cardamom and sugar, chilling it, and decorating it with pistachios and *vark* (edible silver foil). In Britain, too, rice pudding is a traditional dessert, made simply by cooking rice in sweetened milk and serving it with strawberry jelly (see p. 160). In Southeast Asia, sticky rice is often used in desserts. Among the best-known of these is Thailand's sticky rice with mangoes, combining sticky rice enriched with coconut milk with slices of fresh mango to excellent effect.

BIBIMBAP

Serves 4

Preparation 20 minutes

Cooking 20–25 minutes

A hearty Korean favorite, *bibimbap* consists of rice topped with an attractively arranged, colorful mixture of assorted foods, such as fried vegetables and meat. There are numerous recipes—variations on a theme—but key Korean flavorings include garlic, sesame oil, and *gochujang*, Korean's mellow chile paste.

8 oz beefsteak, sliced into short, fine strips

1 garlic clove, chopped

2 tbsp soy sauce

1½ tbsp sesame oil

Pinch of sugar

1½ cups short-grain rice

2½ cups water

Salt

2 carrots, peeled and cut into julienne strips

2 tbsp sesame seeds

4 tbsp sunflower oil

12 button mushrooms, halved

3 tbsp *gochujang* (Korean chile paste)

4 eggs

2 scallions, finely chopped

1 Mix together the beef strips, garlic, 1 tablespoon of the soy sauce, 1 tablespoon of the sesame oil, and the pinch of sugar in a mixing bowl and set aside to marinate.

2 Wash the rice thoroughly in cold water to rinse out any excess starch. Drain, place in a heavy saucepan, and add the water and a pinch of salt. Bring to a boil, reduce the heat, cover tightly, and simmer for around 20 minutes, until the water has been absorbed and the rice is tender.

3 While the rice is cooking, prepare the toppings. Blanch the carrots in boiling water until tender; drain and toss with the remaining sesame oil and the sesame seeds.

4 Heat 1 tablespoon of the sunflower oil in a small skillet. Add the mushrooms and fry until lightly browned. Add 1 tablespoon of the *gochujang* and 1 tablespoon of the soy sauce and fry briefly, coating the mushrooms in the paste.

5 Heat 1 tablespoon of the sunflower oil in a medium skillet. Add the marinated beef strips and fry, stirring often, until just cooked.

6 Divide the freshly cooked rice among four serving bowls. Top each portion with beef strips, sesame carrots, and chile mushrooms.

7 Heat the remaining sunflower oil in a large skillet. Fry the eggs until cooked to taste and top each portion with a fried egg. Sprinkle with chopped scallion and serve at once, with *gochujang* on the side.

CACAO

Of all the plants that humans use as a source of food, *Theobroma cacao* occupies a special place in our affections. Indeed, even its scientific, botanical name suggests its special importance, translating as "food of the gods." From the seeds of its fruit, we make chocolate drinks and—a much more recent development—the sweet version that has become synonymous with the word *chocolate*.

Although the exact origins of the cacao plant are lost in time, we know that the cacao tree is native to the Americas. It is in Mesoamerica that we first find accounts of human beings using cacao. It is thought that the Olmecs, the first of Mesoamerica's major civilizations (1200–400 BCE), used cacao, although details, as with much of this mysterious civilization, remain sketchy. There is no written history of the Olmecs, but traces of the cacao chemical theobromine have been found on Olmec pots and vessels. Cacao, however, undoubtedly played an important part in Maya civilization (250–900 CE). Archaeological evidence, including Mayan hieroglyphic writing and painted scenes on ceramics found in burial chambers, shows that drinks made from cacao were consumed by the Maya elite. It is thought that cacao was used in religious ceremonies in Maya culture and also as a form of currency.

Archaeological evidence, including Mayan hieroglyphic writing and painted scenes on ceramics found in burial chambers, shows that drinks made from cacao were consumed by the Maya elite.

Cacao was also important to another Mesoamerican people, the Aztecs (1300–1521 CE), initially a nomadic people who settled in the central highlands of what is now Mexico and created a sophisticated civilization. In the Aztec Empire, as with the Maya, cacao beans were so valuable that they were used for currency, with trade carried out and tributes paid to the Aztecs in cacao beans. Cacao beans were stored in huge quantities in royal warehouses, used to pay salaries, and consumed in the royal court. Drinks made from cacao beans were used in Aztec rituals of birth, marriage, and death and were drunk ceremoniously. It was a drink enjoyed by Aztec nobility, served at banquets. Cacao had a special status in Aztec society: not simply a luxurious ingredient, it was one with magical and divine powers.

In 1519, the Spanish conquistador Hernán Cortés led an expedition that led to the collapse of the Aztec Empire in 1521, with the death of the Aztec's Emperor Moctezuma II in 1520 and the fall of Tenochtitlán, the Aztec capital, in 1521. The Spanish colonialists had noticed that cacao was valued in Aztec society and used as a currency. Cortés reported on this usage to his royal master, Emperor Charles V: "Cacao is a fruit like the almond, which they grind and hold to be of such value that they use it as money throughout the land and with it buy all they need in the markets and other places." The Spaniards also quickly understood that the drinks made from cacao were consumed by the upper tiers of Aztec society, observing that the Emperor Moctezuma II drank a frothed beverage made from the beans.

Following their conquest of the Aztecs, it was, accordingly, the Spanish who introduced the exotic novelty of drinking chocolate to Europe in the sixteenth century. It was the Spanish who gave the name *chocolatl* to the drink, a word thought to have derived from the Nahuatl *cacahuatl*, meaning "cacao water." From *chocolatl* comes the word "chocolate," which we use today.

Not everyone was convinced of the drink's appeal. The Italian historian and traveler Girolamo Benzoni wrote in *History of the New World* (1565) that "it [chocolate] seemed more a drink for pigs, than a drink for humanity. I was in this country for more than a year, and never wanted to taste it, and whenever I passed a settlement, some Indian would offer me a drink of it, and would be amazed when I would not accept, going away laughing. But then, as there was a shortage of wine, so as not to be always drinking water, I did like the others. The taste is somewhat bitter, it satisfies and refreshes the body, but does not inebriate, and it is the best and most expensive merchandise, according to the Indians of that country."

It was the Spanish who gave the name chocolatl *to the drink, a word thought to have derived from the Nahuatl* cacahuatl, *meaning "cacao water."*

Drinking chocolate, however, became very fashionable among the courts and stately homes of Europe. There it was a high-status beverage made from

TRIPLE CHOCOLATE COOKIES

Makes about 30 cookies
Preparation 15 minutes
Cooking 10 minutes per batch

This classic cookie recipe is a great way to enjoy three types of chocolate in one go. Savor them with a refreshing glass of cold milk or a warming cup of coffee.

1 stick salted butter, softened, plus extra for greasing

¼ cup superfine sugar

¼ cup soft brown sugar

1 egg, lightly beaten

1 cup all-purpose flour

½ tsp baking soda

⅓ cup bittersweet chocolate chips

⅓ cup milk chocolate chips

¼ cup white chocolate chips

1   Preheat the oven to 350°F.
2   In a mixing bowl, cream the butter and two sugars together until they are well mixed. Gradually add the beaten egg.
3   Sift the flour and baking soda into the mixture and stir in. Mix in all the chocolate chips.
4   Place teaspoons of the mixture, spaced well apart, on greased baking sheets. Bake them in batches in the oven for 10 minutes until the cookies have spread and turned golden brown. Remove carefully with a spatula and let cool on wire racks. Store in an airtight container.

expensive, imported cacao, enjoyed by the social elite rather than the masses (see "Chocolate Beverages," p. 188). Importantly for its fashionable success, chocolate was also regarded as a drink with health-giving properties. In the seventeenth century, chocolate was drunk in the Spanish court and also served at spectacles such as bullfights.

One of the issues with regard to drinking chocolate in Catholic countries such as France, Italy, and Spain, where it was popular, was whether consumption of this rich, nourishing beverage was allowed during fast days. In 1662, Pope Alexander VII's declaration that *liquidum non frangit jejunum* (liquids do not break the fast) meant that chocolate could be drunk on fast days, which became another factor in its popularity. Chocolate frequently had noble and influential advocates, who played a part in spreading the word of this new drink. In France, the notable Cardinal Mazarin was a lover of chocolate, bringing with him from Italy two cooks who knew how to prepare coffee, tea, and chocolate. In 1666, King Louis XIV granted to one

David Chaliou the monopoly to make and sell "a certain composition which is called chocolate, the use of which is very healthful" in France. The chocolate-drinking habit spread from continental Europe to England, with the opening in 1657 of a chocolate house set up by a Frenchman in Bishopsgate Street, London, selling "an excellent West India drink, called chocolate."

The noted seventeenth-century English diarist Samuel Pepys, who had a taste for novelties, recorded in 1661 drinking "jocolatte" to settle his stomach the morning after a night of heavy alcohol consumption. A number of chocolate houses were set up in England, including White's Chocolate House, opened by Francis White in 1693. Men gathered in these houses to discuss politics and the affairs of the day and to gamble. Famously, White's is today known as the oldest gentleman's club in the country, an exclusive establishment frequented particularly by members of the Tory party.

In eighteenth-century North America, too, hot chocolate became a fashionable drink, consumed by the elite at breakfast time. It was regarded as having healthy, nourishing properties, and among its champions was Founding Father Thomas Jefferson, who predicted in a letter of 1785 that it would overtake tea and coffee as the United States' favorite drink.

An aspect of the new drink's allure was undoubtedly its reputation as an aphrodisiac. The Spanish royal physician and naturalist Francisco Hernández, who traveled to New Spain (Mexico) in 1570, composed a major work on the region's plants and gave a recipe for chocolate, which, he wrote, "aroused the venereal appetite." The seventeenth-century physician Henry Stubbes prepared chocolate for King Charles II, a monarch noted for his active love life. Writing on the drink made from cacao, Stubbes observed: "The great use of Chocolate in Venery, and for supplying the Testicles with a Balsam or a Sap, is so ingeniously made out by one of our learned Countrymen already, that I dare not presume to add any Thing." Such was

Chocolate's aphrodisiac reputation carried on into the eighteenth century. Madame de Pompadour, the official chief mistress of France's King Louis XV from 1745 to 1751, was known to drink chocolate.

Charles's fondness for chocolate that the royal accounts books reveal that in 1666, £57 18s. 8d. was spent on chocolate, rising to an impressive £229 10s. 8d. in 1669. On tea, in comparison, the king spent much less, usually only around £6. Chocolate's aphrodisiac reputation carried on into the eighteenth century. Madame de Pompadour, the official chief mistress of France's King Louis XV from 1745 to 1751, was known to drink chocolate. The legendary Italian womanizer Giacomo Casanova is said to have been a chocolate consumer, drinking it before lovemaking. To this day, chocolate continues to be associated with love and romance, as witnessed by the large spike in chocolate sales each Valentine's Day.

It was the Industrial Revolution that saw chocolate move from being a drink enjoyed by a privileged few to a beverage that was more affordable and accessible. Key in this process was the invention by the Dutch chemist Coenraad Johannes Van Houten in 1828 of a cacao-pressing method, which could produce a cocoa powder that could easily be mixed with water or milk and turned into a beverage. Chocolate, as Benzoni had noted in 1575, is a teetotal drink. It was this aspect that appealed to Quakers in Britain seeking to find an alternative to alcohol, which they felt caused misery and deprivation.

The advances in machinery that led to the making of cocoa powder also led to the creation of eating chocolate in the form that we know today. Many of the pioneers in this field are company names still recognized. In 1847, J. S. Fry & Son, a Quaker chocolate manufacturer, found a way to mix together cocoa powder, sugar, and cacao butter to create a chocolate paste that could be molded into bars. The world's first chocolate bar had arrived, and in 1849, Fry's exhibited its innovative "Chocolat Délicieux à Manger." Progress in chocolate manufacturing continued apace, with the English Quaker company Cadbury's credited with introducing the first chocolate box in 1868.

In 1879, the first milk chocolate was produced, an invention of chocolate manufacturer Daniel Peter, working with Henri Nestlé, a Swiss chemist who had discovered a process to make powdered milk. The same year saw Rudolf Lindt invent conching, which is a way of mixing chocolate that greatly improves its texture (see p. 183).

In the United States in 1893, the caramel manufacturer Milton Hershey saw a demonstration of new chocolate-producing machinery at the Chicago World's Fair. He built a chocolate-processing plant in 1896 and, in 1900, began manufacturing Hershey Bars. Today, chocolate confectionary is produced on a large scale, readily available in many parts of the world and easily affordable. Chocolate, however, continues to be seen as a treat.

CACAO VARIETIES

It is increasingly realized that the traditional way of classifying cacao varieties is too simplistic. Progress in science, including the ability to trace genotypes, is throwing light on a far more complex scenario. The older way of classifying cacao—a system that is still widely used—splits it into three broad divisions:

Criollo

The word means "native" in Latin American Spanish and is used to refer to a cacao grown in Mesoamerica before the arrival of the Spanish. *Criollo* cacao is highly prized for its quality. *Criollo* trees are fragile, susceptible to pests and diseases, and low yielding, so *criollo* cacao is rare and expensive.

Forastero

The word means "foreign" in Spanish. The vast majority of cacao grown in the world, in places including Africa, Brazil, and Ecuador, is of this variety. It is a hardy cacao, less susceptible to diseases.

Trinitario

A hybrid cacao, named after the island of Trinidad, where it was developed, traditionally considered to be a cross-breed between *criollo* and *forastero*.

A new approach to classifying cacao sees the term *forastero* as an oversimplification, as it covers such a wide range of cacao varieties. Instead, *forastero* is differentiated into eight varieties: *amelonado, contamana, curaray, guiana, iquitos, marañón, nanay,* and *purus. Criollo* is defined as the ancient cacao used by the Maya and Aztecs. Many other genetic types of cacao are in the process of being recognized, among them *nacional*, grown in Ecuador and northern Peru. In the cocoa or cacao market, there are two categories of cacao beans. "Bulk" or "ordinary" beans are the most widely grown cacao. Their flavor lacks the complexity of *criollo* or *trinitario* varieties. Generally speaking, bulk cacao consists of beans from *forastero* varieties. "Fine" or "flavor" beans come from *criollo* or *trinitario* cacao trees. In terms of total world cacao production, only 5 percent per annum is fine or flavor cacao.

HOW CHOCOLATE IS MADE

The long process of solid chocolate production begins with the growing of the cacao fruit to produce the beans from which it is made.

GROWING AND HARVESTING CACAO

Growing cacao is hard manual work and labor intensive, as ongoing care and attention are required during both the growing and the harvesting.

Native to the tropics, the cacao species grows successfully in the world's "tropical belt," a geographic band around the globe spanning 23 degrees north and south on either side of the Equator. In its natural habitat, the 16- to 26-foot-tall cacao tree grows in the shady understory of the tropical rain forest. Cacao trees are delicate, requiring protection from direct sun and wind. In order to encourage their trees to thrive, small-scale cacao farmers often plant seedlings in the shelter of taller trees, such as banana, coconut, or rubber. On large-scale cacao plantations, however, hundreds of cacao trees are planted together. If planted in direct sunlight, without the protection of shade, cacao trees are stressed and more susceptible to pests and diseases, which are easily passed in densely planted plantation conditions.

A cacao tree begins to flower when it is two to four years old. In order to bear fruit, cacao flowers require pollinating, a process that is carried out by tiny midges. It is estimated that only 5 percent of the flowers produced by a cacao tree will start to turn into fruit. It takes around five to six months for a pollinated flower to turn into a mature fruit, known as a cacao pod. Strikingly, these spindly trees bear large fruits that grow on the trunk and on the branches. These are shaped like elongated melons and range in length from 9 to 13 inches. One tree bears around twenty to forty cacao pods, with each pod containing thirty to fifty seeds, which are known as beans. In terms of production, cacao trees usually peak at around seven years, though they can go on producing fruit beyond that time. A single cacao tree bears fruit at different stages of ripeness, so the cacao farmer has to track the ripening progress of individual pods. The pods need to be harvested when ripe but before they begin to germinate, a period of around three to four weeks. Harvesting is done manually, using a machete to cut the heavy fruit cleanly from the stem without damaging the tree, immature fruit, or flowers.

It is estimated that only 5 percent of the flowers produced by a cacao tree will start to turn into fruit. It takes around five to six months for a pollinated flower to turn into a mature fruit, known as a cacao pod.

The ripe cacao fruit are then split open, and both the cacao beans and the sticky sour-sweet pulp that surrounds them are removed from the pod's thick shells and taken to a collection point.

FERMENTING CACAO

The fermenting of the beans is an important stage in developing the chocolate flavor and reducing the level of harsh tannins within the cacao. It is usually carried out in the cacao's country of origin, with the tropical

GRANOLA WITH
CACAO NIBS

Makes 1¼ lb

Preparation 5 minutes

**Cooking 1 hour 5 minutes
to 1 hour 35 minutes**

3 cups porridge oats

1 cup sunflower seeds

1 cup chopped pecans

3½ fl oz sunflower oil

5 tbsp runny honey or
maple syrup

Pinch of salt

1 tsp vanilla extract

3 tbsp cacao nibs

Homemade granola always tastes so much better than that bought in a store. The fun of making your own is that you can tweak the ingredients as you want. Using cacao nibs is a lovely way of adding extra texture and a chocolaty flavor to the mixture.

1   Preheat the oven to 275°F.

2   Mix together the oats, sunflower seeds, and pecans. Gently heat together the oil and honey or syrup in a saucepan, stirring well. Mix in the salt and vanilla extract.

3   Pour the oil mixture into the oat mixture and mix together well. Spread the mixture evenly in a roasting pan and bake for 1 to 1½ hours, stirring now and then, until golden brown and crunchy.

4   Remove, allow to cool, then transfer from roasting pan to a large bowl. Mix in the cacao nibs. Store in an airtight container.

CHOCOLATE POTS

Serves 4
Preparation 10 minutes, plus
  2–3 hours chilling
Cooking 3 minutes

⅔ cup heavy cream
1 cup bittersweet chocolate
  chips
2 egg yolks
¼ cup superfine sugar
Whipped cream, to decorate
Amaretto cookies, to decorate

These small, rich chocolate pots are definitely a dessert for serious chocolate lovers. As they can be made in advance, they are excellent for dinner parties. Serve topped with whipped cream and with a dainty amaretto cookie on the side.

1 Preheat the oven to 275°F.
2 Heat the cream in a saucepan and bring to a boil. Remove from the heat and immediately mix in the chocolate chips, stirring well until melted.
3 Beat the egg yolks and sugar together in a bowl until well mixed. Pour in the hot chocolate cream, stirring constantly as you do so.
4 Divide the mixture among four ramekins or small bowls. Cool, cover, and chill for around 2–3 hours until set.

heat an aid in the process. The cacao beans, together with the soft pulp, are piled together in heaps or placed in containers such as boxes (sometimes called sweat boxes) or hanging bags, covered with leaves (such as plantain or banana leaves), and left to ferment. Spores from naturally occurring yeasts settle on the beans, and the natural sugars in the pulp quickly begin to ferment, turning into acetic acid (a form of vinegar). The temperature of the massed cacao beans rises, softening the beans, allowing the acid to penetrate them and kill the embryo (germ) within each bean, and triggering a series of chemical changes within them, including enzyme activity and the breakdown of proteins into amino acid. As the pulp transforms into acetic acid, it drains off naturally from the beans, leaving them slightly darkened.

The fermenting period ranges from two to six days, depending on the variety, with *criollo* requiring a shorter fermentation time than *forastero*. During fermentation, the cacao is turned or mixed in order to increase aeration and thus encourage the required bacterial activity and ensure even fermentation.

DRYING CACAO
The next stage after fermentation is the drying of the cacao beans, with the aim being to reduce the moisture content from 60 percent to around 7.5 percent. In many countries, sunshine is used to dry the beans, which are spread out on mats, trays, or floors in a sunny location. In some countries where there is a lack of a dry period after harvesting, artificial drying is used. In Papua New Guinea, for example, cacao beans are dried next to wood fires, which gives a characteristic smoky flavor to cacao from there. During the drying period of around five to six days, the beans are regularly raked several times each day to ensure that the drying happens evenly and effectively. Drying the beans thoroughly is important in order to prevent the growth of molds, which would taint the flavor of the cacao. Once drying is completed, the cacao is then graded according to size and quality, weighed, and packed. Most of it is shipped abroad in cargo vessels, sent to brokers' warehouses or directly to chocolate factories to be processed.

ROASTING THE CACAO
Once at the chocolate manufacturer, the cacao beans are first sorted through and cleaned of any foreign matter, such as jute fibers from sacks, twigs, or stones. The beans are then roasted, another vital stage in developing the sought-after "chocolate" flavor, in the same way that roasting coffee beans helps create the "coffee" flavor.

CLASSIC BROWNIES

Makes 16 brownies
Preparation 15 minutes
Cooking 35 minutes

Who can resist a chocolate brownie? There is something about that soft texture that makes them very easy to eat indeed. The walnuts are a classic addition, their slight bitterness contrasting nicely with the sweetness of the chocolate mixture.

1 stick salted butter, plus extra
  for greasing
1⅛ cup dark chocolate chips
2 eggs
1 cup superfine sugar
1 tsp vanilla extract
1 cup all-purpose flour, sifted
½ cup walnut or pecan pieces

1   Preheat the oven to 350°F. Grease and line an 8-inch baking pan with baking paper.

2   Place the butter and chocolate in a small, heavy saucepan. Heat gently over low heat, stirring, until melted. Set aside.

3   In a mixing bowl, whisk the eggs until pale and frothy. Gradually whisk in the sugar, mixing in thoroughly.

4   Fold in the melted chocolate and stir in the vanilla extract. Fold in the all-purpose flour and then add the walnut or pecan pieces.

5   Transfer the mixture to the prepared baking pan. Bake for 30 minutes. By the end of the baking time, the mixture should have formed a crust in the tin and should be set around the edges but still soft in the center. Remove from the oven, let cool for 10 minutes, then cut into 16 squares. Let cool completely before serving.

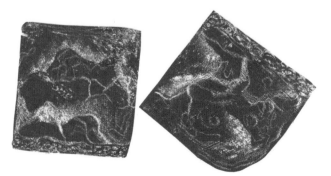

The process of roasting the beans, which makes them darken in color, results in what is known as the Maillard reaction, in which sugars and proteins break down to create more complex flavors in a food. The same process happens when meat is roasted or bread is baked. The heat of the roasting process also destroys remaining tannins, creating chocolate that is far smoother in flavor. Roasting also has a food-safety aspect, as the heat helps to destroy unwanted bacteria within the cacao.

The roasting temperature and the time depend on the type of bean being used and also the effect the chocolate manufacturer is looking for. Large-scale producers with well-equipped factories use different roasting processes than small chocolate makers. In general, though, cacao is roasted at lower temperatures than coffee, and care must be taken not to overroast the beans, destroying flavors in the process.

Fine aromatic cacao beans, such as *criollo*, require a shorter roasting time than *forastero* cacaos. For craft chocolate makers producing their own "bean-to-bar" chocolate (see p. 187) in small batches, the roasting stage is very important, allowing the maker who roasts carefully and skillfully to bring out the flavor potential of the particular cacao being worked with. While artisan makers typically roast whole beans, in the world of large-scale,

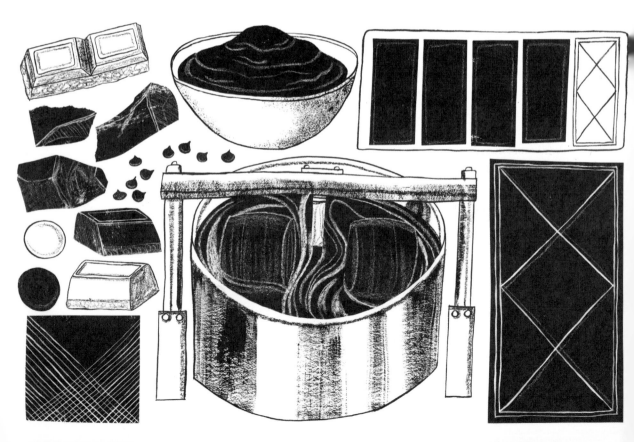

industrial chocolate manufacturing, one also finds nib roasting (the "nibs" being the bits of cacao bean that remain after the hull has been removed) and cocoa mass roasting, in which the paste made from ground cacao beans is roasted.

The roasted whole cacao beans, which are now dry and brittle, are next crushed in order to winnow the shells (hulls) from the broken cacao nibs. The cacao nibs are then crushed and ground in mills to a dark brown, thick paste known as "cacao liquor" or "cocoa liquor" and also as "cocoa mass," which liquefies when heated. The term "liquor" is misleading, as it is solid at room temperature and is not alcoholic at all. At this stage it contains both cacao solids and cacao butter (the natural fat within the cacao beans), though the level of cacao butter will depend on the origins of the bean and seasonal and harvesting conditions.

The heat of the roasting process destroys remaining tannins, creating chocolate that is far smoother in flavor. Roasting also has a food-safety aspect, as the heat helps to destroy unwanted bacteria within the cacao.

A portion of the cacao liquor can be further processed in order to separate the cacao butter from the cacao mass; this is done through the use of hydraulic presses. Usually, the cacao butter—which is added to chocolate and also used to make toiletries—will then be put through a deodorizing process to make it neutral in aroma and taste. It is an expensive ingredient, and some chocolate manufacturers use cheaper fats, such as vegetable oil or palm oil, instead of cacao butter.

The chocolate manufacturer next blends ingredients such as vanilla, sugar, and powdered milk (in order to make milk chocolate) into the cacao liquor. Lecithin, which is widely used as an emulsifier, is also often added. Additional cacao butter might also be mixed in, depending on the texture sought. The cacao content within a chocolate bar—which when declared is usually presented as a percentage on the packaging—consists of the cacao solids together with the cacao butter. A high cacao content is an indicator of quality, although it is by no means the only one. In the world of dark chocolate, for example, a 70 percent cacao content bar might well be considered better than an 80 percent one, as other factors—such as the quality of the cacao used and the care taken when fermenting, roasting, and processing the cacao—come into play.

This gritty, blended cacao mixture is then conched—that is, mixed in a conche for a period of some hours. The conche machine was invented by the chocolate manufacturer Rudolf Lindt in 1879 and was named, supposedly, after the Latin word for "shell" because of its shape. Traditional conche machines, known as longitudinal conches, feature granite rollers that roll back and forth, causing the chocolate liquor to splash back into a trough. The action of the rollers creates friction, which heats the cacao mixture. Conching is regarded as an important stage in chocolate making, as this process of stirring the cacao mixture refines it, reducing the particle size of the cacao and sugar so that the previously gritty mixture becomes noticeably smooth to our palates. Unwanted volatiles and aromas are also driven off during the period of constant movement, and the cacao mixture is aerated. In Lindt & Sprungli's account of its history, Rudolf Lindt, either accidentally or on purpose, left a cacao mixture mixing in the conche machine for a whole weekend, far longer than usual. When he tasted the results, however, he realized that conching for this length of time had produced chocolate that was smoother and creamier than the norm at the time, characteristics that became typical of Swiss chocolate. High-quality chocolate manufacturers have conched for many hours—as much as 72 hours. In contrast, other manufacturers, making lower-grade chocolate on a larger scale, may carry out a brief spell of conching that lasts only a few hours. Modern conches exist in a number of forms; in the quest for efficiency and speed of production, there are now single machines that can grind, mix, and conche the cacao.

Conching is regarded as an important stage in chocolate making, as this process of stirring the cacao mixture refines it, reducing the particle size of the cacao and sugar so that the previously gritty mixture becomes noticeably smooth to our palates.

Once the chocolate has been conched, it is then tempered, a process that realigns the cacao butter crystals (see p. 197); usually this is done in tempering machines. The tempered chocolate is poured into molds to form bars, cooled, and wrapped, usually by machine. The bars are sent from the factory to shops, where the consumer can buy them.

TYPES OF CHOCOLATE

Traditionally, three different types of eating chocolate have been produced by chocolate manufacturers: dark, milk, and white.

Dark chocolate, also known as **plain chocolate**. In Europe, this is made from cacao mass and cacao butter and usually also contains sugar. In the United States, the Food and Drug Administration requirement is that dark, bittersweet, or semisweet chocolate contain at least 35 percent cacao and less than 12 percent milk solids. Within these parameters, in the United States, the terms "semisweet" and "bittersweet" chocolate are used at the manufacturer's discretion. Semisweet is typically understood to have a lower cacao content and to be sweeter than bittersweet chocolate. Chocolate with 100 percent cacao content is a form of dark chocolate made from the cacao mass without any additional sugar; hence its flavor is noticeably more bitter.

Milk chocolate is made from cacao mass, cacao butter, and milk powder; hence the name "milk chocolate." Milk chocolate is often paler than dark chocolate because of the addition of milk powder, and usually sweeter and creamier in flavor. Traditionally, its cacao content is lower than that of dark chocolate. This varies with manufacturers and country of production, but around 25 percent is typical. In the United States, chocolate with more than 12 percent milk solids is labeled as "milk chocolate."

White chocolate is made from cacao butter, sugar, and milk powder, without any cacao mass. It is cream-colored due to the absence of cacao mass and noticeably softer in its texture than either dark or milk chocolate due to its high fat content. In producing these types of chocolate, many manufacturers add soy lecithin, which is used to aid emulsification. Vanilla flavoring is often added to white chocolate.

Dark milk chocolate is a newcomer to the chocolate world. It consists of chocolate that has the high cacao content associated with plain chocolate, but with the addition of milk powder.

Raw chocolate is another recent addition. The "raw" refers to the fact that the cacao beans used to make it are not roasted, as is traditional in chocolate making, although they are sun-dried.

Single-origin chocolate is the term given to chocolate made from cacao sourced from just one country. Most mass-produced chocolate is made from cacao sourced from more than one country of origin.

THE CRAFT CHOCOLATE MOVEMENT

The familiar chocolate bar in the form we know it today is largely a product of the Industrial Revolution, created through technological breakthroughs

LUXURIOUS HOT CHOCOLATE

Serves 2
Preparation 5 minutes
Cooking 5 minutes

Using real chocolate, rather than simply sweetened cocoa powder, makes hot chocolate a truly luxurious drink. The Aztecs used vanilla in their chocolate drinks, so this flavor combination has a venerable history. Serve as a warming and comforting drink on a cold winter's day.

1¾ cups full-fat milk
⅓ cup dark chocolate,
   finely chopped
1–2 tbsp granulated sugar
½ tsp vanilla extract
Mini-marshmallows,
   for topping

1. Place the milk, chocolate, and 1 tablespoon of the sugar in a small saucepan. Gently bring to a boil, stirring often, until the chocolate has melted and the sugar has dissolved.
2. Remove from the heat and stir in the vanilla extract. Taste the hot chocolate and add more sugar if required.
3. Pour into two mugs, top with mini-marshmallows, and serve at once.

in how cacao was processed. Chocolate manufacturers were able to make chocolate bars and chocolate confectionary on a large scale at accessible prices, with Hershey's, Lindt & Sprungli, and Cadbury's becoming household names. Chocolatiers, especially in France and Belgium, continued the tradition of working with high-quality couverture chocolate (see p. 195) to produce delicacies such as chocolate bonbons—filled with ganache (a combination of chocolate and a liquid), pralines, or caramel— and novelties made by molding chocolate (see "The Chocolatier," p. 195).

Recent decades, however, have seen the rise of a new chocolate craft movement in a number of countries, centered on the chocolate bar. In the world of craft coffee, aficionados appreciate filter coffee because it offers an expression of both the coffee beans used to make it and the care taken in making the drink. Similarly, the chocolate bar offers a chance to showcase the cacao used to make it and the skill of its producer.

Historically, cacao grown in the tropics was shipped abroad to be processed into chocolate. Now most of it is sold in bulk via brokers, with future commodity prices per ton set by the New York or London stock exchange. This generic cacao is used to make the majority of mass-produced chocolate. In contrast, the craft chocolate movement has seen the rise of what is called "bean-to-bar" chocolate, made from carefully sourced premium cacao bought directly from farmers rather than anonymously on the open market. At the heart of this movement are chocolate makers. Whereas chocolatiers make chocolates from couverture chocolate, bean-to-bar chocolate makers use raw cacao beans, which they then roast, grind, and turn into chocolate themselves. Controlling the whole process in this way, with care taken at every stage, allows for cacao's rich diversity of flavors to be expressed effectively in the resulting chocolate. Artisan chocolate makers produce chocolate with provenance, showcasing cacao-producing countries such as Bolivia, Venezuela, Peru, Vietnam, and Madagascar. Furthermore,

> *The craft chocolate movement has seen the rise of what is called "bean-to-bar" chocolate, made from carefully sourced premium cacao bought directly from farmers rather than anonymously on the open market.*

chocolate makers experiment with specific varieties of cacao—such as *criollo*, *arriba*, and *trinitario*—offering single-variety bars but also blending together cacao beans to achieve the desired flavor profiles.

In twentieth-century North America, two figures were important early pioneers of bean-to-bar chocolate. The physician Robert Steinberg and the winemaker John Scharffenberger founded Scharffen Berger Chocolate

Maker in California's Bay Area in 1999, making bean-to-bar chocolate from high-quality cacao, which Steinberg sourced with great care, traveling to countries such as Ecuador on his quest for interesting varieties. The influence of Scharffen Berger was considerable, with many contemporary craft chocolate makers inspired to set up in business by what they did. In 2005, Scharffen Berger was acquired by Hershey's. Today, however, their legacy lives on in a dynamic chocolate scene in the United States.

Craft chocolate makers are, in fact, now found in countries around the world, including Britain, France, and Italy. Many of these craft producers work on a small scale—with pounds of beans rather than tons—hence the term "micro-batch" or "small-batch" chocolate. One of the striking trends in recent years has been the rise of quality chocolate being produced in the country where the cacao is grown, rather than in Europe or the United States, as was the historic pattern.

A realization of how fascinating and diverse good chocolate can be is reflected in an increasing connoisseurship. International chocolate competitions have been set up to encourage growers and chocolate makers and to create an appreciative and knowledgeable audience for fine chocolate. The craft chocolate scene is also influencing mass chocolate producers: for example, single-origin bars are no longer the preserve simply of the micro-batch maker but are also offered by larger companies.

CHOCOLATE BEVERAGES

Chocolate, as we have seen, was long predominantly enjoyed as a beverage rather than in solid form. Chocolate drinks made from cacao were very important in Maya culture, used ceremonially in rituals and banquets and drunk by Maya kings and nobility. Similarly, in Aztec culture, chocolate drinks were highly esteemed, and consumed by warriors and Aztec nobility. The fact that chocolate was a nonalcoholic drink seems to have been part of the reason for it being valued over other drinks. An early Spanish account of how the Aztecs made drinking chocolate was written by "a companion of Hernán Cortés," known by scholars as the Anonymous Conqueror, and published in 1556. The anonymous chronicler wrote:

> *These seeds which are called almonds or cacao are ground and made into powder, and other small seeds are ground and this powder is put into certain basins with a point [sic], and then they put water on it and mix it with a spoon. And having mixed it very well, they change it from one basin to another, so that a foam is raised which they put in a vessel made for the purpose. And when*

they wish to drink it, they mix it with certain small spoons of gold or silver or wood, and drink it, and drinking it one must open one's mouth, because being foam one must give it room to subside, and go down bit by bit. This drink is the healthiest thing, and the greatest sustenance of anything you could drink in the world, because he who drinks a cup of this liquid, no matter how far he walks, can go a whole day without eating anything else.

The creation of foam was an important element of chocolate drinks for both the Maya and the Aztecs. Bernardino de Sahagún—the Spanish friar who wrote a remarkable sixteenth-century account of Aztec civilization based on his own observations and extensive interviews—described how Aztec chocolate sellers lifted the drink up high and poured it so as to create a frothy foam. A sixteenth-century post-conquest illustration shows chocolate being poured by a standing woman from a vessel held at shoulder height into another vessel on the ground. Sahagún described a well-made chocolate drink being "such as only the lords drink: smooth, frothy, vermilion, red, and pure." The penchant for frothy chocolate passed on to the Spanish conquistadors. The Spanish are credited with coming up with an ingenious device for frothing chocolate drinks called the *molinillo* during the sixteenth century. This consisted of a wooden stick with rings around it with which to whisk the chocolate and so whip up a foam, an instrument used in Mexico to make hot chocolate to this day.

Both the Maya and the Aztecs used cacao in a sophisticated and nuanced way, creating various beverages from the precious beans. A variety of flavorings were added to chocolate in Mesoamerica, among them chile powder, vanilla, honey, and corn, just to name a few. Sahagún recorded an account of the chocolate drinks served to an Aztec ruler, which gives a sense of their diversity: "Then, by himself in his house, his chocolates were served: green cocoa-pods, honeyed chocolate, flowered chocolate, flavored with green vanilla, bright red chocolate, huitztecolli-flower chocolate, flower-colored chocolate, black chocolate, white chocolate."

Both the Maya and Aztecs used cacao in a sophisticated and nuanced way, creating various beverages from the precious beans. A variety of flavorings were added to chocolate in Mesoamerica, among them chile powder and vanilla.

When chocolate was introduced to Europe, it was initially very much a courtly drink, enjoyed by the social elite of the day. European royalty, among them the French queen Marie Antoinette, employed specialist chocolate makers among their staff in order to enjoy this fashionable beverage freshly made for them.

CHOCOLATE CAKE

Makes one 8-inch cake
Preparation 15 minutes
Cooking 45–55 minutes

⅔ cup dark chocolate, chopped
1¾ cups self-rising flour, sifted
½ tsp baking soda
1 oz cocoa powder
2 sticks salted butter, softened,
    plus extra for greasing
1 cup superfine sugar
4 eggs
2 tbsp milk or brandy

Homemade chocolate cake is always a treat.
Serve slices of the cake with a cup of coffee
or tea or with whipped cream for dessert.

1   Preheat the oven to 350°F. Grease and base-line an
    8-inch round cake pan with baking paper.
2   Put the chocolate in a heatproof bowl suspended over a
    pan of simmering water (making sure that the water does
    not touch the bowl). Heat gently, stirring now and then,
    until the chocolate has melted. Set aside to cool slightly.
3   Sift together the flour, baking soda, and cocoa powder.
4   In a mixing bowl, cream the butter and sugar together.
    Add the eggs one at a time, mixing well between each
    addition. Add a little of the flour if the mixture begins
    to curdle. Mix in the cooled, melted chocolate.
5   Fold in the rest of the sifted flour mixture. Mix in the
    milk or brandy. Transfer the cake batter to the cake pan
    and bake for 40–50 minutes until risen and set. Test
    whether the cake is done by inserting a skewer into
    the center; if it comes out clean, the cake is ready.
    Remove and let cool.

HOMEMADE CHOCOLATE RUM TRUFFLES

Makes 26 truffles

Preparation 25 minutes, plus chilling

Cooking 5 minutes

1¼ cups good-quality bittersweet chocolate chips

⅓ cup heavy cream

3 tbsp rum

Cocoa powder, for coating

There is something very satisfying about making your own chocolate truffles. Make sure to use good-quality chocolate—the results will taste great and really impress your guests.

1   Place the chocolate chips and cream in a heatproof bowl suspended over a pan of simmering water (making sure that the water does not touch the bowl). Heat gently, stirring now and then, until the chocolate has melted.

2   Add the rum and stir to mix together well. Set aside to cool, then chill in the refrigerator for at least 1–2 hours to firm up the mixture.

3   Take teaspoons of the chocolate mixture and, with lightly oiled hands, shape into small, rounded truffles. Coat the truffles lightly in cocoa powder as soon as they have been shaped. Cover and chill in the refrigerator until serving.

At Hampton Court Palace in England, occupied by generations of British rulers, a "lost" royal chocolate kitchen was rediscovered in 2013 and opened to the public in 2014. Records show that it was used during the eighteenth century by King George I's personal chocolate maker, Thomas Tosier, to make hot chocolate for His Majesty.

The way of producing chocolate beverages from cacao beans remained remarkably similar across cultures and across centuries. Cacao beans were first roasted, then ground into a powder or a paste, which was then mixed with a liquid such as hot water or milk (a European innovation), and whisked together to dissolve the cocoa and create the foam. As in Mesoamerica, other flavorings were ground and added to the beverage in Europe. Cacao is naturally bitter, and it was the Spanish who first used sugar, another expensive ingredient, to sweeten hot chocolate. Various spices such as allspice or ginger were added, with cinnamon proving particularly popular. Floral essences, such as orange flower water or rose water, and ground nuts—almonds, hazelnuts, and walnuts—were also added. In order to make hot chocolate even more luxurious and special, costly ingredients such as ambergris or musk were also used.

One famous courtly flavored beverage was the jasmine-flavored hot chocolate enjoyed by Cosimo III de' Medici, the grand duke of Tuscany from 1670 to 1723. The recipe was developed for Cosimo III by the physician and botanist Francesco Redi, who kept the recipe a closely guarded secret during his life; revealed after his death, it used fresh jasmine flowers, musk, vanilla, and ambergris.

Turin in Italy also saw the combination of two fashionable beverages—namely hot chocolate and coffee—with the creation of the *bicerin*. Said to have evolved from an eighteenth-century drink called the *bavareisa*, the *bicerin* is a carefully layered combination of espresso, hot chocolate, and milk, named after the small handle-less glass in which it was served. Among the drink's famous admirers was the French novelist Alexandre Dumas. Visitors to Turin today can visit Caffè al Bicerin, a historic coffeehouse founded in 1763, which has become synonymous with this famous Turinese beverage.

Cacao is naturally bitter, and it was the Spanish who first used sugar, another expensive ingredient, to sweeten hot chocolate. Various spices such as allspice or ginger were added, with cinnamon proving particularly popular.

Such was the social status of hot chocolate in Europe during the seventeenth and eighteenth centuries that the French created special chocolate pots called *chocolatières* to hold the drink. A distinctive feature

of these long, slender spouted vessels was that their lids contained small openings in which to insert a *molinet* (a swizzle stick) in order to keep the drink well blended and frothy. These vessels were often made from silver or porcelain, the value of the materials reflecting the rarity and cost of the drink they contained.

In addition to chocolate pots, special drinking vessels were also produced in countries where hot chocolate was enjoyed. The custom arose in Latin America of using hollowed-out coconuts as drinking vessels, with the most elegant of these decorated with silver rims and handles and resting on silver bases. During the 1640s, the viceroy of Peru, the marquis of Mancera, instructed silversmiths in Lima to construct what became called the *mancerina*, a small plate with a collar-like ring in the center that could safely hold a drinking vessel for chocolate without spillage.

This practical idea was echoed in France in the late seventeenth century with the creation of the *tasse trembleuse*, a deeply curved saucer with a lip to hold its matching cup securely, decorated in patterns inspired by fashionable fabrics. Renowned porcelain manufacturers Sèvres and Meissen produced fine examples of *tasse trembleuses*, which are nowadays collectors' items found in museums and galleries.

In 1828 in Holland, the scientist Coenraad Johannes Van Houten invented a hydraulic press that removed the cocoa butter from roasted cacao, leaving "cocoa," which could then be ground into a powder. It was soon realized that ground cocoa powder could quickly and easily be made into a delicious warming drink by adding either water or milk. Soon sweetened cocoa powder was being produced on an industrial scale, allowing hot chocolate, for so many centuries an expensive luxury, to become an affordable everyday drink.

THE CHOCOLATIER

"Chocolatier" is the term describing a person who makes confections such as truffles from chocolate. It is a French word, which reflects the historic importance of chocolate in French society. There is a long tradition of working with cacao and chocolate in France. Often cited as the oldest chocolate shop in Paris, À la Mère de Famille on rue du Faubourg, Montmartre (established in 1761), still sells chocolates in addition to other confectionary.

During the eighteenth century, the city of Bayonne in southwest France became a center of chocolate knowledge, with a guild of chocolate makers founded there. The knowledge of how to transform cacao beans into hot chocolate was introduced to Bayonne by Iberian Jews fleeing persecution in Spain and Portugal. Chocolate workshops were set up in the city, and by 1875 it was home to more than thirty chocolatiers.

The skills needed to work with chocolate are nowadays passed on to students at institutions, notably the École du Grand Chocolat Valrhona in Tain-l'Hermitage in southeastern France. An appreciative market for good chocolate means that one finds artisan chocolatiers selling their handmade creations in elegant shops throughout France. Successful companies such as the internationally known La Maison du Chocolat, founded by Robert Linxe in 1977, ensure that the craft of working with chocolate continues to survive and thrive in France to this day.

Chocolatiers work with what is known as couverture chocolate. This is good-quality chocolate with a high cocoa butter content, designed to be used professionally by patissiers and chocolatiers to produce chocolate creations. The skill required to transform couverture chocolate into the array

HOT CHOCOLATE SAUCE

Serves 6
Preparation 5 minutes
Cooking 5 minutes

This hot chocolate sauce is a useful one to have in your repertoire, as it can be made very quickly and easily. Serve it with vanilla ice cream for a simple but delicious dessert, or use it to top a homemade banana split.

¼ cup salted butter

¼ cup cocoa powder

⅓ cup semisweet
   chocolate chips

½ cup sugar

½ cup heavy cream

½ tsp vanilla extract

1   Gently melt the butter in a heavy saucepan. Whisk in the cocoa powder thoroughly.

2   Add the chocolate chips, sugar, and cream and cook, stirring over low heat, until the mixture thickens and comes to a boil.

3   Remove from the heat and stir in the vanilla extract. Serve at once.

of chocolates that one finds in a good chocolate boutique is considerable. Among the techniques used by professionals is one called tempering. This process is key to the production of small chocolates, molded chocolate, decorations, and bars. Tempering involves putting chocolate through a series of temperature shifts from heating to cooling to heating, and follows what is called a "tempering curve"; the range of temperatures followed varies according to the type of chocolate—that is, dark, milk, or white—being tempered. This intricate process, far more complex than simply melting chocolate, realigns the crystal structure within the chocolate and allows it to be worked properly. Tempered chocolate has a good snap when broken, can be turned out from molds successfully, and retains an appealing glossiness.

Traditionally, tempering was done by heating chocolate in a bain-marie or water bath until it reached a particular temperature, transferring most of it to a marble slab and working it rapidly with a palette knife until its temperature had cooled to a precise point, then mixing the cooled chocolate with the remaining warm chocolate in order to achieve the final desired temperature point. Some chocolate makers still temper this way, maintaining this artisan tradition and testing that the chocolate has reached the desired temperatures by touching it to their upper lip. Another tempering method is known as the seeding method, a process that involves adding ratios of finely chopped and warm melted chocolate to each other in order to create the required tempering curve. Nowadays, many artisan producers use a tempering machine, which takes the chocolate through the necessary cycle of temperatures.

While traditional ganaches were often flavored with alcohol, such as brandy or champagne, today's chocolatiers play with imaginative flavors, often using savory ingredients such as salt or miso.

The tempered chocolate is used by chocolatiers for varying procedures, such as coating a filling—ganache, caramel, *pâte de fruit*, nuts, praline, or crystallized fruit peel. A fine chocolate coating offers a contrasting texture and flavor to its filling. While traditional ganaches were often flavored with alcohol, such as brandy or champagne, today's chocolatiers play with imaginative flavors, often using savory ingredients such as salt or miso. Tempered chocolate is also used for molding shapes, classically Easter eggs, Christmas-themed shapes such as Santa Claus, and hearts for Valentine's Day. Much to the delight of chocolate lovers, chocolate in the hands of a good chocolatier continues to offer myriad creative possibilities.

CELEBRATORY CHOCOLATE

The rise of eating chocolate, as opposed to drinking chocolate, also saw it being used to create seasonal novelties. Chocolate's remarkable plasticity, which means it can be molded and shaped into myriad forms, lent itself naturally to this use.

The Easter egg, a symbol of fertility, has long been eaten in celebration of this springtime festival. Historically, real eggs were used to mark Easter, from Greece's *kokkina avga* (hard-boiled eggs dyed red to symbolize Christ's blood) to Poland's beautifully decorated eggs. During the nineteenth century, however, Easter eggs started being made from chocolate in Europe. In Britain, the first commercially produced chocolate Easter eggs were made by chocolate manufacturers J. S. Fry & Sons, with their rivals Cadbury's following suit two years later. Initially, Easter eggs were an expensive luxury aimed at the adult market, but from the 1950s onward, chocolate Easter eggs were produced for children. Today, chocolate eggs, rather than real eggs, are regarded as an essential part of Easter. Christmas, the other major Christian festival, has also seen the rise of festive chocolate offerings such as Santa Claus figures, foil-wrapped coins, and chocolate Advent calendars.

In the chocolate calendar, Valentine's Day is another major celebration. Chocolate's long-time sensuous association as an ingredient with aphrodisiac properties means that it is an appropriate gift for a loved one on this romantic day. For this festival, it is the heart shape that dominates, whether in the form of solid or hollow chocolate hearts or in heart-shaped boxes, nowadays usually red, that can be filled with a selection of chocolate truffles. The historic credit for producing the first heart-shaped chocolate box is given to Richard Cadbury of Cadbury's, who produced a decorative "fancy box" in the shape of a heart in 1868. Nowadays, both large chocolate manufacturers and artisan chocolatiers produce a range of imaginative chocolate creations for Valentine's Day, Easter, and Christmas, with the sales during these ancient festivals forming an important part of their annual business model.

CULINARY CHOCOLATE

Chocolate is widely used in both the professional and the domestic kitchen. One of the reasons for chocolate's popularity as an ingredient is its versatility. While possessing a distinctive, recognizable, much-loved flavor, it also pairs well with numerous other flavors, from powerful ones such as

ROCKY ROAD

Makes 12 portions

Preparation 10 minutes, plus cooling and chilling

Cooking 5 minutes

Quick and easy to make, rocky road is always popular with family and friends. The mini-marshmallows and crunchy nuts not only add texture and flavor, but also give the confection its lumpy appearance, which is reflected in its humorous, distinctive name.

⅔ cup semisweet
   chocolate chips

1 cup milk chocolate chips

¼ cup salted butter

2 cups mini-marshmallows

⅓ cup chopped, roasted
   almonds

1 Line the base of an 8-inch-square baking pan with baking paper.
2 Place the semisweet and milk chocolate chips and the butter in a heatproof bowl suspended over a pan of simmering water (making sure that the water does not touch the bowl). Heat gently, stirring now and then, until the chocolate has melted.
3 Let cool slightly, then stir in the mini-marshmallows and almonds, mixing well. Spread the mixture in a layer in the prepared pan.
4 Cover and chill. Slice into 12 even-sized portions when ready to serve.

coffee, mint, or chile to subtle ones such as citrus, vanilla, or raspberry. It is a foodstuff that can be used in a variety of ways, capable of taking center stage as well as being a bit player.

There are, however, only a few classic savory recipes that feature chocolate as an ingredient. One of the best known of these comes appropriately (given chocolate's Aztec ancestry) from Mexico and is called *mole poblano*—a richly spiced sauce, flavored with a small quantity of high-cocoa-content chocolate. In Italy, one finds *agrodolce* (sour-sweet) sauce, often served with venison, which can also contain dark chocolate. On the whole, however, chocolate is used in recipes that are sweet.

Nowadays, of course, chocolate is used to produce a wide range of confectionary, ranging from everyday items sold in supermarkets to exquisite, handcrafted creations sold in exclusive chocolate boutiques. The sheer range available is a tribute to human ingenuity and to our fondness for chocolate. The fact that solid chocolate can be successfully melted into a liquid form, allowed to set and become solid once more, is key to this usage. Chocolate can be molded to form chocolate bars, made simply from chocolate or with additions—such as nuts, raisins, or candied peel—or flavored with essential oils to make chocolate that tastes, for example, of mint, orange, or, a recent addition to the canon, chile. Chocolate bonbons can be made by using melted chocolate to enrobe a variety of ingredients: nuts, wafers, caramels, fondant fillings, raisins, candied fruit, praline, or sugar shells filled with liqueur. A luxurious example of chocolate confectionary is chocolate truffles—rich concoctions traditionally made from a ganache filling (a combination of chocolate and a liquid, usually cream), often flavored with alcohol, such as brandy or champagne, and coated in a layer of chocolate, cocoa powder, or finely chopped nuts (see p. 192).

Chocolate can be molded to form chocolate bars, made simply from chocolate or with additions— such as nuts, raisins, or candied peel—or flavored with essential oils to make chocolate that tastes, for example, of mint, orange, or chile.

In the world of the pastry chef, learning to work with chocolate, using techniques such as tempering (see p. 197) and molding, is one of the skills that must be acquired. Many artisan chocolatiers begin life as pastry chefs, who then become fascinated by the potential offered by working with chocolate.

When it comes to melting chocolate, whether in a professional or domestic kitchen, it is important to know that chocolate is very sensitive to heat. Chocolate requires slow, gentle melting, as otherwise, if it overheats, it becomes thick and lumpy. The safest way to melt chocolate, therefore, is in a bain-marie, suspended over simmering water. Another useful thing to remember is that if melted chocolate comes into contact with water, it will "seize," becoming granular. Dark chocolate with a high cacao content, rather than milk chocolate, is usually used in baking, as it delivers a more powerful chocolate flavor. Despite the technical challenges that chocolate presents, patissiers enjoy the creative options that come with using it.

Dark chocolate with a high cacao content, rather than milk chocolate, is usually used in baking, as it delivers a more powerful chocolate flavor.

French cuisine, with its long and splendid patisserie tradition, offers many amazing chocolate creations. A good French *boulangerie* (bakery) would be expected to offer *pains au chocolat*, made from croissant dough filled with pieces of dark chocolate, an excellent accompaniment to a *café au lait*. The chocolate éclair, made from a tube-shaped choux pastry bun filled with whipped cream and topped with chocolate fondant icing, is another French classic. A Christmas treat is the *bûche de Noël* (Christmas Yule log), a striking log-shaped cake, cleverly coated with brown chocolate frosting so that it does, indeed, resemble a wooden log and decorated with almond-paste holly leaves and meringue mushrooms.

The international world of baking widely employs both chocolate and cocoa powder. Among their popular uses is to make chocolate cakes, with homemade chocolate cakes (see p. 191) a childhood treat in many homes. One particularly elegant take on a chocolate cake is Austria's famous *Sachertorte*—a gateau filled or covered with apricot jam and coated with a glossy chocolate frosting. This was created in 1832 by a pastry chef called Franz Sacher for a dinner held by the German Austrian diplomat Prince Wenzel von Metternich. Sacher's son Eduard introduced the cake to a larger audience through selling it at his establishment, the Hotel Sacher. The cake has become emblematic of Austrian cuisine and, to this day, slices of *Sachertorte* with whipped cream are served in Vienna's historic cafés.

In neighboring Germany, one finds Black Forest gateau, named for the sour cherry liqueur (*Schwarzwälder Kirsch*) of the Black Forest region used in it. This is an eye-catching creation—consisting of layers of chocolate sponge, cherries soaked in kirsch, and whipped cream, decorated with cherries and chocolate shavings—and is as indulgent as it looks.

In the United States, the wonderfully named devil's food cake is another striking chocolate cake, made from three chocolate sponge cakes layered one atop another, filled and generously topped with chocolate frosting. The brownie, described variously as a bar cookie or dessert, is another iconic U.S. baked chocolate creation. The first brownie recipe to be published was Fannie Farmer's, in her influential 1896 *Boston Cooking-School Cook Book*, and it contained molasses. She subsequently published a revised version in 1905, which contained considerably less flour. The ideal texture of a brownie is a source of much discussion, ranging from soft and squidgy in the middle to drier and more cakelike. Brownies continue to be made widely today both in domestic kitchens (see p. 181) and professional ones. Chocolate is also used in cookie recipes in a variety of ways. Chocolate chip cookies (see p. 171) are now popular in many countries outside the United States, while in Britain the chocolate-coated digestive biscuit (made from oats) is much loved.

Chocolate is also widely used in the world of desserts, with the chocolate soufflé being a French classic. Combining a rich chocolate flavor with an ethereal lightness from the addition of whisked egg whites, this is served straight from the oven. Another French dessert made from chocolate and eggs is the chocolate mousse, which, when made well, is at once light in texture yet distinctly luxurious. In classic French style, a *tarte au chocolat* (chocolate tart) combines a velvety chocolate ganache filling with a crisp pastry case. In the world of fine dining, one finds the molten chocolate cake, popularized by the famous French chef Jean-Georges

Chocolate, of course, is a hugely popular ice-cream flavor, found in numerous versions ranging from sophisticated dark chocolate sorbets to dairy-based chocolate ice creams further enriched with chocolate chunks, nuts, or cookie dough.

Vongerichten. This memorable creation requires precise timing in order to ensure that the outside is cooked and set while the filling remains liquid.

Chocolate, of course, is a hugely popular ice-cream flavor, found in numerous versions ranging from sophisticated dark chocolate sorbets to dairy-based chocolate ice creams further enriched with chocolate chunks, nuts, or cookie dough. A simple but effective way of adding a chocolate dimension to vanilla ice cream is to serve it with a chocolate sauce (see p. 196), with the contrast between the two flavors and textures forming part of the appeal.

Although chocolate is today both widely available and much more affordable than it used to be, it continues to retain its status as a treat. It is this "specialness" that sees dinner parties rounded off at the end of the meal with the serving of chocolate truffles, pleasures to be enjoyed and savored with friends.

TOMATO

Nowadays regarded as an everyday ingredient, the tomato started life as a wild plant in South America. The cultivated tomato was introduced across the continents, but acceptance was gradual. This novel plant, with its strikingly colorful fruit, was regarded with suspicion and initially often grown as an exotic ornament rather than as a useful food crop.

The ancestor of the domestic tomato is a wild plant, bearing tiny, red, pea-sized fruit, known as *Solanum pimpinellifolium*, a member of the *Solanaceae* family and related to potatoes, capsicums, and eggplants. It is a vigorous, hardy plant, capable of thriving in a range of climates and weather conditions, that is today still found growing wild in Peru. It is from this plant that the domestic tomato (*Lycopersicon lycopersicum*) is descended. The wild tomato plant was taken north to Mexico, and its first known cultivation was by the Aztecs.

The word "tomato" is a linguistic legacy of the role the Aztecs played in its history. In Nahuatl (the language spoken by the Aztecs), the word *xitomatl* means simply "plump fruit." It was the Spanish, with their conquest of the Aztec Empire in the sixteenth century, who took *xitomatl* as the name for this novel red fruit, deriving the word "tomate" from it. In his monumental work *The General History of the Things of New Spain* (1569), the Spanish priest Bernardino di Sahagún, who traveled to New Spain (as the Spanish called Mexico) in 1529, wrote an eyewitness account of a great market in Tenochtitlán. In it he describes a colorful fruit in assorted shades of yellow and red, a description that is thought to refer to either tomatoes or tomatillos. While it is not known exactly how the tomato traveled from Mexico to Europe, it is assumed that the Spanish introduced the plant to their native continent. The earliest known written European reference to the tomato is by the Italian doctor and botanist Pietro Andrea Mattioli in his *Commentarii* of 1554. He wrote of the recent arrival in Italy of a new plant he called *mala aurea* (Latin for "golden apple"), a name that translates into *pomi d'oro* in Italian. Classifying the plant as a member of the mandrake family, Mattioli described how its fruit was flattened at one end, like an apple, and changed color from green to golden as it ripened. This description is taken to suggest that these early varieties were yellow-fruiting, though in later years Mattioli also mentioned a red variety.

The early history of the tomato in Europe has much folklore and superstition attached to it. The name "golden apple" in herbals links the tomato to the ancient Greek myth of the golden apples found in the Garden of the Hesperides. As with many exotic new ingredients, mysterious powers were attributed to it, including aphrodisiac ones, perhaps through that early association with the mandrake (a plant whose root was thought to be magical and an aphrodisiac). An illustrated herbal (dating from between 1550 and 1560) includes a picture of a tomato plant bearing the caption *Poma Amoris*, meaning "love apple," and this term was used in England for centuries, while the French called the tomato *pomme d'amour* (apple of love).

There was also a distinctly dark side to how the tomato was initially viewed; it was long regarded with great suspicion in many of the countries where it was introduced. As part of the botanical family *Solanaceae*, it resembled deadly nightshade, a member of the same family, and for centuries various parts of the tomato plant—the fruit and its strong-smelling leaves and stalk—were considered to be poisonous. Its botanical name *Lycopersicon* translates as "wolf peach" and is suggestive of its folkloric associations with werewolves. In Europe, it was often cultivated as an ornamental plant, enjoyed for its striking appearance and colorful fruit rather than for its culinary appeal. Even when the fruit was considered edible, there was often a noticeable lack of enthusiasm. The Italian naturalist Costanzo Felici, writing of the tomato in the late 1560s, observed, "To my taste better to look at than to eat." In his influential *English Herball* of 1597, the herbalist John Gerard wrote: "In Spaine and those hot Regions they use to eat the Apples prepared and boiled with pepper, salt, and oile: but they yield very little nourishment to the bodie, and the same naught and corrupt [*sic*]." Slowly, however, the wariness about the tomato plant began to ebb, and during the eighteenth and nineteenth centuries it became more widely grown and eaten in European countries. In French culinary lore, it was the people of Marseille who, when visiting Paris in 1790 for the Fête de la Fédération (a holiday held to celebrate the French Revolution of 1789), urged Parisian market growers to cultivate tomatoes, a plant that was grown and appreciated in the south of France.

GAZPACHO

Serves 6

**Preparation 10 minutes,
plus at least 3–4 hours
chilling time**

1¾ lb ripe tomatoes

1 garlic clove, peeled and
chopped

1 shallot, peeled and chopped

1 red bell pepper, chopped

½ cucumber, chopped

4 tbsp olive oil

2 tbsp red wine vinegar

Salt and sugar, to taste

⅔ cup cold water, to taste

TO GARNISH

¼ cucumber, finely diced

½ green bell pepper, finely
diced

Handful of croutons

This classic Spanish recipe uses raw tomatoes
to create a refreshing chilled soup—perfect food
for a hot summer's day. Use the ripest, tastiest
tomatoes that you can find.

1 Scald the tomatoes by placing them in a heatproof
   bowl, pouring over boiling water, and setting aside for
   a minute. Drain them and peel off their loosened skins.

2 Place the skinned tomatoes, garlic, shallot, red bell
   pepper, and cucumber in a food processor and pulse
   blend until finely chopped, making sure to retain some
   texture. Add the olive oil and vinegar, season with salt
   and sugar, and blend again briefly. Add a little cold water
   to achieve the desired texture if needed. Cover and chill
   for 3–4 hours (ideally overnight) before serving.

3 Serve chilled, freshly garnished with cucumber, green
   bell pepper, and croutons.

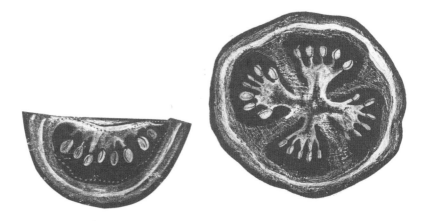

TOMATO

Despite the reservations with which it was often initially greeted, the tomato plant spread around the globe. It was not only to Europe that the Spanish introduced the tomato. It was through their colonies in Florida, New Mexico, Texas, and California that the tomato was initially brought into North America. The first printed reference to the tomato in North America was in the herbalist William Salmon's work *Botanologia* (1710). By the middle of the eighteenth century, tomatoes were being cultivated in the Carolinas, with documentary evidence suggesting that they were grown as an edible crop, not simply as an ornamental plant.

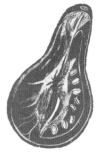

One of the early champions of the tomato in the United States was the forward-thinking Thomas Jefferson, who cultivated tomatoes in his Monticello vegetable gardens between 1809 and 1820. In popular tomato folklore, President Jefferson is credited with eating the first tomato in Lynchburg, Virginia—consuming the exotic novelty in public to demonstrate that it was not poisonous. There is a similar apocryphal story about Robert Gibbon Johnson, a prominent judge in Salem. The tale is that, having planted and grown tomatoes in his garden, Johnson ate a tomato before an audience on his courthouse steps in 1820 to show that it was safe to eat. The survival of these stories, whether true or not, suggests the suspicion with which tomatoes were at first regarded.

By the mid-nineteenth century, the tomato had become a more familiar foodstuff in North America, with recipes for ways in which to cook it—in soups, cooked with chicken, pickled, or baked—appearing in cookbooks of the period.

The development of tomato canning in the United States during the 1840s helped popularize tomatoes, with the industry growing enormously following the end of the Civil War. By the mid-nineteenth century, the tomato had become a more familiar foodstuff in North America, with recipes for ways in which to cook it—in soups, cooked with chicken, pickled, or baked—appearing in cookbooks of the period. Today, of course, the tomato, in the form of tomato ketchup, is taken for granted as part of life.

It was through their colonies that the Spanish and their neighbors the Portuguese also spread tomatoes around the globe. The Spanish introduced the tomato to the Caribbean and to the Philippines, where tomatoes are used in classic Filipino dishes such as fish *tinola* and pork *sinigang*. The Portuguese are credited with bringing the tomato to India, too, through their colonization of Goa. The rise of trade routes between Europe and other countries in the world also contributed to the spread of the tomato around the globe.

The versatility of the tomato in both the domestic and the professional kitchen—aided by the fact that it can be successfully and usefully preserved in so many ways—has made the tomato a global success story. Nowadays, it is widely and successfully cultivated in a huge number of countries, regarded as an everyday ingredient rather than the curious novelty that it once was.

FRUIT OR VEGETABLE?

Any exploration of the tomato and its history will come across the question of whether the tomato is a fruit or a vegetable. Botanically speaking, the tomato is a berry or fruit, as it fulfills the criteria that define a fruit as being a seed-bearing structure, formed from an angiosperm's (flowering plant's) ovary. Writing in 1597, when the tomato was still a novel plant in Europe, the herbalist John Gerard wrote of the "fruit" of the tomato plant; and, as noted earlier, "love apple" was an early name for the tomato in Europe.

The issue of whether the tomato is a fruit or a vegetable took on a legal significance in the United States in the nineteenth century. John Nix was a New York City–based importer of fresh produce, whose wholesale

company was a major player in the fresh produce market. In 1886, Nix began importing tomatoes into New York from the West Indies. The Tariff Act of 1883 imposed a duty of 10 percent on imported vegetables (though not on imported fruit), and Nix was taxed on his tomatoes. Nix protested that the tax was unfair, saying tomatoes were a fruit, not a vegetable. In 1887, Nix filed a suit against Edward L. Hedden, the collector of the port of New York, for reimbursement of the tariff duties. The *Nix v. Hedden* case made its way through the legal system to the Supreme Court. In 1893, Justice Horace Gray delivered his Supreme Court ruling on the case in the following terms:

> *Botanically speaking, tomatoes are the fruit of a vine, just as are cucumbers, squashes, beans, and peas. But in the common language of the people, whether sellers or consumers of provisions, all these are vegetables, which are grown in kitchen gardens, and which, whether eaten cooked or raw, are, like potatoes, carrots, parsnips, turnips, beets, cauliflower, cabbage, celery, and lettuce, usually served at dinner in, with, or after the soup, fish, or meats which constitute the principal part of the repast, and not, like fruits generally, as dessert.*

Nix had lost his case, and the tomato is legally considered to be a vegetable.

TOMATO VARIETIES

Over the centuries, humans have bred tomatoes, encouraging commercially useful traits such as heavy yields, hardiness, and an ability to resist disease, as well as sensory aspects such as sweetness, good color, and flavor. Today, there are thousands of different tomato varieties, with this impressive range adding to its culinary flexibility. When it comes to size, for example, cooks are spoiled for choice. Small, sweet cherry tomatoes are excellent for snacking on, adding to salads, or used, halved or sliced, to garnish canapés. Regular-sized tomatoes or plum tomatoes are great for cooking, classically for use in a tomato sauce or soup. Large tomatoes, such as beefsteak tomatoes, lend themselves to being stuffed and cooked. Furthermore, tomatoes come in an array of colors. One can find pale yellow, bright yellow, pink, green, and purplish "black" tomatoes in addition to the familiar red tomato.

Horticulturally, tomatoes are categorized into determinate and indeterminate and hybrid and heirloom. Determinate (also called bush) tomatoes grow to a set, short height and cease flowering once their fruit sets on the top bud. All their tomatoes will ripen over a brief period, usually one

SUGO AL POMODORO

Serves 4–6
Preparation 5–8 minutes
Cooking 10–15 minutes

Made using canned tomatoes, this simple, easy pasta sauce is a useful standby for a quick family meal on a busy working day. Serve it with spaghetti and grated Parmesan cheese.

1 tbsp olive oil

1 onion, peeled and finely
 chopped

1 fresh or dried bay leaf or
 2–3 sprigs of basil

1 garlic clove, peeled and
 chopped

4 cups canned chopped
 tomatoes

Salt and freshly ground
 black pepper

1   Heat the olive oil in a skillet. Add in the onion and bay leaf, if using. Fry gently, stirring often, for 2–3 minutes, until softened. Add in the garlic and fry briefly, stirring, until fragrant.

2   Add the chopped tomatoes and fresh basil, if using. Bring to a boil, reduce the heat, and cook for about 5–10 minutes, stirring often, until just slightly reduced. Season with salt and pepper. Discard the bay leaf, if used.

3   For a smooth-textured sauce, blend using a stick blender or in a jug blender.

to two weeks, after which the plant will decline and no longer produce any tomatoes. In contrast, indeterminate (also called vine or cordon) tomatoes grow their flowers along their length and continue blooming, setting new fruit and ripening them until their activity is curtailed by frost or pruning.

Hybrid tomatoes (also known as F1 hybrid tomatoes) are cultivars created by cross-pollinating the seeds of two pure lines. These are valued by growers for the consistency and quality of their crop. On the other hand, F1 hybrid tomato seeds tend to be more expensive, and any seeds saved from F1 hybrid plants will not grow true to type—in fact, they may not even germinate, which makes them a riskier plant to grow.

HEIRLOOM TOMATOES

"Heirloom tomatoes" (as well as "heritage tomatoes") is a term applied to traditional, open-pollinated tomato cultivars. The term "open-pollinated" means that seeds from these plants breed true, so that if one saves seeds from an heirloom tomato and sows them, the plants that grow from those seeds will bear tomatoes that are true to type. Saving seed and planting from it was the historic way in which farmers and gardeners grew crops from year to year.

The terms "heirloom" or "heritage" are taken to mean an old or historic variety that has been grown over generations, but, in fact, there is no legal meaning attached to these descriptors. Instead, there is much debate as to how many years a tomato cultivar should have been grown before it can be called an heirloom.

One reason for the interest in heirloom tomatoes among growers and consumers is a simple but fundamental one—they are perceived as tasting better than contemporary hybrid ones. These old varieties were valued by growers for their flavor and color; hence their seed was saved and passed down over the generations to keep the strain going.

One reason for the interest in heirloom tomatoes among growers and consumers is a simple but fundamental one—they are perceived as tasting better than contemporary hybrid ones.

In contrast, F1 hybrids are seen as having been developed by agribusiness to enhance commercial traits such as heavy cropping or the ability to travel well, with the actual flavor of the resulting tomatoes not a priority. Influential chefs such as Alice Waters of Chez Panisse, a pioneer of farm-to-table restaurant cuisine, have helped create an interest in heirloom tomatoes through their inclusion in recipes. There is now a perceived culinary cachet to using heirloom tomatoes in the kitchen, and consumers can buy them in farmers' markets and upmarket food shops.

A profound desire to preserve biodiversity also underlies the heirloom vegetable movement. There is an awareness that becoming overly dependent on a single variety of a food can lead to disaster should disease strike that variety, as happened for example, in the Irish Potato Famine in the 1840s, which led to the death or emigration of around 1.5 million people. Furthermore, there is also a desire to conserve the rich diversity of an agricultural inheritance.

In 1975, a young couple in Missouri, Diane and Kent Whealy, founded Seed Savers Exchange, a nonprofit organization that preserves heirloom varieties through regeneration, distribution, and seed exchange. The starting point was a desire to save the plants Diane's grandparents had cultivated from seed that they grew and saved. When her grandfather died, Diane realized that this seed heritage would be lost unless she acted to save it and share it. The first two plants in Seed Savers Exchange were a German pink tomato and a purple morning glory, brought to the United States by Diane's great-grandparents when they immigrated to Iowa from Bavaria in the 1870s and given to her as a wedding present by her grandfather shortly before he passed away. Diane wanted to save not only the seeds but the stories that went with them—which in turn represented a connection to the past and a sense of place carried down by gardeners and farmers.

Today, Seed Savers Exchange is based on 890 acres at Heritage Farm in Winneshiek County, Iowa. The organization has around 13,000 members and conserves over 20,000 different varieties of heirloom and open-pollinated plants. It is the largest nongovernmental seedbank in the United States. Among the numerous heirloom tomato varieties that Seed Savers Exchange maintains are tomatoes such as the Brandywine, which traces its origins to 1889 in Ohio and is named after Brandywine Creek in Chester County. It produces large, deep-red tomatoes, each weighing between 8 to 12 ounces and noted for their flavor.

Today, with interest in heirloom tomatoes high among growers, restaurateurs, retailers, and consumers, many seed companies offer heirloom tomato seeds, with their catalogs filled with evocative names such as African Queen and Dixie Golden Giant. Such is the affection in which tomatoes are held that a number of tomato festivals, celebrating heirloom varieties, are held in the United States each year.

HEIRLOOM TOMATO SALAD

Serves 4
Preparation 5 minutes

This simple but attractive salad is a pleasure for both the eye and the palate. For the best results, choose good-quality, ripe heirloom tomatoes, ideally in a range of colors and shapes.

8–10 assorted heirloom
  tomatoes, ideally at room
  temperature
3 tbsp olive oil
1 tbsp sherry or white wine
  vinegar
Pinch of sugar
Salt and freshly ground
  black pepper
Handful of basil leaves or
  1 tbsp finely chopped chives
  or parsley

1 Slice the tomatoes into fine slices and arrange in a serving dish.
2 Make a dressing by mixing together the olive oil, vinegar, and sugar. Season well with salt and pepper.
3 Pour the dressing over the tomatoes, tossing together lightly. Scatter with the basil leaves or chives or parsley, and serve at once.

CULTIVATING TOMATOES

The scale on which the tomato is grown is noteworthy, with tomatoes coming in high on the list of most produced vegetables in the world. Recent estimates put global tomato production at around 130 million tons, of which 88 million are destined for the fresh market and the remaining 42 million to be processed. Five countries or regions alone account for 70 percent of the world's entire tomato production: China, the European Union, India, the United States, and Turkey. Within the European Union, the tomato is the largest fresh vegetable crop being grown. In the United States, it is California that is the major supplier of tomatoes, growing 90 percent of the nation's processed tomatoes.

The development of modern industrial agricultural techniques has allowed tomatoes to be grown on this large scale. As a subtropical plant, the tomato requires full sunlight; hence its cultivation in places that possess warm, dry, sunny climates such as Spain, Italy, and California. Growers in temperate climates can successfully raise tomatoes by using greenhouses or (a more recent development) polytunnels, which protect them from the elements and give the plants the warmth they require. Whatever their location, commercial growers cultivate tomatoes speedily, either growing them outdoors or under glass or plastic, with the latter enabling the growers to control the environment in which they are grown. They are often grown hydroponically—that is, without soil, in sand, gravel, or liquid with added nutrients. Often the tomatoes are harvested while firm and unripe, placed in cold storage, and then ripened through the use of ethylene gas. Like all farmers, tomato growers face challenges from pests and diseases such as blossom end rot, tomato blight, and pythium root rot. Crop monitoring, chemical and biological controls, efficient sanitation, good ventilation for indoor-grown plants, and the use of resistant cultivars are all methods used within tomato agriculture to minimize these threats.

Growers in temperate climates can successfully raise tomatoes by using greenhouses or (a more recent development) polytunnels, which protect them from the elements and give the plants the warmth they require.

At the more specialist end of the supply chain, there are growers working to produce high-end tomatoes—with the emphasis on achieving excellent levels of taste and texture—that are sold to restaurants and upmarket food shops. An interesting development among Sardinian growers has been the rise of what are called winter tomatoes, created by growing Camone (a variety developed by a Swiss agribusiness) during the mild winter,

rather than in the heat of the summer. This long, slow growing in cool temperatures with minimal watering—and the stress the plants are placed under—results in distinctive eating tomatoes characterized by crisp flesh and a rich complexity of flavor.

For the home gardener with a fondness for tomatoes, growing your own is an appealing and accessible option. To begin with, especially if you are growing from seed, you can choose an interesting variety, such as an heirloom tomato that would not be readily found in the supermarket. Furthermore, ample space is not required for tomato growing; they can be grown successfully in a large pot or grow-bag.

One of the first decisions to make as a grower is whether to opt for indeterminate tomatoes or determinate ones (see p. 210). If you are growing from seed, the seedlings need to be pricked out into small pots. If you do not have space to grow tomatoes from seed, then young tomato plants can be bought from garden centers. In late spring, after the last frost, young tomato plants should be planted in the ground, in a sunny, sheltered spot. If you are growing tomatoes in a container, place it in a sheltered spot. Tomatoes are hungry plants, requiring regular feeding, especially when grown in a container. Regular watering, too, is important, as irregular water can cause the tomatoes to split and also lead to blossom end rot, caused by a lack of calcium. The care required is rewarded when you're able to pick and eat a truly fresh tomato—one of life's simple but most satisfying pleasures.

PRESERVING TOMATOES

When tomato plants bear fruit, they do so prolifically, offering their growers a glorious abundance of ripe, fresh tomatoes that require harvesting. The question then arises of how best to deal with this highly perishable glut. Across the centuries, humans have responded to this question with a range of solutions, preserving tomatoes in a variety of ways.

Italian cuisine is particularly rich in methods of preserving tomatoes. This reflects not just the affection with which *pomodori* (tomatoes) are held in Italy, but also the profound Italian respect for ingredients and deep-rooted dislike of any waste of food. During the summer months in Italy, as the tomatoes grown in people's gardens and smallholdings ripen in the sunshine, one common household activity is the making of tomato *passata*. This involves large quantities of fresh tomatoes being passed through a food mill and transformed into thick, smooth tomato sauce. Each family will have its own *passata* recipe, with variations regarding

TOMATO SALSA

Serves 4
Preparation 12 minutes

10½ oz ripe tomatoes
1 fresh jalapeño chile
½ onion, peeled and diced
1 garlic clove, peeled
  and chopped
4 tbsp chopped cilantro
Juice of 1 lime
½ tsp cumin powder
Salt and freshly ground
  black pepper

This piquant tomato and chile relish is a great way to add a lift to recipes such as grilled meats, enchiladas, and egg dishes. Alternately, serve it as a dip with tortilla chips.

1   Halve the tomatoes. Deseed them by using a small, sharp knife to cut out and discard the seedy pulp. Finely dice the remaining firm-flesh tomato "shells."

2   Cut the jalapeño in half lengthwise. Using a small, sharp knife, cut out and discard the white pith, seeds, and core inside the chile and trim off its stem. Finely chop the deseeded chile.

3   Mix together the chopped tomato, jalapeño, onion, garlic, cilantro, lime juice, and cumin in a bowl. Season with salt and freshly ground pepper. Serve at once or, ideally, cover and set aside at room temperature for an hour before serving.

flavorings and procedure. In some versions, a fresh tomato purée is strained, bottled, and then simmered in hot water to sterilize it, while other recipes require the tomatoes to be cooked and passed through a mill (or passed and cooked), then stored while still hot in sterilized jars, with the tomato's natural acidity levels an important factor in the success of this preserving process. Whatever the means, the idea is always to preserve the summer's tomato harvest, allowing it to be consumed—in the form of pasta sauces, soups, stews, and bean dishes—during the cold, dark winter months.

In countries with a warm climate, one simple, effective way of preserving tomatoes is to dry them in the sunshine. The hot southern regions of Italy, notably Puglia and Sicily, are known for their sun-dried tomatoes, a traditional delicacy. The tomatoes are halved, then sprinkled with salt to draw out their excess moisture and keep away bacteria, and finally dried for a number of days in the hot open air. This desiccating process not only changes the texture of the tomatoes from soft and moist to a tough, chewy leatheriness, but also intensifies their flavor, transforming them into a food that can be safely stored for months. Before cooking with sun-dried tomatoes, they should be rehydrated in warm water to soften them. One popular Italian way of storing sun-dried tomatoes is to cover them with oil and flavorings such as garlic and herbs; these *sott'olio* ("under oil") sun-dried tomatoes can then be served as an antipasto. For those who do not live in hot, sunny countries, it's possible to achieve an effect similar to sun-dried tomatoes by slowly drying out salted tomato halves in a cool oven for a number of hours. Sun-blush tomatoes—a popular delicatessen item— are created by partly drying out tomatoes, giving them a juicier texture than the traditional sun-dried ones. Another classic Italian way of preserving tomatoes by removing their moisture is by drying tomato sauce, historically by leaving it out in the sun, or nowadays by cooking down sieved tomatoes for hours until the mixture forms a thick, dry-ish, dark-red mass—namely, tomato paste—that keeps well. This long, slow reduction also concentrates and intensifies the flavor, so only a small amount of the paste is required in recipes for many dishes such as stews or sauces.

> *In countries with a warm climate, one simple, effective way of preserving tomatoes is to dry them in the sunshine. The hot southern regions of Italy, notably Puglia and Sicily, are known for their sun-dried tomatoes, a traditional delicacy.*

In Britain, making tomato chutney is a traditional way of using up an excess of fresh, ripe tomatoes. The word "chutney" is derived from the Indian word *chatni*, used for a spicy relish; both the word and the dish were

TOMATO SOUP

Serves 4
Preparation 15 minutes
Cooking 32–35 minutes

1 tbsp olive oil

1 tbsp butter

1 onion, peeled and finely
   chopped

1 celery stick, finely chopped

1 carrot, finely chopped

1 sprig of thyme

Splash of dry white wine

1½ lb ripe tomatoes, roughly
   chopped

2½ cups chicken or vegetable
   stock

Salt and freshly ground
   black pepper

Bread and butter or hot
   buttered toast, to serve

TO GARNISH
Heavy cream
Chopped chives

With its bright orange-red color and pleasant
flavor, there is always something appealing about
homemade, warming tomato soup.

1   Heat the olive oil and butter in a large saucepan. Add the
    onion, celery, carrot, and thyme and fry gently, stirring
    often, for 2–3 minutes, until the onion has softened and
    is fragrant. Add the white wine and cook off over a high
    heat for 1–2 minutes.

2   Add the tomatoes, stirring to mix in, and the stock.
    Season with salt and freshly ground pepper.

3   Bring to a boil, cover, reduce the heat, and simmer for
    about 25 minutes.

4   Allow the mixture to cool slightly, then transfer it to a
    jug blender or a food processor and blend until smooth.
    Strain the soup through a fine strainer and heat through
    gently. Garnish each serving with a swirl of cream and
    a sprinkling of chives. Serve with bread and butter or
    hot buttered toast.

TOMATO

brought back to Britain via its colonial presence in India. British chutneys use sugar, vinegar, and spices to transform perishable produce such as apples, tomatoes, and cucumbers into rich, soft-textured preserves, usually with a mellow flavor, that are eaten as an accompaniment to cold meats, cheese, or pies. In French cuisine, sugar is also used to preserve fresh tomatoes by making tomato jam. Whereas tomato chutneys are flavored with onions and spices, in effect masking the flavor of the tomatoes, the French jam tradition allows the delicate flavor of ripe tomatoes to come through in the final conserve.

Inexpensive, convenient, and easy to use, canned tomatoes have become an everyday cupboard staple in kitchens around the world. The origins of commercial canning can be traced back to the experimental work carried out during the late eighteenth and early nineteenth centuries by the French confectioner Nicolas Appert. In 1810, Appert published his seminal work, *L'Art de Conserver*, a guide to his new method of preserving food, which was soon translated and published in England and the United States. Such was his breakthrough that he was awarded a financial prize by the French government for work in this area, as France was then seeking ways of preserving food in order to feed the French army. Appert's method involved placing food in jars, sealing them well, then heating the jars in water baths. His ground-breaking preserving technique was quickly adopted and played a central part in the rise of commercial bottling and canning during the nineteenth century. Initially, due to the labor and costs involved, it was luxurious foods such as asparagus or oysters that were preserved in this way. As the technique became more widespread and production more affordable, vegetables, including tomatoes, were canned.

In Italy, a young agricultural exporter, Francisco Cirio, developed *appertization* as a way of preserving fruit and vegetables, establishing his first canning factory in Turin in 1835. As the Cirio company grew, it invested in the south of Italy, where the climate and rich soil lend themselves to tomato agriculture, and became known for its tomato canning. Plum tomatoes, with their elongated shape and greater ratio of solid to liquid content, are the favored type for canning. The nineteenth and twentieth centuries saw the rise of tomato canning in southern Italy, providing an important source of work for local communities. The period between 1880 and 1915, after the unification of Italy in 1861, was a time of great hardship in the south of Italy. Driven by harsh economic necessity, millions of Italians, often from poor, rural communities, emigrated. It is estimated that during the early twentieth century around 4 million Italians emigrated to the United States. With them they brought the foods of their homeland, including pasta, olive oil, and canned tomatoes—the latter an affordable, easily transportable, long-lived food that allowed them to recreate dishes, such as pasta with tomato sauce, for which they were nostalgic. The hot, sunny climate with which the south of Italy has been blessed is ideal for growing flavorful tomatoes, and to this day Italian canned tomatoes are a popular export.

With regard to the United States's own canning industry, around the mid-nineteenth century, one Harrison Crosby did much to promote commercially canned tomatoes. A shrewd businessman with an eye for publicity, he sent samples of his novel canned tomatoes to celebrities, including President James K. Polk and Queen Victoria. The American Civil War (1861–65) is credited in playing a part in popularizing canned tomatoes, as during it many soldiers were introduced to canned vegetables for the first time. Tomato canning became big business in the United States; by 1870, tomatoes were one of the three main vegetables to be preserved in this way, together with corn and peas. As canning developed, canned tomatoes became widely available and affordable. The tomato's ability to be successfully preserved in so many useful ways—extending its availability and culinary range—has undoubtedly played a part in its success.

THE SAN MARZANO TOMATO

Among canned Italian tomatoes, one particular variety above all others is especially prized by chefs and discerning cooks alike, namely the San Marzano tomato. This is a distinctive-looking tomato, rich red in color, with a long, narrow shape that tapers to a point. It is a delicate tomato with a thin, easily peelable skin, appreciated for the complexity of its flavor, which contains bittersweet notes; its low acidity; and its firm-textured flesh, which contains only a few seeds. All these elements combine to make it an excellent tomato for canning, as it retains flavor and texture through the process.

The San Marzano tomato traces its origins to the small town of San Marzano sul Sarno in Italy. Historically, it was grown in the rich volcanic soil of Vesuvius. The proximity of this tomato-growing area to Naples, from which pizza originates, is also significant; traditionally, it is these tomatoes that are used to make an authentic Neapolitan pizza margherita.

So important is the San Marzano tomato in Italian culinary heritage that it was granted a Designated Origin of Protection (DOP) in 1996, with its rules enforced by the Consorzio di Tutela del Pomodoro San Marzano

dell'Agro Sarnese-Nocerino (the San Marzano Consortium). These rules stipulate that San Marzano tomatoes must be grown only in specific areas close to Naples and detail how they are grown, when they are picked, how they are harvested (only by hand), and how they are packed. The fertile, mineral-laden soil in which San Marzano DOP tomatoes are grown plays an important part in creating their distinctive flavor. Growing and preparing these tomatoes is a costly business because of the labor involved, with only a few companies maintaining the tradition. So desirable are San Marzano tomatoes that there is a trade in counterfeit ones. Genuine canned San Marzano DOP tomatoes are accordingly labeled "Pomodoro San Marzano dell'Agro Sarnese-Nocerino" and carry the DOP symbol.

THE MEDITERRANEAN TOMATO

The phrase "the Mediterranean diet" immediately evokes certain simple ingredients: olive oil, olives, pulses, whole grains, fish, fresh fruit, and vegetables, including the tomato. Once regarded with suspicion, the tomato now occupies a central role in the Mediterranean. In this warm, sunny

region, the tomato plant grows well, producing fine, flavorful tomatoes with a natural sweetness. Here tomatoes are an important crop, grown on a large scale by commercial growers but also in gardens and smallholdings by domestic gardeners for family consumption. Eaten raw or cooked, fresh or processed, the tomato appears in recipes throughout the Mediterranean, adding color and flavor to dishes from fragrant Moroccan tagines to robust Italian pasta dishes such as Bologna's famous *tagliatelle al ragù*.

Such is the importance of the tomato around the Mediterranean that it is also celebrated with annual festivals. The best-known celebration is Spain's La Tomatina festival, held each year in the summer heat of August in the small town of Buñol, Valencia, and dating back to the 1940s. Valencia is a major tomato-growing area, so throwing a festival to celebrate the locally cultivated *tomate* is natural. Rather than focusing on the culinary delights of the tomato, however, this riotous event sees soft, ripe tomatoes thrown through the air by participants, with predictably messy results, and the streets running red with tomatoes and their juice. The statistics are impressive: around 140 tons of tomatoes are brought into the town by truck in order to be used as "ammunition." In the era of social media, word has spread, and this traditional event now brings in around 50,000 attendees, who are advised to don swimwear and goggles in order to take part in what is billed as the "World's Biggest Food Fight."

Italy sees a more conventional tomato-centric festival happen, an event at which eating tomatoes, rather than throwing them, is at the heart of the celebration. Italy—with its intensely regional cuisine—has a tradition of small, community festivals known as *sagre*, often centered on foods, typically local specialties of the region. The Sagra di Pomodoro (Tomato Festival) is held near Naples to celebrate the locally important San Marzano tomato.

TOMATO KETCHUP

Nowadays, bright red, sweet, thick tomato ketchup is taken for granted as a ubiquitous U.S. condiment—an essential topping for popular fast foods such as hamburgers, hot dogs, and French fries. Its origins, however, can be traced back centuries to Asia, with the word coming from the Chinese (Amoy dialect) *ketsiap*, meaning a fermented fish sauce; this, in turn, entered Malay as *kecap*, describing a fermented sauce. It is thought that during the eighteenth century, European traders, who had come across the sauce in Southeast Asia, introduced the idea of a salty, spicy condiment called "ketchup" to Europe.

PAN CON TOMATE

Makes 8 slices
Preparation 5 minutes
Cooking 5 minutes

In this classic Spanish recipe, a few simple ingredients—fundamentally, bread and fresh tomatoes—are transformed into an irresistible snack. Serve as an appetizer with drinks.

8 medium-thick slices
  of sourdough bread
1 garlic clove, peeled
4 ripe tomatoes, halved
Extra-virgin olive oil, for
  drizzling
Sea salt flakes, for sprinkling

1   Preheat the broiler to high. Toast the bread slices under the broiler until lightly golden on top, then turn and toast until the other side is lightly golden, too. Alternately, thoroughly heat a ridged griddle over a medium-high heat and cook the bread slices in batches until griddle marks appear, turning over to cook on both sides.

2   Rub the garlic clove firmly over the top of each freshly toasted or griddled slice of bread. Rub the cut side of a tomato half firmly over each slice of bread, so that the juice from the tomato soaks into the bread.

3   Drizzle each slice with a little olive oil and sprinkle with a pinch of sea salt. Serve at once.

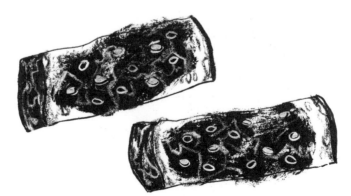

FRIED GREEN TOMATOES

Serves 4
Preparation 5 minutes
Cooking 4–6 minutes

If you are wondering what to do with those unripe tomatoes on your plants, frying firm-textured green tomatoes in this way transforms them into a tasty dish. Serve with bacon and eggs for a simple but excellent breakfast.

4 green tomatoes
3 tbsp fine cornmeal
1 tbsp plain flour
1 tsp granulated sugar
Salt and freshly ground
   black pepper
2 tbsp vegetable oil
1 tbsp butter

1   Cut the green tomatoes into thick slices. Mix together the cornmeal, flour, and sugar. Season the mixture well with salt and freshly ground pepper.

2   Heat the oil and butter in large skillet over medium heat until they are frothing. Dip the tomato slices in the cornmeal mixture, coating well on all sides, shaking off the excess coating from each slice.

3   Add the freshly coated tomato slices to the pan and fry for 2–3 minutes, then carefully turn them with a spatula and fry for a further 2–3 minutes until golden brown on both sides. Serve at once.

In 1747, the English cook Hannah Glasse published a bestselling cookbook, *The Art of Cookery Made Plain and Easy*, a work that went on to be popular in the United States. In the first edition, in the chapter "For Captains of Ships," she included a recipe for "catchup," a sauce made from beer, anchovies, mushrooms, shallots, and spices that could be bottled and kept for months; hence its usefulness on voyages. Ketchup was traditionally made from a variety of ingredients, including mushrooms, oysters, and walnuts. It is from this culinary tradition of creating spiced condiments that ketchup made from tomatoes arose.

After the American Civil War, there was a marked increase in the amount of commercially made ketchups being produced, and tomato ketchup became the most popular of them.

The first known recipe for tomato ketchup, entitled "Tomatoes or Love-Apple Catchup," was published in the United States in 1812 by James Mease, a scientist and doctor from Philadelphia. Rather than vinegar, it contained brandy, which would have helped preserve the sauce. William Kitchiner's English cookbook *The Cook's Oracle* (1817) contained a recipe for "Tomato Catsup," made from anchovies and tomatoes, while the following year, he published a recipe without anchovies but containing vinegar. Tomato ketchup recipes then began to appear more frequently. In 1824, Mary Randolph published her influential U.S. cookbook, *The Virginia Housewife*. It contained the following recipe for "Tomato Catsup:"

> *Gather a peck of tomatos* [sic], *pick out the stems, and wash them; put them on the fire without water, sprinkle on a few spoonfuls of salt, let them boil steadily an hour, stirring them frequently; strain them through a colander, and then through a sieve; put the liquid on the fire with half a pint of chopped onions, half a quarter of an ounce of mace broke into small pieces; and if not sufficiently salt, add a little more—one table-spoonful of whole black pepper; boil all together until just enough to fill two bottles; cork it tight. Make it in August in dry weather.*

These early recipes for tomato ketchup varied a great deal, both in terms of ingredients and in regard to the methods used, such as straining or not straining the sauce. Sugar as an ingredient in tomato ketchup appeared only in the mid-nineteenth century.

The nineteenth century saw tomato ketchup being produced commercially as well as within domestic kitchens. After the American Civil War, there was a marked increase in the amount of commercially made ketchups being produced, and tomato ketchup became the most popular of them. The production of tomato ketchup was historically closely linked to the United States' thriving tomato canning industry; initially, ketchup was only a by-product of tomato canning, a way for manufacturers to use up tomatoes that would otherwise be discarded. In 1876, the H. J. Heinz Company began making its own tomato ketchup, producing a preservative-free version in 1906. Hugely popular, Heinz ketchup—with its distinctive octagonal glass bottle (patented in 1890), keystone label, and screw cap—has become an iconic food. It remains the United States' best-selling tomato ketchup, far outselling any of its competitors, while its recipe for thick-textured, salty-sweet sauce remains a closely guarded secret. An 1896 article in the *New York Tribune* described tomato ketchup as the United States' national condiment—found "on every table in the land"—and that statement remains valid today.

THE CULINARY TOMATO

Despite the initial skepticism with which tomatoes were regarded when they were first introduced as an exotic novelty, today the tomato features in many cuisines around the world. The tomato's distinctive combination of both natural acidity and sweetness, combined with its juiciness, makes it a useful ingredient in the kitchen, often used to lift dishes. It is also an ingredient that can take center stage—one thinks of tomato salads, stuffed tomatoes, or tomato soups—or be a bit player, discreetly present, used to add a touch of color, texture, or flavor. The many forms that the tomato takes—fresh, canned, dried, tomato paste—undoubtedly contribute to its usefulness.

It is a remarkably versatile ingredient, which can be enjoyed raw or cooked. When eating raw tomatoes, one simple way to maximize their flavor is to remove them from the fridge well before eating to give them time to come to room temperature, as the chilling process mutes their flavor. When made from ripe, flavorful tomatoes—ideally, freshly picked—even a simple salad is a pleasure to eat. The natural colorfulness of tomatoes—usually red, but also found in yellow, green, or dark red—makes it a vivacious presence in salads. Italy's well-known *insalata tricolore* combines sliced green avocado, white mozzarella cheese, and bright red tomatoes to patriotically recreate the colors of the Italian flag.

The tomato's juicy texture is central to many of its culinary uses. In Mexico, where the tomato was first cultivated, the tomato plays an important role in many recipes, characteristically chopped and used in salsas. Finely diced deseeded tomato is often added to guacamole, where its fresh acidity contrasts with the creamy richness of the avocado.

TOMATO CROSTINI

Makes 16
Preparation 10 minutes
Cooking 15–20 minutes

In Italy, these dainty tomato-topped morsels are a popular appetizer, traditionally served as an accompaniment to a glass of chilled prosecco or wine.

8 slices of ciabatta bread

2 tbsp olive oil

10 cherry tomatoes, quartered

2 Roma tomatoes, diced

1 tsp balsamic vinegar

8 basil leaves

Salt and freshly ground
   black pepper

1   Preheat the oven to 400°F. Cut each slice of ciabatta in half. Place the 16 pieces of ciabatta on a baking sheet. Using 1 tablespoon of the olive oil, brush the top of each piece of ciabatta lightly with olive oil. Bake the bread for 15–20 minutes until golden brown, turning the slices over halfway through the cooking time to color both sides. Remove and set aside to cool.

2   Prepare the tomato topping. In a bowl, mix together the cherry tomatoes, Roma tomatoes, remaining olive oil, and balsamic vinegar. Shred the basil leaves and mix in, reserving a little for garnish. Season with salt and freshly ground black pepper.

3   Spoon a little of the tomato mixture on top of each baked piece of bread, dividing it evenly among them. Garnish with the remaining basil and serve at once.

There is an interesting tradition of recipes, such as Spain's *pan con tomate*, that combine bread, often dried, with fresh, raw tomatoes, so that the natural juices of the tomatoes soak and soften the bread (see p. 227). On the Greek island of Crete, the dish known as *dakos* consists of hard barley rusks topped with chopped ripe tomatoes, onion, feta cheese, and olives, and set aside to stand for a short while before serving in order to allow the juices to penetrate the dry rusk. In Italy, one finds *panzanella*, a bread and tomato salad in which cubes of bread are tossed with tomatoes, onions, and an olive oil–based dressing. It, too, is set aside for a time before serving.

Countries with warm climates use fresh, raw tomatoes in many ways, with the dishes designed to offer refreshment during the hot summers. In Sicily, one finds the local specialty *pesto alla trapanese*, named after the town of Trapani on the western coast of the island. This regional version of pesto is made by combining ripe tomatoes, blanched almonds, garlic, and basil into a paste, traditionally using a mortar and pestle, which is then tossed with freshly cooked pasta. *Salsa di pomodoro crudo* is another Italian pasta sauce that is made from raw tomatoes, simply chopped or crushed and flavored with garlic, olive oil, and basil. In Spain, the famous chilled soup gazpacho uses the juiciness of raw tomatoes to create a dish that is meant to be enjoyed on a hot day (see p. 207).

> *In Sicily, one finds the local specialty* pesto alla trapanese, *named after the town of Trapani on the western coast of the island. This regional version of pesto is made by combining ripe tomatoes, blanched almonds, garlic, and basil.*

The natural juiciness of tomatoes also lends itself to cooked dishes. Usefully for those without access to ripe, juicy, tasty fresh tomatoes, canned tomatoes make a handy substitute. Soups—whether a smooth-textured cream of tomato soup made with a béchamel sauce, a refined consommé, or a chunky Italian minestrone—are an excellent way to make the most of the tomato's natural moisture. A Tuscan specialty is *pappa al pomodoro*, a thick soup with a porridge-like texture that is made from stale rustic bread, tomatoes, garlic, and stock. Sauces, too, including Italy's *sugo al pomodoro* (see p. 211), are often flavored simply with onion and garlic. A southern Italian version of this recipe flavors the tomatoes with crushed dried chiles and salted anchovies, serving it tossed through spaghetti and topped with dried breadcrumbs. In Spanish cuisine, *salsa romesco* is made by blending roasted or grilled tomatoes, almonds or hazelnuts, garlic, and grilled *nora* peppers with wine vinegar and olive oil. The resulting roughly textured, piquant sauce is served with fish, vegetables, or meat. And, of course, pizza usually comes with a red smear of tomato sauce over the dough (see p. 234).

PIZZA MARGHERITA

Makes 4 pizzas

Preparation 25 minutes,
plus 1 hour dough resting

Cooking 10–15 minutes
per pizza

4 cups all-purpose flour, plus
extra for dusting

1 tsp salt

1 tsp granulated sugar

1 tsp fast-action dried yeast

1¼ cups lukewarm water

2 tbsp olive oil

1¼ cup tomato sauce or 12–16
tbsp tomato paste

3 fresh buffalo or cow's milk
mozzarella cheeses, torn
into pieces

2 handfuls basil leaves

Freshly ground black pepper

Reputedly created by chef Raffaele Esposito
in Naples to honor Queen Margherita of
Savoy in 1889, this classic pizza patriotically
combines the red, white, and green colors
of the Italian flag.

1   Make the pizza dough by mixing the flour, salt, sugar,
and yeast together. Gradually add the lukewarm
water and the olive oil, mixing together to form a sticky
dough. Transfer the dough to a lightly floured, clean
work surface and knead vigorously until the dough
becomes smooth and supple. Place the dough in an oiled
bowl, cover with a clean dish towel, and set aside in a
warm, sheltered place to rise for 1 hour.

2   Meanwhile, preheat the oven to 475°F.

3   Working on a lightly floured, clean work surface, break
down the risen dough, roll out finely to around ⅛ inch
thickness, and shape into four circular pizza bases.

4   Place each base on a lightly floured pizza stone or
baking sheet. Spread each base lightly and evenly with
the tomato sauce or paste. Dot each pizza with pieces of
mozzarella cheese and half the basil leaves. Season well
with black pepper.

5   Bake the pizzas, in batches if need be, in the preheated
oven for 10–15 minutes, until the dough has turned
pale gold and the mozzarella has melted. Serve at once,
garnished with the remaining fresh basil.

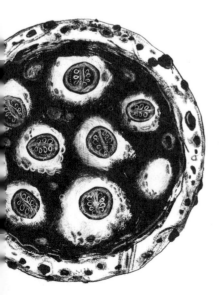

Certain ways of preparing tomatoes allow them to be used in different ways in recipes. Some tomato recipes require the removal of the skin. This is classically done by blanching tomatoes in very hot water to loosen the skin, then simply peeling it off. In a classic recipe for Piedmontese peppers, for example, red peppers are filled with fresh, peeled, whole tomatoes, garlic, and anchovies, then baked until cooked through.

In contrast, another way to use the tomato in the kitchen is to scoop out the soft, juicy seeded heart of the tomato, creating a firm shell. This natural, colourful container can then be filled with ingredients, ranging from vegetables to tuna fish. France has a fine range of traditional stuffed tomato recipes, including *tomates farcies chaudes à la bonne femme*, in which hollowed-out tomatoes are filled with a hearty sausage-meat mixture. In Greece, a popular taverna dish consists of tomatoes filled with a mixture of rice, onion, and herbs, baked slowly and gently until the rice is cooked.

The tomato's high water content and distinctive flavor means that it is also consumed in liquid form as tomato juice. A chef named Louis Perrin, working in 1917 at the French Lick Springs Hotel in Indiana, is credited with first squeezing tomatoes to serve their juice as a beverage. The Kemp family in Indiana began producing tomato juice commercially in 1929, followed a few years later by the H. J. Heinz Company and the Campbell Soup Company as the United States acquired a taste for this new red beverage. It was during the 1920s or the 1930s that an iconic cocktail made from tomato juice—the Bloody Mary—was invented. Its exact origins are disputed. The French barman Ferdinand "Pete" Petiot claimed he mixed tomato juice and vodka together in Harry's Bar in Paris in 1921. Later, he introduced the drink to New York while he was working at the city's St. Regis

A chef named Louis Perrin, working in 1917 at the French Lick Springs Hotel in Indiana, is credited with first squeezing tomatoes to serve their juice as a beverage.

Hotel, and it was here he added flavorings of salt, black pepper, cayenne pepper, and Worcestershire sauce. Other contenders include bartender Henry Zbikiewicz at New York's 21 Club and the comedian George Jessel, who was a regular at the bar and is said to have come up with a mixture of vodka and tomato juice as a pick-me-up. Whatever its origins, the Bloody Mary has become one of the most popular cocktails in the country.

The cheerful-looking tomato, gloriously useful and noticeably versatile, has earned its place as a much-loved vegetable—one that is both eaten and drunk—and is enjoyed around the world.

INDEX

OCT -- 2018